PROBSTHAIN'S ORIENTAL SERIES

VOL. XVI

THE WORKS OF HSÜNTZE

THE WORKS OF HSÜNTZE

荀　　　子

TRANSLATED FROM THE CHINESE, WITH NOTES

BY

HOMER H. DUBS, Ph.D.

(Author of Hsüntze, the Moulder of Ancient Confucianism)

Sole distributors in the USA & Canada
PARAGON BOOK GALLERY, LTD.
14 EAST 38th STREET
NEW YORK, N. Y. 10016

Original Edition Published By

ARTHUR PROBSTHAIN
(LATE PROBSTHAIN & CO.)

41 GREAT RUSSELL STREET, LONDON, W.C.

1928

Republished by

PREFACE

THIS work contains a translation of all the writings of Hsüntze that are both genuine and important. Hsüntze's writings were much more voluminous than those of either Confucius or Mencius, and consequently contain much repetition. To be sure to give a complete view of Hsüntze's teaching, I have not hesitated to include some writings whose authenticity is doubtful, and some which are not so important. Matters of authenticity are discussed in the notes. Since Hsüntze was primarily a philosopher, and our aim is to understand his teaching, I have felt that it is more important to make the translation accurate and even literal than to make it literary. I hope, nevertheless, that it will be found to be readable.

Matters of textual criticism and explanation of the text have been so admirably summed up by Wang Hsien-Ch'ien [1] that I have felt free to omit such matters from the notes except where I have differed from him. To aid in reference to that work I have indicated the paging or foliation of that edition by numerals in the margin of the translation. The paragraph division is my own, though Hsüntze's mind was so orderly that his writing falls naturally into paragraphs. The paragraph headings placed in the margin are also mine, but the paragraph titles placed in the middle of the page are original in the Chinese text.

Should the reader prefer to begin with the most important

[1] 荀 子 集 解. A photographic reprint is published by the Commercial Press, Shanghai. The sinologue is referred to this work for matters of textual emendation and further elucidation of matters implied in the text.

parts of Hsüntze's work, he will find them in Books XVII,
XIX, XXI, XXII, and XXIII, together with Book IX.

This translation is throughout a new one, although I have
not hesitated to make use of whatever partial translations
have been made.[1] As in the case of the first translation of
every philosopher, there are probably mistakes, and no one
will welcome corrections or emendations more than I. The
translations of the quotations from the *Odes* and *History* are
also my own; I have compared them with Legge's translation and have quoted them by his numbering, but have
ventured to make a new translation in order to bring out
the point Hsüntze uses them to prove. In matters of textual
criticism I have generally followed the Chinese commentators,
who have done wonders in clearing up the difficulties of the
Chinese text. The best edition is that of Wang Hsien-ch'ien,[2]
and I have indicated in the notes any variations from the
emendations he proposes. Matters of historical criticism have
also been taken up in the notes. While what we have now as
Hsüntze's works are mostly genuine, there are undoubtedly
large spurious passages. Such can only be tested by the
canons of historical criticism. In the transliteration of
Chinese names I have followed in the main Wade's system
as that best known ;[3] though I have not hesitated to depart
from it in the interests of clearness or convenience, especially
in the case of common words, where there can be no misunder-

[1] Cf. *H.*, p. 47, note 3, for a list of these.

[2] Cf. *H.*, p. 46, and note 2.

[3] The pronunciation of Chinese names is always a stumbling block to
those unversed in the Chinese language. However, they can take courage
from the fact that because of the tonic character of the Chinese language,
it is impossible to get even an approximately exact pronunciation without
prolonged practice under the direction of a Chinese teacher. Indeed, in

standing of the Chinese character meant. A few Chinese
moral concepts, such as *Tao, Li, Yi, Jen,* which, more particularly than other terms, have no exact equivalent in
English, and which are translated differently by different
translators, are indicated by the transliteration in brackets
placed after an approximate translation.[1] It is hoped that
the notes to the text will help to clear up difficult points
in Hsüntze's writings. Nothing is more irritating than
an unexplained allusion or an unresolved obscure
sentence. Chinese texts are full of commentary, the commentary often amounting to several times the length of the
text. Because an English translation is very largely an interpretation, and because I have omitted matters of textual
criticism,[2] I have tried to avoid very copious notes which
interrupt the course of the thought.

different parts of China there are greatly varying pronunciations for the
same character. So perhaps the best way is to make a brave attempt to
pronounce the word as it stands and stick to what one gets. Vowels should
be given the Italian pronunciation, i.e. the English short *ă* and long *ī* should
be avoided. After *Ch, K, T,* and *Ts* an apostrophe indicates the presence
of a strong aspirate, and the absence of an apostrophe changes the pronunciation of *Ch* to *Dzh, K* to *G, T* to *D,* and *Ts* and *Dz.* By following these
directions the reader can come near to some one of the Chinese pronunciations.

The name of this author, for example, Hsüntze, is pronounced in the
north shü-in-tz, with a German umlaut *ü* and a short *ĭ.* The sound of the
last syllable can be approached by pronouncing *tzĭ* (giving the *z* its full
sonant value) and leaving off the vowel. In the south, this name is pronounced sŭn-tz, with a short *u* ; this pronunciation is probably nearer that
of the time of Hsüntze.

[1] On the difficulty of translating Chinese philosophy, cf. J. Percy Bruce's
translation of *The Philosophy of Human Nature,* the Preface, pp. xii–xv,
with whose remarks I am in full sympathy.

[2] Which forms a large part of the Chinese commentary. For matters
of textual criticism and emendation, cf. Wang Hsien-ch'ien's edition of
Hsüntze.

One of the foundations of Hsüntze's philosophy is his conception of history, and consequently his writings abound in historical allusions. I have prefaced the translation with a sketch of Chinese history and cosmology as presupposed by Hsüntze, in the hope of making more systematic the reader's conception of this essential to the understanding of this great thinker. More detailed matters are explained in the notes to the text.

Hsüntze was one of the greatest of Chinese philosophers, the Aristotle of China. Yet his importance for us consists not only in his original contributions, but in the fact that he gave the earliest complete and systematic presentation of Confucianism, and so presents it in its primitive purity, uncorrupted by Buddhistic influences. His orderly mind and the fullness of his expositions served to bring out the implications of Confucius' teaching as nowhere else, and make a study of his writings indispensable for a knowledge of ancient Confucianism. For a systematic elucidation of that philosophy, the reader is referred to the companion volume to this translation, *Hsüntze, the Moulder of Ancient Confucianism*. In the notes this work is referred to by the abbreviation " *H.*" It is hoped that this translation will aid in the comprehension of the philosophy which has been the most powerful moulding force in one great centre of human culture for over two thousand years, and thereby to an understanding and sympathy with one of the greatest of human civilizations.

HOMER H. DUBS.

CHICAGO, ILL.
　　3rd July, 1925.

TABLE OF CONTENTS

BOOK VII

BOOK XX

BOOK XXI

BOOK XXII

BOOK XXIII

INTRODUCTION

A SKETCH OF CHINESE HISTORY

ANCIENT Chinese cosmology begins with two primordial principles, the *Yin* and the *Yang*, negative and positive respectively, through whose perpetual combination and mutation everything exists. Through these two were produced Heaven and Earth. By Heaven [1] was meant Nature, especially in its astronomical phenomena, the seasons, the weather, etc. By Earth was meant Nature as the producing and sustaining power, especially as shown in the growth of plants.[2] Through the combination of Heaven and Earth,[3] the Ten-Thousand Things were born, by which are meant everything between Heaven and Earth, especially living and movable objects. From them man arose.[4] Thus there was a metaphysical dualism. But the principle of action of the *Yin* and *Yang*, Heaven and Earth, is that of *Tao*, which is not only a cosmological and metaphysical principle, but also a moral one. Thus there was also a monism. This cosmology is stated in the Classics and is presupposed in Hsüntze, but plays no important rule in his philosophy. He accepted it together with the rest of the Confucian history.

Chinese received history goes back to fabulous ages. But Hsüntze wrote : " Previous to the Five Emperors, there was

---

[1] This is the meaning given the term by Hsüntze. Other writers sometimes use it as synonymous with " God ". Cf. the discussion of this term in *H.*, p. 60 f.

[2] But this growth required the assistance of Heaven (rain) too.

[3] Heaven was Yang and Earth Yin.

[4] Cf. p. 235 for Hsüntze's own account.

no record." [1] He also mentions Sui-ren,[2] the inventor of fire (probably a culture hero), who, according to one account, selected Fu-Hsi or T'ai Hao from among four of his disciples to be the first of these Five Emperors.[3] He is dated by present historians somewhere about the beginning of the third millennium B.C., although the best Chinese historians do not give any dates in such remote antiquity. The second of these Five Emperors was Shen-Nung, the "Divine Farmer", and the third was Hwang-ti or the "Yellow Emperor". The other two emperors are less distinct. They were very indistinct figures even in Hsüntze's time. He writes, "Of the period of the Five Emperors there is no record of their government, . . . because of the length of time intervening." [4] They were probably only culture heroes.

Yao, Shun and Yu.

Following them came three rulers, Yao, Shun, and Yu, who have since been among the most popular figures in Chinese history and models for all subsequent rulers. Eulogized in the *Book of History*, they have been held up by Confucius and all subsequent Confucians as Sages or Sage-Kings, combining the virtue and wisdom of the Sage with the power of the king—the most perfect combination to be found. After a reign of seventy years, Yao [5] wished to abdicate. He offered the throne to one of his trusted ministers, who

[1] p. 74.

[2] p. 203.

[3] According to another account, Sui-ren followed Fu-hsi, which would seem to be Hsüntze's opinion, since he held that there was no record previous to Fu-hsi. Cf. Hirth, *The Ancient History of China*, for a fuller account of this history.

[4] Cf. p. 74.

[5] Supposed to have reigned 2357–2258 B.C. Cf. *Book of History*, I, iii.

declined it as being unworthy. Finally a young man named Shun, who had exhibited his filial piety by living at peace with an obstinately unprincipled father, an insincere step-mother, and an arrogant half-brother, and who by his filial piety had induced them to live together harmoniously, was pointed out as the most qualified; and the monarch sent for him and married him to his two daughters. Upon the death of Yao, Shun mourned three years, and then ascended the throne.[1] He organized the government, and passing over his own son, he appointed Yu,[2] who had been successful in curbing the great floods, as his successor. Yu founded the first dynasty, that of Hsia. This dynasty began with a virtuous Sage, but gradually degenerated to end in the person of Ch'ie,[3] a tyrant and immoral wretch, the description of whose vice and cruelty surpasses everything recorded in the history of the world, not excepting the darkest periods of imperial Rome.

The Hsia Dynasty.

Ch'ie.

The reaction set in under T'ang, Prince of Shang, who gathered the righteous forces of the country, defeated and banished Ch'ie to his ancestral home, where he was kept prisoner, and founded a new dynasty, that of Shang. Later the capital was changed to Yin, and the dynasty was called by that name. But this dynasty too degenerated. The last emperor was Chou or Chou-sin,[4] who was spurred on in his crimes by a beautiful concubine, Ta-ki. Punishments were made severe; a new form of torture was invented, in which

T'ang.

The Shang or Yin dynasty.

Chou-sin.

---

[1] Supposed to have reigned 2258–06 B.C.
[2] Supposed to have reigned 2205–2198 B.C.
[3] Dated at 1818–1766 B.C.
[4] Dated 1154–22 B.C.

a greased copper pillar was laid across a pit of live charcoal, and the culprit was made to walk across it ; when he slipped and fell into the fire, Ta-ki was greatly delighted. When a relative and high official, Pi-kan, remonstrated with Chou upon his excesses, Chou cried out, "They say that a Sage has seven orifices in his heart (the seat of the understanding). Let us see if this is the case with you." He then caused Pi-kan to be disemboweled before him. Likewise one of the foremost of the nobles, the Viscount of Chi, was imprisoned for remonstrating.

The Chou dynasty.

King Wen.

King Wu.

In the west, the state of Chou [1] had been growing strong. T'an-fu, known as King T'ai, had established it securely. His grandson, who is known best by his posthumous title, King Wen,[2] developed the state by devoting himself entirely to its administration, so that he changed it into a model of good government. By making war on neighbouring states which the emperor had asked him to subdue, he increased his military power. His son King Wu,[3] found himself at the head of a revolutionary party created by the cruelties and misgovernment of Chou. After a bloody battle the forces of Chou were completely defeated. He took refuge in his palace, and set fire to it in order not to fall into the hands of the enemy. King Wu, hearing of this, hastened to the palace to convince himself of the fact, shot three arrows into the Emperor's corpse, descended from his chariot and stabbed the corpse

---

[1] Not to be confused with the Emperor Chou. In Chinese the emperor is 紂 and the dynasty 周, a clear distinction ; but in pronunciation they are similar.

[2] Ruled 1184–35 B.C.

[3] Ruled 1134–16 B.C., became Emperor 1122 B.C.

with his dagger, after which he severed the head from the body and suspended it from a crimson standard. This picture of King Wu, given by the historian, is quite different from the idealized description given by the Confucian theorists.

King Wu now became emperor, and founded the dynasty of Chou which lasted until 249 B.C. After only six years as emperor, King Wu died, and his son and successor, King Ch'eng,[1] was only a minor. King Wu's brother, known as the Duke of Chou, was appointed as Regent, and the Con- *Duke Chou.* fucians (indeed Confucius himself) laud him as one of the great Worthies or even as a Sage, especially for his guardianship of the young emperor and his refusal to take advantage of the opportunity to make himself emperor. To him was due the organization of the new government. It was a feudal kingdom, and Duke Chou saw to it that most of the feudatories were members of the Imperial Clan. Thus most of China came to be ruled by a small group of interrelated families with the same culture and traditions.

But this new dynasty was no more permanent than the *Degeneration of the Chou dynasty.* preceding ones. The feudatories increased their power at the expense of the emperor, and the northern barbarians attacked, so that in 770 B.C. the capital had to be moved for fear of these barbarians. From this time the weakness of the dynasty began. Its sovereignty became merely nominal. At first the King of Chou was still nominally honoured as suzerain; then he became merely the pontifex maximus, as Son of Heaven, which title the emperor always

---

[1] Reigned 1115–1079 B.C.

had,[1] and finally he was totally disregarded. Without any powerful outside enemies, China had no necessity to remain unified, and was torn between the dissensions of the feudal states.

The feudal states.

These feudal states now occupy the foreground of the stage, and in the classical period of Chinese literature and philosophy they were all powerful. We must remember that the civilized China of that day was but a fraction of what is now China. Very little was known of the regions south of the Yangtze river. To the east was the ocean and the mountains of Shantung, with their barbarians; to the north were the barbarians, and to the west were the mountains. Four seas were supposed to surround the continent. China was merely a group of states situated around the Yellow river. In the centre was Lu,[2] the cultured state from which was to come Confucius. To the west was Sung,[3] chiefly noteworthy because it was established by King Wu with the object of providing

Lu.

Sung.

The Emperor's Title.

[1] Lit. 天子. This title distinguished the emperor as pontifex maximus. The term now used for emperor, 皇帝, did not come into use until appropriated by the first Ts'in emperor. The Chou emperors styled themselves "King", 王. But as their power deteriorated and that of the feudatories increased, the larger of the feudatories assumed the title of King too, until there were many Kings. Emperors previous to the Chou dynasty are usually spoken of by their name, without any title, showing that the use of " King " by the Chou emperors represents an advance in the process of magnifying the Son of Heaven. But in their temple name, these earlier rulers were entitled 帝, which is half of the later title for Emperor, and may be translated " Potentate " or " Emperor ". It was a posthumous title given them. For the sake of uniformity, we may call them all " Emperor " though the titles applied to them vary. Cf. Parker, *Ancient China Simplified*, p. 55 f .

[2] 魯 In what is now the south of Shantung.

[3] 宋 In the east of Honan, south of the Yellow river.

someone who should carry on the sacrifices to the monarchs of the deposed line of Shang. After the rebellion of Wu-ken, the son of Chou-sin, Wei-tze Ch'i, a prince of the house of Shang, was enfeoffed with this state and given the title of Duke, so that he should be able to carry on the ancestral sacrifices, and that the deceased monarchs should not be neglected. These, together with a number of other states, were all small, and formed the centre of the ancient civilization. It was the states surrounding this centre which could expand at the expense of the surrounding uncivilized country, and which became most important towards the close of the Chou period. To the east was Ts'i,[1] which became wealthy Ts'i. because of its salt and iron industries, although it could not expand as much as the others because it was hemmed in by the sea-coast. Under Duke Huan,[2] his great prime Duke Huan. minister, Kuan Chung, first stimulated commerce, enriched the state through a tax on the iron and salt, and then partly by diplomacy and partly by military expeditions, raised the state to the pre-eminence among the feudatories. The Emperor's power had waned, and Duke Huan assumed the presidency of the feudal powers, called conferences of the feudal chiefs, and used his power for peace and concord in the empire. He was rewarded by the Emperor with the title of Lord Protector,[3] and even exercised a deciding voice in such matters as the succession to the imperial throne. But at the death of Kuan Chung he devoted himself to excesses, and died neglected by all, in the fight over the succession.

---

[1] 齊 In the north of present Shantung.

[2] Ruled 685–643 B.C.

[3] Lit., 霸 .

There were five of these Lords Protector, as five different states successively acquired the pre-eminence in the empire.

Tsin.

On the north-west was Tsin,[1] once the largest of all the feudal states. One of its Dukes became the third of the Lords Protector. But it was torn by internal dissensions, and finally divided into three states, Han,[2] Chao,[3] and Wei,[4] each of which became powerful. On the south was the semi-barbaric state of Ts'u,[5] which had the whole Yangtze valley in which to expand, and so grew to be one of the largest and most powerful of the states. It was originally outside the limits of the original Chinese civilization, and this fact may account for the different character of the philosophy of Laotze, who was a native of Ts'u, from that of the rest of China. The eastern end of this territory developed a separate state, that of Wu,[6] which became important, but engaged in a bitter struggle with its southern neighbour, Yueh,[7] and was finally annexed by Yueh,[8] only to be swallowed up in turn by Ts'u.[9]

Han,
Chao, Wei.

Ts'u.

Wu.

Yueh.

Ts'in.

The largest state of all, the final conqueror of all the others,

---

[1] 晉 The southern part of present Shansi.

[2] 漢 South Shensi and western Honan. The division occurred in 376 B.C.

[3] 趙 North Shansi and western Chihli. The ancestral home of Hsüntze.

[4] 衛 Southern Chihli and western Honan.

[5] 楚 Occupying the Yangtze valley. Cf. p. 217 for Hsüntze's description of its boundaries. His final home was in this state.

[6] 吳 In the south of Kiangsu.

[7] 越 Chehkiang.

[8] 473 B.C.

[9] 334 B.C.

was Ts'in, located in the west.[1] Beginning as a very small state, it acquired power and territory through wars with the barbarians. Unlike the others, its people remained simple and uncorrupted by the luxury and cultural influences of civilized China, and it never produced a single scholar of note, devoting its strength instead to military purposes. Yet its rulers took advantage of clever Chinese scholars who lent themselves to the aggrandisement of Ts'in, and by a combination of military aggression and husbanding of its strength, it finally conquered all the other states of China, then under its King Chen (known in history as Ts'in Shih Hwangti, or the First Emperor) it unified the country and abolished the feudal system. That a prince of a state which had yielded least of all to the cultural influences of the Confucian (Chinese) civilization and which disregarded the Confucian code, should eventually conquer and attain the position which belonged by rights only to the most thoroughly virtuous, hence most thoroughly Confucian state—this fact was a shock to every thoughtful man of the time.

This history forms the background and foundation of the Confucian philosophy. A great many more characters and places than are here mentioned are referred to by Hsüntze. The foregoing is what constituted history as the Chinese knew it, and the glory of rule continued to be the pinnacle of attainment, even to such a sophisticated philosopher as Hsüntze. In endeavouring to think this long period of history in terms of cultural development, we must remember that the stone

Cultural Development.

---

[1] 秦 The south of Kansu. Expanded to include the greater part of Shensi. It should be distinguished from Tsin, 晉.

age in China probably lasted down until about 2500 B.C.,[1] which would be about the time of Hwang-ti. The copper age, inaugurated at that time, lasted down to about 2200 B.C., which would be the time of Yu, from which would date the bronze age. The common use of iron came relatively late, about 600 B.C., only a short time before the birth of Confucius. At the same time we must remember that dates prior to 800 B.C. are doubtful, and that we cannot be sure of any details prior to the Chou dynasty. However, the Chinese have always been extremely tenacious of the past, and thereby have made some surprisingly accurate deductions of the course of cultural development.[2]

Literature.

Evidently there was a slow advance in culture and in the development of writing, which was scratched or painted on strips of bamboo. At first literature consisted in brief, dry historical records and some poetry—all for the use of the governing classes. Thought was stereotyped by custom. But with the development of culture there came a breakdown of the central authority, enabling the different states to set themselves up as practically independent, and at the same time there was a good deal of intercourse, especially among the governing classes and travelling merchants. Under these circumstances it was not surprising that literature and

[1] These dates are taken from a paper by Dr. V. K. Ting.

[2] I refer to the statement made by a writer of the Han dynasty, that " In Shen-nung's time, magical power resided in stone implements ; in Hwang-ti's time this magical power passed to jade with which weapons were made ; in the great Yu's time that power passed to bronze (or copper, the character may mean both), thanks to which the great canals were excavated ; but now the magical force is found in iron." Cf. also Hirth, p. 236.

philosophy should develop. The same phenomena appeared as in ancient Greece—a group of sophists covertly attacking the received morality ; serious philosophy seeking for a firm basis upon which to found morals, and the development, in the most brilliant age of the nation, of a galaxy of thinkers and of a classical age in philosophy together with the dying out of this philosophical impulse at the end of the Chou period. But there was this difference from the situation in Greece— classical China was not a new country with only a few hundred years of background, but it already possessed a hoary past, with traditions of thousands of years of development, and stories of ancient kings and emperors, who, although doubtless they had been greatly idealized, yet presented ideal figures of whom any nation might well be proud, not figures whom later generations criticized as did the Greeks the characters of Homer. These ancient Worthies greatly influenced the time. Ancient China was already ancient in its own eyes, and the traditions and customs of the past possessed a tremendous hold upon the rulers and people.[1]

With the contentions of the various states for supremacy, a new age for thought began. In politics there were bewildering sets of changes, when boundaries of states changed radically every year. The central authority was no more, and with the development of many states, each practically independent, freedom of thought became possible. Constant warfare compelled the feudal chiefs to take account of the latest developments in military science, and even seek for new inventions in military machinery or strategy. The new, not the old, became valuable. A group of sophists arose,

Break up of the old.

[1] For other aspects of history, cf. *H.*, chap. ii.

learned in the art of persuasion, which they used to insinuate themselves into high position, without any scruples as to whom they served. The philosophers of the day went from court to court as did Confucius, until they found a master willing to employ them. Every custom, every inherited idea was subjected to criticism. There was the clever twisting of arguments, which in the absence of any formal logic or dictionaries, enabled the sophist to prove that white was black. There was the same training in the art of persuasion regardless of right or wrong which we find in ancient Greece. There was the subjectivism by which Chuangtze doubted whether he was the man he knew himself when awake, or the butterfly which he dreamed he was when asleep. There was the more than Cyrenaic individualistic selfishness in which Yangtze subordinated the whole world to his own enjoyment. And there was the repudiation of the past and its heritage by Micius [1] and the endeavour to formulate everything anew on the basis of utility and universal love.

Confu-
cianism. Among these currents of thought, Confucianism represented the conservative tendency. Confucius spoke of himself as " A transmitter and not a maker, believing in and loving the ancients " [2] and to an extent seldom realized by the Western world that was the case. He did not seek to create anything new ; he merely re-edited the ancient records of his race and thus embued them with his own spirit. For him history was the vehicle of moral instruction, and besides his editing of the ancient works, his sole original composition was a history of his native state of Lu, which has ever since been extravagantly

[1] Or Mo Ti 墨 翟 or 墨 子.
[2] *Analects*, VII, i.

admired for the subtle way in which, although living in an age when the passing of judgments upon rulers was not yet possible, he combined moral lessons with history. Learned in the traditions of his race, he passed them on to his pupils by word of mouth, and they saw everything through the medium of his remarkable personality. After him his pupils carried on the tradition, and some of them wrote short treatises, now found in the *Great Learning, Doctrine of the Mean, Book of Rites, Classic of Filial Piety*, etc. In Mencius, Confucianism found an able and brilliant supporter, who carried on the doctrine and was a powerful defence against all attacks. It is with a younger contemporary of Mencius, Hsüntze, that we are concerned. The Confucians were the conservers of the heritage of the race. They attempted to preserve and teach the best that had been developed in the past history of the nation. Their original emphasis was not upon their own writings, but upon the ancient Classics, the ancient heroes, and ancient ways. In the writings of Hsüntze we find clear evidence that in that day Confucius was looked upon only as the greatest expositor and master of the ancient Way or *Tao*, a Sage, but not an original genius.

"Confucius possessed the qualities of benevolence and wisdom and was not prejudiced, hence his scholarship and mastery over all teachings were sufficient to make him equal with the ancient Kings. He possessed the whole of the right Way (*Tao*); he brought it to people's notice and he used it; he was not prejudiced nor unable to carry it out." [1]

But the Confucians could not remain stationary in this time of rapid development. They had to reformulate the

[1] p. 265.

ancient doctrines ; they had to systematize and develop their teachings to meet new attacks, and they were forced to counter-attack their opponents. In Hsüntze we find this process going on. Consequently he is of great significance in the history of the development of Confucianism on its way to become the dominant and sole philosophy of China. In Confucianism we are not studying *a* Chinese philosophy, but *the* Chinese philosophy, which has and always will exercise a profound influence over this great nation. And in Hsüntze we find ancient Confucianism coming to its fullest expression, and are able to understand this powerful force better than in any other writer.

BOOK I

AN ENCOURAGEMENT TO STUDY

The superior man says : Study should never stop. Green [1][1]
dye is taken from blue, but it is nearer the colour of nature [2]
than is blue. Ice comes from water, but is colder than
water.[3] If wood is straight, it conforms to the plumb-line ;
steam it and bend it, and it can be used for a wheel, but its
curvature must be in accord with the compass. Although it
were dried in the sun it would not again become straight—
the bending made it that way. For wood must undergo the
use of the plumb-line to be straight ; iron must be ground on
the whetstone to be sharp ; the superior man must make his
learning broad and daily examine himself in order to have his
knowledge exact and his actions without blemish. If a [2]
person does not ascend a high mountain, he will not know
how high heaven is ; if he does not descend into a deep ravine,
he will not know the depth of the earth ; if he never hears
the wisdom handed down from the former Kings, he will
not know the greatness [4] of knowledge. The children of
the states of Kan,[5] Yueh,[6] Yi,[7] and Ho,[8] all make the same

---

[1] These numerals in the text refer to the pages (folios) of Wang Hsien-
ch'ien's edition of Hsüntze, 荀 子 集 解.

[2] Green.

[3] I.e., through study, one's ability can be increased.

[4] The commentator, Yang Liang, comments : " Its benefit to men."

[5] A small feudal state in Kiangsu, later engulfed by the state of Wu.

[6] A feudal state in Chehkiang.

[7] [8] Two barbarian tribes on the north and east of China.

sounds when born, but when grown have different customs—
teaching makes them thus. The ode says :—

> " Alas ! Gentlemen !
>> You will not rest for long ;
>> Quietly fulfil your official duties ;
>> Love correctness and uprightness :
>> Then the spirits will hear you
>> And help you to great happiness." [1]

The spirits are not greater than the Way (*Tao* [2]) which
influences and reforms men ; no happiness is greater than
being without unhappiness.

3 Confucius said : I have already meditated for a whole day.
It is not as good as a moment's learning.[3] I have already
stood on tiptoe to see ; it is not as good as going up on a
high place and looking all around. If a person goes up on a
high place and beckons, his arm does not get longer, but it
can be seen at a distance. If he shouts with the wind,
his voice does not gain strength, but it can be heard
more plainly. If he borrows a horse and carriage, it does not
aid his feet, yet he can travel a thousand *li*.[4] If he
borrows a boat and oars, even though he cannot swim, he
can cross rivers or seas. The nature of the superior man is
no different ; he needs to use implements.

In the south there is a bird, called the little tailor bird,
which uses feathers to make its nest, weaves it with hair,

Meditation not as good as learning.

Carefully select what you study—avoid heterodoxy.

[1] The *Book of Odes* (quoted according to Legge's numbering), II, VI,
iii, 5. Advice given to an absent official by his friends.

[2] 道

[3] Probably an expansion of *Analects*, XV, xxx.

[4] A *li* is a third of a mile. A thousand *li* was the distance that certain
famous legendary horses were supposed to be able to travel in one day.

and attaches it to reeds. When the wind blows, the reeds snap, the eggs break, and the birdlets die. It is not the fault of the nest, for it is well-made ; it is the fault of the reeds to which it is attached. In the west there is a plant called the She-kan. Its stalk is four inches long and it grows on high mountains. But if you look at it from the right angle at the edge of an eighty foot gulf, it seems to span the gulf. Not that its stalk grows longer, but the angle at which you view it makes it seem thus. Raspberry vines growing among hemp are straight without being supported ; white sand in black mud at the bottom of a pool is black too, because of the mud.[1] The root of the Lan-huai[2] is called Chih.[3] If it is soaked in manure, a gentleman will not come near it and nobody will like it. It is not because its own substance is not excellent, but because it is soaked in manure. So when the superior man settles down, he should carefully select his dwelling-place ; when he travels for study, he should seek out a real scholar ; he should avoid heretical doctrines and pursue doctrines that are truly orthodox. When classifications of things are made, there must be the things from which the classification is made ; when honour or shame comes, they necessarily reflect a man's goodness.

Spoiled meat produces worms ; rotten fish gives birth to maggots ; laziness, remissness, neglectfulness of one's person cause misfortune and calamity. An overbearing attitude of itself brings downfall ; a humble attitude brings success. Personal impurity brings hatred in one's path. Pile firewood

Do not be lazy or careless.

---

[1] I.e., good and evil depend on one's associates.
[2] A fragrant plant.
[3] Also a fragrant root.

together in one place and the fire will burn violently. If land is perfectly level, and water is put on it, it will all be wet. Herbs and trees spring from their own kind; birds and beasts live in flocks; each follows its own kind. 5 When the target is set up, bows and arrows will fly towards it;[1] if the forest is flourishing, the axe will approach.[2] If trees make shade, numbers of birds will rest there; if the condiments are put on the table,[3] the guests will gather. So a person's talk can call misfortune upon him; his actions can call shame upon him. The superior man is careful of that whereon he stands.[4]

Necessity of industry.

By gathering earth and making a hill, the wind and rain originate; by gathering water and making a pool, the crocodile and dragon are brought forth; by gathering [5] goodness and making virtue, wisdom equal with that of the gods is obtained, and the heart of the sage is perfected. For unless a person adds steps and half-steps to each other,[6] he cannot go a thousand *li*; unless little streams are gathered, rivers and seas cannot be formed. A fast horse in one leap cannot go a thousand paces; but an old broken down nag can do it in ten days—its merit consists in not losing time.[7] If you lose your sickle, you cannot cut down a rotten tree; if you do not lose your sickle, you can carve metal or stone.

[1] Archers will come for target practice when the target is set up.

[2] A flourishing forest is ripe to be cut down. The point is that there is always a reason for the advent of misfortune; people call it upon themselves.

[3] Preparation for a feast.

[4] His learning.

[5] Cultivating.

[6] We should say, goes a step at a time.

[7] Cf. the fable of the hare and tortoise.

The earthworm has not the benefit of claws or teeth, **6**
nor has it the strength of sinews or bones : on the one hand
it eats dirt and on the other it drinks muddy water ; it has
only one thing—diligence. The crab has six legs and two
pincers. It has not a hole like the earthworm, nor has it any
place it can trust for security ; but it pays strict attention to
being fierce. Therefore he who has not a very deep purpose,
nor a very clear perception, nor very continuously strives
towards a goal is without illustrious merit.

The man who tries to travel along both paths of a forked   Necessity of
road will never get there ; he who serves two masters will   tion.
not be employed. The eye cannot look in two directions at
once and see clearly ; the ear cannot hear two things at
once and hear clearly. The T'eng-she dragon has no feet but
flies ; the squirrel has five talents, but cannot perform any
one of them to perfection.[1] The ode says : [2]

> " The turtledove is in the mulberry tree ;
>> Its little ones are seven.[3]
> The virtuous man, my prince,
>> Is uniform in his deportment.

[1] Thus explained : the squirrel can fly but cannot fly over a house ; it
can climb but cannot go to the tip of a tree, it can travel but cannot cross a
gulf ; it can dig but cannot cover itself ; it can walk but cannot go faster
than man. It cannot do anything really well, though its talents are many ;
the T'eng-she dragon can only do one thing, fly ; but it can do that well—
it concentrates.

[2] *Book of Odes,* I, xiv, iii, 1.

[3] But the turtledove has only two young at one time ! Do we have
" seven " because it rhymes with " one " ? Or is this a piece of natural
history fabricated to point a moral ? Some commentators explain that in
the morning the turtledove feeds its young in order, beginning with the
biggest down to the littlest ; but in the evening it begins with the littlest
up to the biggest ; hence it is uniform, because it equalizes things !

> He is uniform in his deportment ;
> His heart is as a knot." [1]

So the superior man [2] too knots everything into one. [3]

7   In ancient times Hu-pa played the lute so that fishes

Learning and orthodoxy lead to fame. swimming along came out to listen. P'e-ya played the lute so that the six horses of the imperial chariot looked up from their feed. For there is no sound so small that it is not heard ; there is no action so secret that it does not leave traces. [4] " If there is jade in the mountain, the trees on it will be flourishing ; if there are pearls in the pool the banks will not be parched." [5] How could it be that the man who is virtuous and thoroughly orthodox should not be famous ? [6]

Study what ? The Classics. What should one study ? How should one begin ? The art begins by reciting the Classics and ends in learning the rites (*Li*). [7] Its purpose begins with making the scholar, and ends in making the sage. [8] Sincerely put forth your efforts, and finally you will progress. Study until death and do not stop before. For the art of study occupies the whole of life ; to arrive at its purpose, you cannot stop for an instant. To do that is to be a man ; to stop is to be a bird

8 or beast. The *Book of History* records political events.

---

[1] Tied to one aim.

[2] The same word as " prince ".

[3] i.e., concentration and unity of aim are essential.

[4] Cf. " What is said in the secret chamber shall be shouted from the housetops."

[5] A proverb still current.

[6] By simply following the Confucian Way, fame and success is certain.

[7] Or, " rules of proper conduct," 禮.

[8] Hsüntze has three grades of virtue and wisdom : scholar, superior man, and sage.

The *Book of Odes* [1] regulates sounds so that they should attain the normal and not go beyond it. The *Book of Rites* (*Li*) deals with the great distinctions of society through rules; it is the unifying principle of general classes of action. Study advances to the *Book of Rites* (*Li*), and stops there. [2] This is what is meant by the extreme of virtue. The reverence [3] and love of elegance [4] of the *Book of Rites* (*Li*), the harmony of the *Book of Music*, the broad knowledge of the *Book of Odes* and *Book of History*, the subtleties [5] of the *Spring and Autumn* [6] are the completion of all creation.

This is the manner of the superior man's learning; it goes into his ears, it is taken into his heart, it spreads through his entire body, it shows itself in every movement. Speaking in low tones and moving gently are his ways of action. This is the manner of the little-minded man's learning; it goes into his ear and comes out of his mouth; between mouth and ear there are only four inches; how can that be sufficient to make his seven feet [7] of body beautiful? The purpose of the scholarship of the ancients was to improve themselves; the purpose of the study of men at present is to exhibit it to others. The study of the superior man is to beautify himself; the study of the little-minded man makes him a bird or calf. [8] To give instruction where it is not asked for is heedless [9]

The manner of the learning of the superior man and the little-minded man.

---

[1] From the context, it should be the *Book of Music* instead of the *Odes*. Probably there is some primitive error here.

[2] As the extreme and end of study.

[3] Bowing and yielding the precedence.

[4] Carriages and clothes.

[5] Subtle praise and blame, criticism and exhortation.

[6] A history of his native state composed by Confucius himself.

[7] The ancient foot was shorter than the modern.

[8] He is not big enough even to be a beast!

talking. To tell about two things when a person asks for one is tiresome. Needless talking is wrong ; to be tiresome is wrong ; the superior man is like an echo.[1]

The Importance of the teacher.

In studying there is nothing better than being intimate with a worthy teacher. The *Rites* (*Li*) and *Music* give principles and no false teaching. The *Odes* and *History* tell about the ancients, and are not familiar.[2] The teaching of the *Spring and Autumn* is suggestive rather than expressed. Associate yourself closely with the teacher ; familiarize yourself with his teaching ; reverence it as universal and common to every age. Hence it is said : in studying there is nothing better than being intimate with a worthy teacher. According to the laws of learning there is nothing which gives quicker results than esteeming a worthy teacher. The exaltation of the 10 rules of proper conduct (*Li*) is the second essential. If a person is neither able to love a worthy teacher nor to exalt the rules of proper conduct (*Li*), how can he obey the teaching of the *Odes* and *History* by putting special emphasis upon heterogeneous subjects ? To the end of his days he will not be able to be more than an ignorant scholar.

The Importance of Li.

In the beginning, the ancient Kings founded their rule on benevolence (*Jen*[3]) and Justice (*Yi*[4]) ; the rules of proper conduct (*Li*) controlled their ingoings and outgoings, their entire path. If a person lifts his fur neck wrapper, bends his fingers, rubs it with his hand, the hairs which follow his 11 action are innumerable.[5] To try to act according to the *Odes* and *History* without making the rules of proper

---

[1] He replies only when and about what he is asked.
[2] Not forward.   [3] 仁.   [4] 義.
[5] So a perfect ceremony is likewise beautiful.

conduct (*Li*) your pattern, is like sounding a river with the fingers or using a spear to pound millet or using an awl in eating from a pot—it will not succeed. For if a person exalts the rules of proper conduct (*Li*), although he may not be renowned, he will be a learned man of principle. If he does not exalt the rules of proper conduct (*Li*), although he should investigate and discuss, he would be a useless scholar. If a person asks something evil, do not tell him ; if he wants to tell something that is evil, do not ask ; if he speaks about what is evil, do not listen [1] ; if he wishes to quarrel, do not discuss with him. If a student comes in the right way (*Tao*),[2] then only should he be given instruction. If he does not come in the right way (*Tao*), avoid him. For one must first reverence the rules of proper conduct (*Li*), and then only can he speak of the means of obtaining virtue (*Tao*) ; his speech must accord with the rules of proper conduct (*Li*), and then only can he speak of the principles of virtue (*Tao*) ; his demeanour must conform to the rules of proper conduct (*Li*), and then only can he speak of attaining to virtue (*Tao*). For talking about what one is not able to talk is heedless talking ; not talking about what one is able to talk is secretiveness ; talking without observing the listener's countenance is blindness. The superior man is not heedless, nor secretive, nor blind ; he is careful to adapt his speech to his audience The ode [3] says :—

12

[1] Cf., " If not right and proper, do not look : if not right and proper, do not listen ; if not right and proper, do not speak ; if not right and proper, do not move." *Analects*, XII, i. This saying has been cleverly embodied in the figures of the three monkeys.

[2] According to the rules of proper conduct.

[3] *Book of Odes*, II, VIII, ix, 3.

" They are neither discourteous nor are they negligent,
        Hence the Son of Heaven [1] has gifts for them " [2]—
this expresses my meaning.

Scholarship is to know things thoroughly.

To miss once in a hundred shots is sufficient to prevent a person from being classed as an expert shot ; to fail to go the last half step in a thousand *li* is enough to prevent a person from being classed as an expert driver ; to fail to understand the niceties of human relationships and to fail to concentrate on benevolence (*Jen*) and justice (*Yi*) is sufficient to prevent a person from being classed as an eminent scholar. Scholarship is to know things thoroughly and to unify them ; to be unified in learning and unified in teaching. The goodness of the man on the street is little, his lack of goodness is great ; as for example, Ch'ie, Chou,[3] and the robber Chih.[4] Scholarship must be complete and exhaustive.

The perfection of scholarship leads to the emperorship and satisfaction of all desires.

The superior man knows that his knowledge is not complete or perspicuous, insufficient to be classed as fine ; so he recites the Classics sentence by sentence in order to make them a part of himself,[5] he seeks to search into them in order to understand them ; [6] he puts himself into the places of the writers in order to understand their viewpoint ; he expels any wrong from his nature in order to grasp and mature

---

[1] The usual term for the emperor.

[2] Referring to the appearance of the feudal princes at the imperial court, at which time the Emperor gave them gifts as well as received their tribute.

[3] Two tyrant emperors.

[4] A rebel.

[5] Lit., he passes himself through them as a string passes through a " string " of cash.

[6] Lit., to go through them.

his knowledge : he makes his eye unwilling to see what is not right ; he makes his ears unwilling to hear what is not right; he makes his mouth unwilling to speak what is not right ; he makes his heart unwilling to think what is not right ; until he obtains what he most desires— the five colours his eyes love, the five sounds his ears love ; **13** the five tastes his mouth loves, the empire [1] which rejoices his heart. For this reason, he cannot be overturned by force ; mobs of common people cannot change him ; the country cannot move him. His life will be according to this, and his death will be according to it. This is what is meant by firmly grasping virtue. When he has firmly grasped virtue, he will be able to fix his mind without distraction ; when he has fixed his mind, he will be able to respond to the situation. When he can fix his mind and can respond to the situation, he can be classed as a perfect man. Heaven exhibits its brilliance ; Earth exhibits its vastness ; the superior man values his own completeness. [2]

[1] Being emperor ; the theory was that a perfectly virtuous man would inevitably obtain the highest honour—become emperor.

[2] His complete virtue. This is the Confucian trinity—Heaven, Earth, and Man.

BOOK II

SELF-CULTIVATION

When you see the good, you should be respectful and **13** investigate yourself to see if you have this virtue or not ; when you see evil, you should be anxious and examine yourself to see if you have it.[1] If you possess this goodness, you should be firm in it and prize it. If you possess **14** this evil, you should feel it as a calamity and hate yourself. Hence he who criticizes me and does so correctly is my teacher ; he who tells me that I am right and does so correctly is my friend ; he who flatters me mistreats me. Therefore the superior man exalts his teacher, clings to his friend, and greatly hates the man who mistreats him. If a man prizes and seeks for the good without ever being self-satisfied, and if he receives the admonitions of others and is able to be warned thereby, even though he did not desire to make progress, could he fail to do so ?

The small-minded man is just the opposite of this. He is extremely disorderly, but hates that others should criticize him ; he is extremely unworthy, but desires that others should consider him a Worthy ; his heart is like a tiger or wolf,[2] his actions are bestial, but yet he hates that others should consider him a public injury. He associates closely with those who flatter him, and is distant from those who

---

[1] Cf. *Analects* IV, xvii, for an identical statement.

[2] Avaricious.

would reprove or differ from him. The correction of error is for him a laughing matter, and great faithfulness is mistreatment. Although he does not desire to be ruined, can he avoid it ? The ode says :

"Now they agree, now they slander one another ;
　Things are in a very sad plight.
If they are given good counsel,
　They all oppose it ;
If they are given bad counsel,
　They all accord with it."

This is what I mean.[1]

Action should be according to Li.

The man who controls his feelings and cultivates his character by the method of everywhere and always doing right, although he may not live as long as Peng,[2] yet if he is strong in cultivating himself, his fame will equal that of Yao 15 and Yu.[3] That which enables a person to act appropriately to the occasion, that which enables him to be successful when in office,[4] and to bear poverty when out of office, is the rules of proper conduct (Li) and faithfulness. Whenever a person deals with flesh and blood,[5] purposes and plans, when it is according to the rules of proper conduct (Li), then his government will be successful. If he does not

---

[1] *Book of Odes*, II, v, i, 2. This ode refers to the perversion of judgment in the country ; good counsel is rejected and evil counsel is taken—which is the inevitable result when the government is in the hands of small-minded men.

[2] Who lived to be 700 years of age.

[3] Sage-Kings.

[4] The only gainful occupation for a Chinese gentleman is government office.

[5] Lit., blood and breath.

act according to the rules of proper conduct (*Li*), he is either wrong.[1] and confused, or careless and negligent. Food and drink, clothing, dwelling places, and movements, if in accordance with the rules of proper conduct (*Li*), will accord to the situation ; if not in accordance with the rules of proper conduct (*Li*), they will meet with ruin and calamity. A person's appearance, his bearing, his advancing and retiring when he hastens or walks slowly, if according to the rules of proper conduct (*Li*), is beautiful ; if not according to the rules of proper conduct (*Li*), then he will be haughty, intractable, depraved, banal, and rude. Hence a man who has no sense of what is proper (*Li*) is without a means of livelihood ; a matter which is not proper (*Li*) will not be brought to accomplishment ; a government without *Li* will not be peaceful. The ode says :

" Every rite (*Li*) is according to rule,

Every smile and word is as it should be "—
this is what I mean.[2]

To lead the people according to the right is to give them teaching ; to follow [3] the right is obedience. To lead people according to the wrong is to mislead them ; to follow the wrong is sycophancy. To know that the right is right and that the wrong is wrong is wisdom ; to think that the right is wrong and that the wrong is right is stupidity. To injure the virtuous is slander ; to maltreat the virtuous

Sundry ethical definitions.

16

---

[1] Unreasonable, or against nature.

[2] *Book of Odes*, II, vi, vi, 3. A sacrificial ode. The reference is to the promise of good fortune and success when the sacrifices are properly performed, as set out in the rest of the verse. Cf. p. 227.

[3] The metaphor is that of a leader and followers in singing.

is oppression. To say that the right is right and the wrong is wrong is uprightness. To steal goods is theft. Hidden actions are deceit. Easy talk is boasting. By turns showing alacrity in doing things and neglecting them is inconstancy. To hold fast to the motive of gain and to discard justice (*Yi*) is to be the most injurious possible kind of person. To have heard much is to have a wide knowledge; to have heard little is to be shallow; to have seen little is to be ignorant. To progress with difficulty is to be slow-going; to forget easily is to be leaky.[1] A little and ordered is to be well-controlled; much and in confusion is to be disorderly.

THE METHOD OF CONTROLLING THE BODY AND NOURISHING THE MIND [2]

Control oneself by *Li*.

17

If a person's animal feelings are strong and severe, then let him weaken them so that he may harmonize himself. If his thoughts are crafty and secretive, then let him unify them so that they may be easily good. If he is bold and violent, then let him guide his feelings, so as to control them. If he is hasty, talkative, and seeking for gain, then let him moderate himself so as to be large-minded. If he is inferior, tardy in important matters, and avaricious, then let him raise himself to a high purpose. If his talents are ordinary or inferior, then let him be importunate to make friends with a teacher. If he is impertinent and proud,

[1] Metaphor of a leaky house.

[2] This seems to be a title to the section given by Hsüntze himself. The methods of controlling the body and nourishing the mind were much sought after by the superstitious of the day, and later by the Taoists; long life and happiness were thought to be secured by this means. Here Hsüntze annexes this interest to Confucianism.

then let him reflect on the calamities that will ensue. If he is simple, sincere, upright, and ingenuous,[1] then let him make himself harmonious by the rules of proper conduct (*Li*) and music. Of all the methods of controlling the body and nourishing the mind, there is none more direct than proper conduct (*Li*), none more important than getting a teacher, none more divine than to have but one desire. These are what I mean by the methods of controlling the body and nourishing the mind.

If a person's will is cultivated, then he can be prouder than the rich and the honourable; if he has emphasized the right Way (*Tao*) and justice (*Yi*), then he can despise kings and dukes; he can contemplate that which is within him and despise outer things. It is said: the superior man employs things; the small-minded man is the servant of things—this expresses what I mean. To work hard **18** but to have his mind peaceful—do that! To have small gain but much justice (*Yi*)—do that! To serve an unjust (*Yi*) prince and obtain high position is not as good as serving a poor prince [2] and being able to follow the right. The good farmer will not refuse to plough because there is no rain: the good merchant will not refuse to trade because he loses money. The scholar or superior man is not remiss concerning the right Way (*Tao*) because of poverty. *Cultivate the will.*

If a man's deportment is respectful, his heart loyal and faithful, his methods according to the rules of proper conduct (*Li*) and justice (*Yi*), and his ruling passions love and *The virtuous are kept in office, and the evil are rejected.*

[1] A type of character combining stupidity and honesty still recognized as common among the Chinese.

[2] Of a little, harassed country.

benevolence (*Jen*), were he to rule over the empire, although he were harassed by the four barbarian tribes, people would not fail to honour him. If he presses forward to perform an arduous undertaking, but is willing to yield to others an affair that is readily done or pleasant to do, if he is upright and sincere, if he holds to his undertakings and is careful of details, were he to rule over the empire, although he were harassed by the four barbarian tribes, the people would not fail to keep him in office. If his deportment is haughty and prejudiced, his heart scheming and deceitful, his methods those of Shentze [1] and Micius, [2] and his ruling passions

19 unregulated and vile, were he to rule over the country, although he were successful in all directions, the people would not fail to despise him. If he is careless, timid, and if, when there is an arduous undertaking, he turns it over to another, if he is persuasive and keen for it and if, when there is an affair readily done and pleasant, he shows no indirection in seeking it, if he is depraved and not upright, if he becomes careless when he has to do difficult things, were he to rule over the whole country, although he were successful in all directions, he would not fail to be rejected.

Manner of walking.

In walking be reverend and upright and do not get stained by mud. In walking do not bend your head as though

20 you were going to hit something. If you meet a companion, bow first; do not be afraid. For if a gentleman only wishes to cultivate himself, he is not offended at meeting a commoner.

[1] 慎子, lived during the time of King Süan of Ts'i, 342–24 B.C. Taught that the worthy need not be advanced.

[2] 墨子, who opposed *Li*.

The bay Chi [1] could go a thousand *li* in a day; an old broken-down horse can make that distance in ten days too. If you wish to exhaust the inexhaustible, to pursue the illimitable, even if you go so far as to break your bones and utterly destroy your sinews, to the end of your days you will not be able to reach your goal. But if there is a limit, then, although a thousand *li* [2] are a great distance, whether slowly or quickly, whether first or last, how could you fail to arrive at your goal? But the person who does not know the Way (*Tao*), can he exhaust the inexhaustible or pursue the illimitable? Can his purpose ever see its fulfilment? Hence there is no reason why the problems of "hardness and whiteness", [3] "likeness and unlikeness," [4]

---

[1] A famous legendary horse.

[2] Meaning a great distance.

[3] Doctrines of the Neo-Micians, Kung Sen-lung and Huei Shih. Kung Sen-lung's "Discussion of Hardness and Whiteness", reads: "Can 'hardness', 'whiteness', and 'stone' be three things? No. Can they be two things? Yes. The eye seeing a stone, perceives it is white, but it does not perceive it is hard, so calls it a 'white stone'. The hand feeling a stone perceives it is hard, but does not perceive it is white, so calls it a 'hard stone'. This shows that hardness and whiteness cannot be united into one." Because they are perceived by two different senses. Among the ancient Chinese, as among the ancient Greeks, the concept of a "soul" or "consciousness" into which the secondary qualities of things could be put and by which they could be synthesized had not been developed.

"Likeness and unlikeness" refers to the investigation into similarities and differences or it may refer to the Neo-Mician doctrines found in Chuang-tze 天下篇, of the difference between being similar in the large and similar in the small. Being alike in being between heaven and earth is called being alike in the large. Things are of different kinds, what is alike is called being alike in the small. This is the difference between being similar in the large and similar in the small. In this passage it is also said: All things are completely alike and completely dissimilar. This is what is called being similar and dissimilar in the large. We say that all things

E

" whether there is thickness or no thickness " [1] should not be investigated, but the superior man does not discuss them; he stops at the limit of profitable discussion. Wonderful and gigantic conduct is certainly difficult, but the conduct of the superior man stops at the limit of what is profitable. 21 For the scholar says, " Wait," and he [2] stops and waits for me; I go on and catch up with him. Then how can it be that either slowly or quickly, either first or last, he [3] cannot reach the goal together with him ? [4] For a lame tortoise can go a thousand *li* by not resting a half step; by heaping up earth and not stopping, a mound or hill can be made high. By stopping its source and opening its channel, a large or small river can be dried up; by alternately advancing and retreating, going to the left and the right, the six noble steeds [5] could not arrive at the goal. The ability of two men may be greatly different; how could it be that a lame tortoise could be equal to the six noble steeds ? Yet

are nevertheless things, all are alike in this respect, hence all things are similar. If you separate and distinguish them, then a man's ears, eyes, nose, mouth, face, members, the branches, leaves, and flowers of herbs and trees are really all dissimilar; hence things are completely dissimilar. This teaching is one form of relativism.

[1] In Chuangtze, 天 下 篇, it is also said : What has no thickness cannot be increased in thickness. If its size is a thousand *li*, it has no thickness ; meaning that which is the limit of thickness cannot have thickness. A thousand *li* here means the limit of thickness. Because that which has no thickness cannot be increased in thickness, that which has infinite thickness also has no thickness, since it cannot be increased in thickness.

For other examples of such logical puzzles, cf. *H.*, p. 219 ff.

[2] The teacher.

[3] The scholar.

[4] The teacher.

[5] A famous legendary team of horses.

the lame tortoise arrives at the goal and the six noble steeds do not. There is no other reason for it than that the one keeps on and the other does not.

Though the road (*Tao*) be short, if a person does not travel on it, he will never get there; though a matter be small, if he does not do it, it will never be accomplished; if a man takes many days of leisure, he will not show much progress. He who loves to follow the Way and carries it out is a scholar. He who has a firm purpose and treads the Way is a superior man. He who is inexhaustibly wise and illustrious in virtue is the sage.[1] *Necessity of the Way (Tao).*

22 A man who is without a rule for action is bewildered; if he has a rule, but does not understand it, he is timid; if he relies upon the rule and knows of what kind it is, then only is he calm. *Necessity of a rule.*

The rules of proper conduct (*Li*) is that whereby a person's character is corrected; a teacher is that whereby the rules of proper conduct (*Li*) are corrected. Without rules for proper conduct (*Li*) how can I correct myself? Without a teacher how can I know what particular action is according to the rules of proper conduct? If a person is to live according to the rules of proper conduct (*Li*), then his emotions must be naturally those that go with the rules of proper conduct (*Li*); if he is to speak like his teacher, then his knowledge must be equal to that of his teacher. When a person's emotions are naturally in accordance with the rules of proper conduct (*Li*), and his knowledge is equal to that of his teacher, then he is a sage. For to go contrary to the rules for proper action *The rules of proper conduct and the teacher.*

---

[1] These are the three grades of virtue and wisdom regularly mentioned by Hsüntze.

(*Li*) is the same as to be without a rule for action; to go contrary to one's teacher is the same as to be without a teacher. Not to hold as right the ways of one's teacher and to prefer one's own ways, is like a blind man distinguishing colours or a deaf man distinguishing sounds; there is no way of getting rid of confusion and error. Hence the student follows the rules of proper conduct (*Li*) and the ways of his teacher. But the teacher considers himself to be the correct measure of all things and honours that which nature has implanted within him. The ode says:

> " He has not learned, he did not know,
>   But he followed the laws of God "—

this expresses what I mean.[1]

Character-istics of good and bad men. Upright, honest, obedient, and reverent to elders—such an one can be said to be a good young man. Add to that a love of study, respectfulness, brilliancy, and not feeling himself superior to his equals—such an one can become a superior man. Weak, stupid, afraid to work, without humility or a sense of shame, but fond of eating and drinking—such an one can be called a bad young man. Add to that the qualities of being dissolute, overbearing, disobedient, dangerous, injurious, and disrespectful—such an one can be called an unfortunate young man, who, when led into wrong, may suffer capital punishment.

Heaven rewards the virtuous. If a person treats the aged and honourable as they should be treated, men in middle life will give him their allegiance.

---

[1] *Book of Odes*, III, I, vii, 7. The meaning of this passage is that the way of the teacher secretly agrees with the way of Heaven, as King Wen unconsciously followed the laws of Heaven, although he had not studied them.

If he treats leniently the unworthy, then those who are wise will gather to him. If in his actions he does not pay attention whether others know of them or not, and gives without seeking for a return, then the worthy and unworthy will unite in honouring him. If a man has these three characteristics, although he had great misfortunes, would Heaven fail to do as he wished ? [1]

23

The superior man only slightly seeks for profit ; he is quick to keep away from evil. He is timorous in fleeing shame and courageous in doing the right (*Tao*).

Only slightly seek profit.

The superior man, when poor, has a profound purpose ; when rich or honourable, he is respectful ; when retired, he does not become lazy ; when working hard or fatigued, his bearing is not careless. When angry, he does not go to the extreme and snatch things away ; when happy, he does not go to the extreme and give things away. The superior man, when poor, has a profound purpose, because he stresses benevolence (*Jen*). When rich or honourable, he is respectful, because he humbles himself. When retired, he does not become lazy, because he carefully selects the principles of his life. When working hard or fatigued, his bearing is not careless, because he esteems the beautiful.[2] When angry he does not go to extremes and snatch things away ; when happy, he does not go to extremes and give things away, because in this way he overcomes selfishness. The *History* says—

The characteristics of the superior man when poor,

24

rich, retired, fatigued, angry, and happy.

---

[1] The Chinese implies the answer, No.
[2] Not the beauty of painting, sculpture, or music, but the beauty of perfect action.

> " Without any selfish likings
>   Reverence the Way (*Tao*) of the Kings ;
> Without any selfish dislikes,
>   Reverence the path of the Kings." [1]

This speaks of the superior man's ability to make public spirit overcome selfish desires.

[1] *Book of History*, V, IV, 14. Also quoted on p. 185.

BOOK IV

ON HONOUR AND SHAME

The general distinction between honour and shame
depends on the usual circumstances attendant on being
peaceful or uneasy, beneficial or injurious to others.[2]
The man who first thinks of justice (*Yi*) and secondly of gain
is honourable; he who first thinks of gain and second of
justice (*Yi*) is shameful. He who has this honour ordinarily
keeps his office; [3] he who has this shame is ordinarily out of

The general
distinctions
between
being
honoured
and shame-
ful.

---

[1] The first half of the present text of this book does not relate to the
subject of the book; which fact would seem to indicate that it is spurious
or added subsequently to the original writing. The various books of Hsüntze's
writing are usually quite unified compositions, and the first section always
relates to the subject of the book. The usual Chinese practice is to entitle
a book by its first words, as with some books of the Bible; in this case
that criterion would indicate that the book should begin with the words,
"Honour and shame," thereby eliminating the first half of the book. The
omitted portion is similar to Book III, which also does not seem to be genuine.
Its vocabulary is similar but simpler than that of Hsüntze; it does not
contain anything new or significant; it contains a description of the superior
man on the lines of that in the last part of Book II; an exaltation of
sincerity; a classification of court officials as learned officers, public-
spirited officers, upright officers, and mean-minded men; the evils of
prejudicedness, etc. The omitted portion of Book IV contains homilies
on the subjects of respectfulness, brawling, courage, and grumbling, in the
Confucian manner. There is a difference in the literary quality of the two
parts of the books.

[2] Cf. Mencius, II, I, iv for a saying that benevolence brings glory and
the opposite brings disgrace, and Mencius, VI, I, xvi for distinguishing
human nobility and Heaven's nobility.

[3] In ancient China the only "gentleman's" occupation was to be a
government official. Although there was a feudal nobility, theoretically
anyone of merit could win his way to high office and distinction. However,

office. The man in office rules others ; the man out of office is ruled by others. This is the general distinction between honour and shame. He who is honest and upright is ordinarily at peace in his mind and beneficial to others ; he who is dissolute and overbearing is ordinarily uneasy in his mind and injurious to others. He who is at peace in his mind and beneficial to others is ordinarily joyous and calm ; he who is uneasy in his mind and injurious to others is ordinarily in grief and dangerous circumstances. He who is joyous and calm ordinarily has a long life [1] ; he who is in grief and danger ordinarily dies young.[2] These are the usual circumstances of being peaceful or uneasy, beneficial or injurious.

Characteristics of men, from the emperor down to the evil-minded man.

Though Nature produced all men, there are distinctions whereby they take different stations in life. The emperor takes his station over the empire because his virtue and character are great, his wisdom and power of thought are very illustrious. The feudal nobles [3] take their station over their dukedoms because their government is lawful, their calling the people up for public service is timely,[4] their hearing of law-suits and their judicial decisions are fair ; on the one hand they are

---

the situation was not as ideal as Hsüntze makes it to be ; his word " ordinarily " covers a multitude of exceptions. The general tendency of the Confucians was to idealize history, with a view to making it a moral lesson for posterity.

[1] Esteemed as a great happiness, not only because of the extended span of days, but because of the honours and authority in the hands of the patriarchal head of the clan.

[2] The Chinese word means " under thirty ".

[3] Dukes and marquises.

[4] Military service should not interfere with agriculture, especially with the times for planting and harvesting the crop.

willing to obey the orders of the emperor and on the other
they are willing to protect their subjects.[1] The officers and
prefects [2] hold their lands and cities because their purpose
and actions are cultivated ; they are skilled in meeting
officials ; on the one hand they are willing to obey their
superiors and on the other hand they are willing to take
their responsibilities. The officials and all the government
servants receive their emoluments and rank because they
preserve the laws and regulations, the weights and **16**
measures, capital and other punishments, local maps, and
Domesday books, without knowing their meaning, but they
carefully guard them, not daring to decrease or increase them,
and hand them down from father to son [3] for the use of the
king or duke—in this way, although the three great dynasties
are gone, their methods of government are preserved.
Ordinary people get warm clothes, full stomachs, long life,
and plenitude of days, and escape from capital and other
punishments when they show filial piety and are reverent
to their elders, when they are honest, when they act
carefully and toil laboriously, when they manage their
affairs but do not dare to be indolent or proud. Evil men
gain uneasiness, shame, death, and punishment because
they excuse false doctrines and gloss over evil speech ;

[1] This was a period when the emperor was a mere figurehead and the
feudal nobles did as they pleased. Hsüntze is speaking of the ideal, not the
real. No wonder the philosophers were called impractical by their own
generation !

[2] 士 大 夫, two grades of high officials who governed minor divisions
of territory. They were not part of the feudal nobility, but were selected
by the heads of the various states.

[3] Not so much the oral tradition as the cumbersome pieces of bamboo
then used for books.

bĕcause they do strange things [1]; they slander, boast, assault and rob; they are dissolute, overbearing, proud, and oppressive; they change from one party to another [2] to save their lives shamefully in the midst of a turbulent world. They gain uneasiness and danger because their reflections 17 are not deep, their choices are not careful, their decisions as to what to take and what to refuse are inferior and dilatory.

Characteristics of the superior man and the mean-minded man.

The superior man and the mean-minded man may be the same in ability, original nature, knowledge, and capacity; they love honour and hate shame; they love what is beneficial and hate what is injurious—this is that wherein the superior man and the mean-minded man are alike. If, however, you compare the way (*Tao*) by which they seek their goals, then they are different. The mean-minded man is strong at boasting, yet desires that others should believe in him; he is strong on imposing on people, yet desires that people should be attached to him; his actions are those of birds and beasts, yet he desires that others should consider him virtuous. In thought he finds it difficult to know things; in action he finds it difficult to find peace; and in what he supports he finds it difficult to be established. In the end he will certainly never get what he wants and will certainly meet with what he hates. On the other hand, the superior man is faithful, and so desires that others should believe in him; he is loyal, and so desires that others should be attached to him; he cultivates uprightness; in ruling he is

---

[1] This prejudice of an age of custom against novelty has been perpetuated by Confucianism.

[2] Act as turncoats.

discriminating, and so desires that others should consider him good. In thought he finds it easy to know things, in action he finds it easy to find peace ; in what he supports he finds it easy to be established. In the end he will certainly gain what he wants, and will certainly not meet with what he hates. For this reason, when out of office, he cannot be unknown ; when in office, he will certainly be greatly illustrious. If he should die, his name would yet be illustrious. The small-minded man always stretches his neck and stands on tiptoe and likes to say, "That man's knowledge and ability is certainly superior to that of ordinary men."[1] For he does not know that he himself is no whit different from that other man. Thus the superior man looks at things rightly, but the small-minded man looks at things wrongly. For if a person thoroughly investigates the knowledge and capacities of the small-minded man, it will be seen that he has more than appears, and that he could do what the superior man does. For example, the man of Yueh[2] is satisfied with Yueh ; the man of Ts'u[3] is satisfied with Ts'u ; the superior man is satisfied with central China.[4] This is not because of his knowledge, capacity, **18** ability, or original nature ; it is because of differences in looking at things and in habits. Benevolent, righteous, and virtuous acts are ordinarily safe methods of action ; however, it is possible that they may be dangerous.[5] Filthi-

---

[1] I.e., " that man " is not an ordinary man, but a Worthy.

[2] A semi-barbaric state on the south-east border of China.

[3] A less barbaric feudal state south of the rest of China.

[4] The central and more civilized states. Lit. 夏. (A textual emendation.)

[5] Hsüntze admits this possibility, b,ut passes on and disregards it. This act did not alter in his mind the Confucian doctrine (which was not original with him) that virtue brought prosperity and vice failure.

ness, lying and cheating, assault and robbery are ordinarily dangerous methods of action; however, it is possible that they may be safe. The superior man considers (*Tao*) what is usual; the small-minded man considers (*Tao*) what is unusual.[1]

People fundamentally alike.

Everyone has characteristics in common with others. When hungry he desires to eat; when cold he desires to be warm; when toiling he desires to rest; he wants what is beneficial and hates what is injurious—with these attitudes man is born; he has them without waiting to learn them; in these respects Yao [2] and Ch'ie [3] were alike. The eye distinguishes white and black, beautiful and ugly; the ear distinguishes clear and confused tones and sounds; the mouth distinguishes sour and salt, sweet and bitter; the nose distinguishes perfume and fragrance, strong-smelling and rank odours; the bones, body, the skin, and the wrinkles distinguish cold and hot, sickness and itching. Man is born with these senses too; he has them without waiting to learn them; in these respects Yao and Ch'ie were alike.

Becoming a Yao or a Ch'ie is dependent on cultivation.

A person can become a Yao or a Yu; he can become a Ch'ie or a Chih [4]; he can become a day labourer or an artisan; he can become a farmer or a merchant; it depends on what training he has accumulated [5] from his ways of

[1] Therefore the small man thinks of the few who are successful in evil, and hopes to be successful like them.

[2] A great and good emperor.

[3] An evil tyrant.

[4] A notorious robber.

[5] Lit. " what he has accumulated." The Chinese language does not distinguish between things which can be counted and those that cannot, between the many and the much; virtue and other accomplishments are commonly spoken of as capable of quantitative increase or 積.

looking at things and his habits. To be a Yao or **19**
a Yu ordinarily brings peacefulness and honour ; to be a
Ch'ie or a Chih ordinarily brings danger and shame ; to be
a Yao or a Yu ordinarily means pleasure and ease ; to be a
labourer, artisan, farmer, or merchant, ordinarily means
trouble and toil ; but most men are the latter and few are
the former. Why is it ? Because their natures are low.
Yao and Yu were not born great [1] ; but they began in trouble,
and completed their development by artificial cultivation ;
they had to wait and strain all their resources and then
only could they be perfect.

Man by birth certainly is a small-minded man. Without **Man by birth**
a teacher or a set of principles, he can only think of profit.[2] **is small-**
Man by birth certainly is a small-minded man. If in addition **minded.**
he meets an evil age, and is influenced by bad customs, from
the small he will repeat their smallness, from the evil he will get
evil. Unless the superior man gains skill to meet the situation,
he will not have the means wherewith to open up a way for
goodness to enter his heart. Now, how are men's mouths
and minds to know the rules of proper conduct (*Li*) and
justice (*Yi*) ? How are they to learn courtesy ? How are
they to learn modesty and shame, firmness of principle and
the accumulation of virtue ? But they only eat and chew,
find things good and fill themselves full. If a man has no
teacher or set of principles, his mind is just like his mouth
or belly.[3]

---

[1] Lit., " wholly as they were."
[2] As the goal of his activities.
[3] There is a play on words ; the word for belly also means " the seat of
the mind ", and is used in the latter sense above.

Parable of
the man who
had never
seen good
food.

Now suppose that a man from birth had never seen meat or grain, but had only seen pulse, coarse greens, and bran, then he would be very well satisfied with them. But if suddenly he should clearly discern someone holding meat and grain coming to him, in astonishment he would gaze at it and

20 say "How funny these things are!" He would smell them and they would gratify his nostrils; he would taste them and they would be sweet in his mouth; he would eat them and they would be pleasant to his body. Then he would certainly get rid of his old diet and take the new food.

Men do not
take to the
Way of the
Kings,
although it is
good, because
their natures
are bad.

Now with this parable compare the Way (*Tao*) of the ancient Kings, the unifying principles of benevolence (*Jen*) and justice (*Yi*). By them people live in society; by them they can preserve and nourish themselves; by them they can make their ways elegant and beautiful: by them they can be peaceful and secure. Now compare the Way (*Tao*) of Ch'ie and Chih—it is unlike the other. Is it not just as unlike as the meat and grain is unlike bran? But most men follow the latter and few follow the former. Why? Because their nature is low. This lowness is the common misfortune of the world, the great calamity and great injury of man. Hence it is said, The benevolent (*Jen*) man likes to tell men the Way. He tells them of it; he proclaims it to them; he spreads it abroad; he repeats it; he hands it down; he emphasizes it; then the man who was unintelligent will suddenly become intelligent; he who was narrow will suddenly be broad; he who was stupid will suddenly be

21 wise. If this be not so, what benefit will there be if T'ang or Wu were over the people, what harm will

there be if Ch'ie and Chou were over the people ? [1]   While
T'ang and Wu lived, the country obeyed, was well-governed
and prosperous ; while Ch'ie and Chou lived, the country
obeyed, was ill-governed and suffered calamity.[2] Looking
at it in this way, how can it be that this was against the
disposition of man ?   Certainly he can be either like the
latter or like the former !

THE DESIRES OF MEN

For food they want to have meat.[3] They want to have Natural
their clothing beautiful and embroidered. In travelling Desires.
they want to have carriages or horses. In addition they
desire abundant riches and stored up wealth. However,
when a man is poor for many years together, he does not
realize that his desires are not satisfied—these are the facts
of man's nature.

Now in real life, man knows how to raise chickens, dogs, Riches come
pigs, and swine, and also how to raise cattle and sheep ; yet in from curbing
eating he does not use wine and pork ; he may have a surplus desires by
of money [4] in storehouses, yet for his clothing he dares not forethought,
and poverty
use silk. The economical man may have baskets and boxes from the
opposite.
of stores, yet in travelling he does not use carriages or horses.
Why is this ?   Not because he does not desire these things.

---

[1] Unless a good ruler can bring about the prosperity which naturally
follows upon virtue, he is worthless.

[2] The people follow the disposition of their leader to good or evil. Cf.
Great Learning, IX, 4.

[3] This term for meat 芻豢 (which is so translated throughout this
chapter) refers to the flesh of the domestic animals—horse, sheep, ox, and
dog ; pork, which is the preferred meat of the Chinese to-day, is not included.

[4] Lit., " knives and cloth."

It is because he thinks far into the future and is afraid that he will not have the means whereby to perpetuate his wealth. Hence he both economizes and controls his desires. He gathers in and stores his wealth in order to perpetuate it. Is not this thinking far into the future very fine ? Now people who live carelessly and who are of shallow knowledge do not realize this. In their food they are very extravagant ; **22** they do not think of the future ; suddenly they are in difficult circumstances and are poor. This is why they do not escape freezing, starvation, using gourds for money-bags,[1] and becoming the putrid carcasses [2] in the ditches.

The Way of the Kings is great and produces forethought.

Now what about the Way (*Tao*) of the former Kings, the unifying principles of benevolence (*Jen*) and justice (*Yi*), the function of the *History*, the *Odes*, the *Rites* (*Li*), and the *Music* ? [3] They are certainly the greatest thoughts of the world ; they will make all people who are born into the world think far into the future, and they will protect all generations for ever. Their influence is vast ; their accumulated virtue is great ; their effects reach out very far.

Guide yourself by the Classics.

Unless a person thoroughly cultivates himself so as to be a superior man, he cannot have knowledge.[4] Hence it is said : A short rope cannot draw water from a deep well ; he whose knowledge is limited cannot converse with those who

[1] Being beggars.

[2] Of beggars.

[3] The Classics ; in Hsüntze's day the canon had not yet been officially formed, and the character 經 was not used with them, only the single characters 書 詩 禮 樂, so I have translated by a single English word. The *Book of Music* is now lost.

[4] This sentence is a doublet in one in Book XIX.

reach to the status of a Sage.   Then the function of the *Odes*,
the *History*, the *Rites* (*Li*), and the *Music* is certainly not
for the ordinary man to understand.   Hence it is said :
Concentrate on them [1] and then you can know more ; possess
them, and you can be enduring [2] ; be versed in them and you
can be successful ; think on them and you can be peaceful ;
repeatedly follow and investigate them and you will love
them the more.   By them control your passions and **23**
you will gain benefit ; by them make a reputation, and
you will have honour ; by them live in society and you
will have harmony ; by them live alone and you will be
satisfied.

What is man's pleasure and purpose ?   To be honourable
as the emperor, to be so wealthy as to own the country [3]—
this is what men's passions alike desire.   But if men's desires
are given rein, then their authority could not be endured,
and things would not be sufficient to satisfy them.   Hence
the ancient Kings invented the rules of proper conduct
(*Li*) and justice (*Yi*) for men in order to divide them [4] ;
causing them to have the classes of noble and base, the
disparity between the aged and the young, and the distinction
between the wise and the stupid, the able and the powerless ;
all to cause men to assume their duties and each one to get
his proper position ; then only can the amount and grade
of their emoluments be made fitting to their position.   This is
the way (*Tao*) of living in society and having harmony and

The desires of everyone cannot be satisfied ; hence control them by Li and Yi.

[1] These Classics. For Hsüntze's part in forming the canon of the Classics,
cf. *H.*, p. 188 ff., 69 f.

[2] Not drop out of the path of learning.

[3] All the land belonged to the emperor and was held from him.

[4] Into social grades ; everybody cannot be emperor.

unity. For when the benevolent (*Jen*) man is in control, the farmers by their strength will be expert at the fields; the merchants by their knowledge of values will be expert at using wealth; all kinds of artisans by their skill will be expert at using tools; none of those above the grade of Officer and Prefect, up to the Duke and Marquis will fail to fulfil the duties of their office according to benevolence (*Jen*), generosity, wisdom and power—then this will be called the Great Equableness. Then whether a man's emolument is the whole empire, he will not think it too much for himself; or whether he is gate-keeper, receiver of guests, keeper of the gate bar, or night watchman,[1] he will not think it too little for himself. Hence it is said: Irregular but uniform, oppressive but favourable, unlike but alike—these are the human relationships. The ode says:

" He received the tribute of the States, large and small,

He was very generous to those states under him "—
this expresses what I mean.[2]

---

[1] Very humble posts.

[2] *Book of Odes*, IV, III, iv, 5. This is the next to the last ode—hence the canon must have been complete in the time of Hsüntze. But Hsüntze also quotes some lost odes. This ode is an eulogy of King T'ang, founder of the Shang dynasty. When the feudal princes brought tribute, the Emperor gave them gifts in return.

BOOK V

AGAINST PHYSIOGNOMY

Physiognomy [1] did not exist in ancient times [2]; a student **1** should not consider (*Tao*) it. Among the ancients there was Ku-pu-tze-ch'ing; at the present time there is Tang Chü of Liang [3] who physiognomizes men's figure and features, and tells their good or bad fortune. The common people praise them—the ancients did not have this practice, and the student should not speak (*Tao*) of it. For to physiognomize a person's appearance is not as good as to consider his heart; [4] considering his heart is not as good as to select his principles. The appearance is subordinate to the heart; the heart is subordinate to the principles. When a person's principles are upright and his heart obeys them, although his physiognomy be repulsive, yet if his heart and principles are good, his physiognomy will not hinder him from being a superior man. Although his physiognomy be good, yet if his heart and principles are evil, his physiognomy will not

Evil and virtue are according to the state of the heart, not the physiognomy.

---

[1] There were and still are in China men who profess to tell fortunes by the looks or " bumps " of persons. These are the " Physiognomists ". This practice is more than physiognomy in the Western sense of the word in that it professes to foretell the future, as well as indicate the character of a person. The Han dynasty index to the Imperial library includes twenty-four volumes on this subject. This book is an example of how Hsüntze attacked superstition.

[2] An appeal to the prejudice against anything new—characteristic of Confucianism. But Hsüntze backs up this appeal by arguments against the inadequacy of the method.

[3] A state whose capital was at the present Nanking.

[4] Chinese uses the " heart " meaning the " mind ".

revent him from being a small-minded man. The superior
man is called fortunate ; the small-minded man is called
unfortunate ; hence to be tall or short, small or big, handsome
or ugly in physiognomy does not prognosticate good or evil
fortune. The ancients did not have this practice, and the
student should not regard (*Tao*) it.

Examples
from history.
For the Emperor Yao was tall, and the Emperor Shun
was short ; King Wen was tall, and Duke Chou was short ;
Confucius was tall, and Tze Kung [1] was short. Formerly
there was an official of Duke Ling [2] of Wei, named
Kung Swen-lü, whose body was seven feet long [3] and his
face three feet long and three inches wide, with nose, eyes,
and ears all there ; yet his fame filled the whole empire.
2 Swen Shou-ao of Ts'u was a countryman from the district
of Chi-sze [4] ; he was bald,[5] his left leg was longer than
the other, but by his virtue and without using military force
he took his place as the virtual ruler of Ts'u. Duke She
Tze-kao [6] was very small, short, and thin ; he walked as
though he could not support his clothes ; but during the
rebellion of Duke Pe [7] he caused **Yün Tze-si** [8] and Sze-ma

[1] Probably Chung Kung, a distinguished disciple of Confucius. Also
mentioned on p. 110, q.v.

[2] 534–493 B.C.

[3] The ancient foot was shorter than the present one.

[4] Now called Kuang Chou in Honan.

[5] In China baldness is considered shameful.

[6] Viscount of Ts'u.

[7] The heir-apparent of Ts'u. In Ts'u the oldest son did not necessarily
succeed to the throne of his father. This man was the grandson of King
P'ing, who reigned 578–516 B.C. The ruler of Ts'u had only the title of
Viscount ; but within his own state he was called " King ", and so the heir-
apparent was styled " Duke ", whereas in other states he would only be
entitled " Prefect ".

[8] The oldest son of King P'ing.

Tze-chi [1] both to be put to death. Duke She Tze-kao came in, seized Ts'u, killed Duke Pe, and tranquillized the state of Ts'u like turning over his hand.[2] His benevolence (*Jen*), justice (*Yi*), merit and fame overshadows all down to later ages.

In ancient times, people did not estimate tallness and measure bigness nor consider weights ; were not they nevertheless successful ? [3] Can it be that they considered whether a person's physiognomy was short, small or big, handsome or ugly ? Yet the physiognomy of King Yen of Hsü [4] was such that he was very short-sighted and had to look up to see a horse ; the physiognomy of Confucius was such that his face was like a rumpled square [5] ; the physiognomy of Duke Chou was such that his body was like a broken tree [6] ; the physiognomy of Kao Yao [7] was such that his complexion was like a peeled melon [8] ; the physiognomy of Hung Yao [9] was such that the skin of his face could not be seen [10] ; the 3 physiognomy of Ch'uan Shuo [11] was such that his body was as

[1] Another son of King P'ing.

[2] So easily.

[3] Without physiognomy they produced many great men.

[4] Another writer says of this cripple that he could not look down, and had no bones. He lived in the time of King Mu (1001–947 B.C.).

[5] The meaning of this character is uncertain. It is also interpreted as meaning " hairy in the face " or " two eyed ".

[6] Humpbacked.

[7] Minister of Shun.

[8] Yang Liang says that this means light green ; we may conjecture that it means hairless, without even any down.

[9] Minister of King Wen.

[10] Too hairy.

[11] Minister at the close of the Yin dynasty.

if the dorsal spines of a fish were sticking out [1]; the physiognomy of Yi Yin [2] was such that on his face there was no beard or eyebrows. Yu was lame and T'ang was paralysed [3]; Shun had two pupils in one eye. [4]

Should the student discuss people's purposes and compare their scholarship; or should he directly consider their differences in size, distinguish whether they are handsome or ugly and be cheated and scorned? The ancients Ch'ie and Chou [5] were very tall, attractive, and handsome, the greatest heroes in the world. Their sinews and muscles were agile and strong; they could stand up against a hundred men. Yet they were killed, their dynasty was destroyed; they became the greatest criminals in the country, and later ages called them evil—this too must be considered. These evils were not because they suffered from their features but from a narrow knowledge and low ideas.

The " clever fellows " of the day.

Suppose we consider one of the " clever fellows " of the villages of the present confused age, none of whom fail to be handsome and attractive, and have unique clothes and womanish ornaments, and who resemble a girl in physical constitution and behaviour; no woman would be unwilling to have such an one for her husband; no unmarried girl

[1] Humpbacked.

[2] Prime Minister in the Shang dynasty.

[3] Partially paralysed.

[4] One Chinese commentator says that this is merely saying that he was doubly wise. In the present text Yao is also said to have had two pupils; but the addition of his name spoils the regular recurrence of the four character lines of which this passage is exclusively composed. The *History* records this fact of Shun, but not of Yao; hence this character should probably be dropped from the text.

[5] Two tyrant emperors, who were the incarnation of everything evil.

would be unwilling to have him for her fiancé, to leave her father's house and be glad to elope with him, and stand shoulder to shoulder with him; yet an average prince would err in making him an official, an average father would err in taking him for a son, an average older brother would **4** err in taking him for a younger brother, and an average man would err in taking him for a friend. Soon he will be bound and taken before the magistrate, and slain before a great crowd.[1] He will not fail to call upon Heaven and weep and cry, bitterly grieving over his present situation and remorseful over his younger days. This is not because he suffered from his features, but from a narrow knowledge and low ideas. Then which would the student rely upon?[2]

    *   *   *   *   *

Wherein is it that man is truly man? Because **5** he makes distinctions.[3] When he is hungry he desires to eat; when he is cold he desires to be warm; when he is tired he desires to rest; he likes what is helpful and dislikes what is injurious—man is born with these ways of acting; he does not have to wait to get them.[4] In these matters Yu and Ch'ie were alike. However, man is not truly man

Man is truly man because he makes distinctions.

---

[1] He will become a great criminal.

[2] This chapter should end here, though in the present text there is added three times as much. But the subject of physiognomy is dropped, and while the remainder of this book might belong to the preceding book, I consider it probably spurious, especially in view of the common tendency to add to ancient manuscripts. The next section deals with: Three sources of misfortune and three sources of poverty. The next section is translated here; from its subject matter, it appears genuine: at least, if not by Hsüntze, it is thoroughly in harmony with his teachings.

[3] Between different classes and relationships.

[4] They are not acquired characteristics.

more particularly in that he has two feet and no feathers,[1] but rather in that he makes distinctions. Now the yellow-haired ape [2] also has two feet and no feathers ; but in contrast the superior man sips his soup and carves his slices of meat.[3] Hence man is not truly man more particularly in that he has two feet and no feathers, but in that he makes distinctions. The birds and beasts have fathers and sons, but not the affection between father and son ; they are female and male, but they do not have the proper separation between males and females.

6 Hence the path (*Tao*) of human life cannot be without its distinctions ; no distinction is greater than social divisions ; no social division is greater than the rules for proper conduct (*Li*) ; the rules for proper conduct are not greater than the Sage-Kings.[4]

Follow the later Kings. But there were many [5] Sage-Kings [6] ; which one shall I follow ? When rules of nice conduct are preserved too long, they are lost. There are officers to preserve the arts and rules of proper conduct (*Li*) ; but if preserved to a great age, they are relaxed. Hence it is said : If you wish to see the footprints of the Sage-Kings, then look where they are most clear ; that is to say, at the later Kings.[7]

---

[1] In his physical characteristics. Cf. the definition of man in these very words by a Greek philosopher

[2] Known for its intelligence.

[3] He eats politely.

[4] Because they established *Li* and *Yi*.

[5] Lit., " a hundred."

[6] The Sage-Kings were the great emperors, such as Yao, Shun, Yu, T'ang, Wen, Wu, Duke Chou. Micius had argued that his teaching accorded with that of the earlier Sage-Kings.

[7] This term " later Kings " is used once in this book, once in Book III, twice in Book VIII, thrice in Book XXII, and once in Book XXV. It

These later Kings were the princes of the whole country. 7
To give up the later Kings and follow those of the extremely
ancient times is like giving up one's own prince and serving
another's prince.   Hence it is said : If you wish to know
a thousand years, then consider to-day [1] ; if you wish to
understand ten or a hundred thousand, then examine one
and two ; if you wish to know the ancient times, then
examine the Way (*Tao*) of the Chou dynasty; if you wish
to know the way of the Chou dynasty, then examine its men,
what princes it honours.   Hence it is said : By the present
you can understand the past ; by one you can understand
a myriad ; by the subtle you can understand the clear—
this saying expresses what I mean.

But abandoned incorrigible people say : Ancient and
present times are different in nature ; the methods (*Tao*)
of good or bad rule were different,[2] and many people are
thus misled.   Those people are stupid and without learning,
ignorant and without perception.   What they see is like a
deception, and yet the right Way has been handed down
for a thousand ages.   The abandoned sophist thus shuts
people up within their doors and halls and cheats them ;

*Ancient and
present times
are alike.*

refers to the great kings (or emperors) of the then reigning dynasty, i.e. Kings
Wen and Wu, and probably Duke Chou, who were the ideals of the Confucians ; it is used in contrast with Yao, Shun, Yu, etc., who were so
ancient that little was known about them.   By extension it would mean
the great kings of whichever dynasty a person was living under, especially
the ruler who founded the dynasty.

[1] This statement is the consequence of Confucius' saying : "Ruminate on
the ancient and you will know the present."

[2] From those applicable to-day.   Cf. *Chuangtze* XIV, II, vii, 4, where
this view is expressed.   This paragraph interrupts the argument and may
be an interpolation.

and so overcomes the tradition of a thousand ages. Why cannot the Sage be cheated ? The Sage measures things by himself. Hence by present men he measures ancient men ; by the events of his day he measures their events ; by his classifications he measures their classifications ; by his doctrines he measures their merit ; by the right Way of life (*Tao*) he can completely comprehend things ; the ancient times and the present are alike. If the classification is not violated, although it is old, the principle remains the same.[1] Hence to consider wrong doctrines (*Tao*) and not be misled, to look at a heterogeneous lot of things and not be confused, can be done by this way of measuring.

Previous to the Five Emperors[2] there is no record ; not that there were no worthy men, but because of the length of time intervening. Of the period of the Five Emperors there is no record of their government ; not because they did not have a good government, but because of the length of time intervening. Of Yu and T'ang[3] there is a record of their government, but it is not as good as that of the Chou dynasty to investigate[4] ; not because there was no good government, but because of the length of time intervening.[5] The longer things have been handed down, the more in

---

[1] Just as " horse " and " cow " in ancient and present times mean the same, so human principles do not change.

[2] Preceding Yao. Cf. p. 17 f.

[3] The first rulers of the Hsia and Shang dynasties respectively.

[4] Not so detailed.

[5] Hsüntze has no conception of progress ; nothing is said of any change in social conditions ; indeed such a supposition would nullify Hsüntze's whole philosophy, which presupposes a static world. It is supposed that

outline they are ; the more recent they are, the more detailed they are. When in outline they merely mention the big things ; when detailed, they mention the small things. The stupid man hears the outline, but does not know the details ; or else he hears the small things and does not know the big things.[1] This is destroying rules of conduct by preserving them too long, losing ceremonials by collecting them too long.[2]

the same principles of government and action as applied in ancient times could be used unchanged to-day ; only the way they were applied by the ancient Worthies is not known in detail.

[1] He fails whether he studies the ancient or the present.

[2] These "later Kings" were not so recent even to Hsüntze ; Kings Wen, Wu, and Duke Chou were more than 800 years earlier than he ! But Hsüntze thought that was better than going back 2,000 years for the ideal of government !

The remainder of the book seems spurious. This subject is dropped, and the book speaks of the speech of the superior man—which must agree with that of the earlier Kings and with Li ; it is pleasant because it is right ; the superior man correctly estimates and uses all kinds of men ; disputation of the Sage, scholar, superior man, and evil man are compared ; not as in Book XXII, but according to the amount of preparation needed for a true disputation ; the evil dialectician is worse than a robber and there is no hope of change for him. So ends the book.

BOOK VI

AGAINST THE TEN PHILOSOPHERS [1]

They take advantage of the present generation [2]; they 13 gloss over unorthodox teachings; they beautify evil ideas, To Hsiao and Wei Mou. so that they make the country wicked and confused; they are hypocritical and deceitful, paltry and insignificant; they cause the country to be chaotic, not knowing that there is anyone who preserves the distinction between right and wrong, good and bad government; they give rein to their passions; they are satisfied to be supercilious; they perform bestial actions [3]; they are insufficient to be classed with the

[1] The present text of the title says: " Twelve Philosophers." But the 韓 詩 外 傳 which quotes this passage states " Ten Philosophers ", omitting Tze-Sze and Mencius. There are several reasons for thinking that that text is right. Hsüntze, who was the leader of the Confucian school of his day, and a polished gentleman who emphasized courtesy and moderation, would hardly stoop to such abuse of these two prominent Confucians as in this book. (Cf. *Mencius* II, 1, ii for how one Confucian would treat other disciples of Confucius, and pp. 273, 147 note 1, 193 note 1, for Hsüntze's attitude of approval of Mencius.) While Hsüntze criticizes Mencius elsewhere, he nowhere abuses him; instead Hsüntze is a follower of Mencius in most matters. In addition, there are stylistic differences between the part of this book which I have translated and the latter part; the usual formula which sums up the criticism is absent from the criticism of Tze Sze and Mencius. The text of the 韓 詩 外 傳 is probably preferable here, as the present text can only be traced to the commentator Yang Liang, A.D. 818.

[2] The time of the " Contending States," when everything, philosophies, customs, morals, political ideals, and especially the political situation was in a state of flux.

[3] Moral wickedness, not observing the rules of proper conduct and justice which distinguish human beings from beasts.

accomplished or with those who know how to govern rightly ;
yet what they support seems reasonable, their teachings are
plausible, sufficiently so to deceive and mislead the ignorant
multitude—such are To Hsiao [1] and Wei Mou. [2]

Ch'eng Chung and Shih Ch'iu.

These repress their passions ; they are very deep ; they
4 leave the world to stand alone ; they wrongly think
that if they are different from others they are superior ;
but they are unworthy to be classed with the general run
of people or to make clear the great duties [3] ; yet what
they support seems reasonable ; their teachings are plausible,
sufficiently so to deceive and mislead the ignorant multitude—
such are Ch'eng Chung [4] and Shih Ch'iu. [5]

Micius and Sungtze.

These did not know how to unite the empire nor how to
establish the power and reputation of a state ; they honour
utility and exalt economy, but do not have any ranks in
society [6] ; they are not really sufficient to endure distinctions
nor to distinguish prince and vassal ; yet what they support
seems reasonable, their teachings are plausible, sufficiently
so to deceive and mislead the ignorant multitude—such are
Mo Ti [7] and Sung Hsin. [8]

[1] 它 囂 Unknown.

[2] 魏 牟 Contemporary of Chuangtze, a Taoist.

[3] Loyalty (for a vassal) and filial piety (for a son), etc.

[4] 陳 仲 A man of Ts'i who lived among the hills, would not take money
from his older brother, refused riches or honour, and unselfishly took care
of others' orchards. He was known for his honesty. Also called T'ien Chung.

[5] 史 鰌 A Prefect in Wei.

[6] They made no distinction of classes or ranks ; they would have the
rulers work together with the ruled.

[7] 墨 翟 Micius, who preached universal love and equality, and stressed
economy and utility.

[8] 宋 鈃 Also called Sung K'en, a native of Sung ; a contemporary
of Mencius and mentioned by him.

These honour the law and yet are without law ; they do not follow the old laws but love to make new ones ; when they talk to the upper classes they get a hearing from them ; when they talk to the lower classes, they get a hearing from them. They talk for a whole day ; they write essays ; but if one turns round and investigates them, they are a law to themselves and cannot be pinned down. They cannot 15 manage a country nor establish people's duties. Yet what they support seems reasonable ; their teachings are plausible, sufficiently so to deceive and mislead the ignorant multitude—such are Shen Tao [1] and T'ien P'in.[2]

Shentze and T'ien P'in.

These do not follow the early Kings ; they do not hold that the rules of proper conduct (*Li*) and justice (*Yi*) are right ; yet they like to deal in strange teachings, and weary people with curious ideas. They are very critical but do not care about its usefulness ; they debate but impractically. They make much fuss but accomplish little ; their doctrines cannot be the unifying bond of good government. Yet what they support seems reasonable ; 'their teachings are plausible, sufficiently so to deceive and mislead the ignorant multitude —such are Huei Shih [3] and Teng Si.[4]

Hueitze and Teng Si.

[1] 慎 到 Shentze.

[2] 田 駢 A native of Ts'i ; his writings were collected in fifteen books. A Taoist.

[3] 惠 施 Prime Minister of Liang, contemporary of Chuangtze. A leader of the Neo-Micians.

[4] 鄧 析 Prefect of Cheng ; liked to propound dilemmas. Also a Neo-Mician. It is curious that Kung Suenlung is not mentioned with Huei Shih ; possibly because he was only a contemporary of Hsüntze and not a predecessor.

From this point on the rest of the book is probably spurious. It begins by abusing Tze Sze (grandson of Confucius) and Mencius, as only partially following the ancient Kings ; their knowledge is confused, very perverted ; they forge Confucius' words, etc. Confucius and Tze Kung are uncriticizable ; kings and dukes cannot vie with them in reputation. If people would only imitate Shun and Yu, Confucius and Tze Kung, and stop listening to the talk of these twelve philosophers, all the trouble in the world would stop. Then a paragraph speaks of the evils (chiefly unorthodox teaching), the Sage-Kings prohibited ; the virtues that make Worthies and honourable people praise a man. Ancient officials are praised and present ones condemned. The superior man does not seek for fame but for right. The proper hat, clothes, and deportment of various types of men. Abuse of Tze Chang, Tze Hsia, Tze Yu (three disciples of Confucius) closes the book. A good deal of the opprobrium from which Hsüntze has suffered is due to this abuse of Tze Sze, Mencius, and other Confucians contained in the spurious part of this book.

BOOK VII

THE CONFUCIANS [1]

THE CONFUCIANS ARE ONLY IMMATURE [2] MENIALS
THEIR TALK RARELY MENTIONS THE FIVE LORDS
PROTECTOR [3]

Why was this the case ? Because they really could only Duke Huan.
be rarely mentioned. [4] Huan [5] of Ts'i [6] was the greatest

---

[1] The title of this book is taken from its first words, not from its subject. It is composed of four sections, each with a title.

[2] Lit., " five-foot ". In ancient times the foot was shorter than at present and an adult was ten feet tall.

[3] A criticism of the Confucian school. These Five Lords Protector were historical characters who took the lead in the empire when the authority of the Chou emperor weakened. Duke Huan was the first of them, and probably the best. The Confucians stood for the legitimacy of the ancient political organization, in which the emperor was supreme in authority and power ; they disliked that anyone else should have the power that should belong to the emperor, even though the emperor had lost his power by his own pusillanimity, and Duke Huan used his power to bolster up the authority of the Emperor and was recognized as Lord Protector by the Emperor himself. To the Confucians theory was everything, historical events ought to adapt themselves to the theory ! Confucius himself criticized Duke Huan. The five Lords Protector were (1) Duke Huan of Ts'i (685–643 B.C.), (2) Duke Siang of Sung (650–637 B.C.), (3) Duke Wen of Tsin (636–628 B.C.), (4) Duke Mu of Ts'in (659–621 B.C.), (5) King Chuang of Ts'u (613–591 B.C.). In this passage they are further stigmatized by being called the " five Earls " instead of " Lords " ! Cf. *Mencius* VI, II, vii.

[4] The Confucians only discoursed of the good ; hence they could not speak of the five Lords Protector. Cf. *Mencius* I, I, vii, 2.

[5] Duke Huan of the feudal state of Ts'i in present Shantung. His prime minister, Kuan Chung, raised Ts'i to the leadership of the feudal states, but Huan himself was addicted to the pleasures of the table and the harem. Cf. p. 23.

[6] In feudal China, the feudal principalities were spoken of as 國, " countries " ; and the whole country was spoken of as 天下, " all under

of the five Lords Protectors. In his earlier days he killed his older brother and wrested the state from him. In his internal affairs, he did not marry off seven women, aunts and sisters [1]; in his inner apartments there was dissipation and extravagance; he caused the state of Ts'i to contribute half of its wealth as taxes and was not satisfied. In external affairs he deceived Chü,[2] made a secret attack on Chü,[3] and absorbed thirty-five states.[4] If his actions were so bent on evil, depraved, licentious, and extravagant, how could he be really great enough to be placed in the same class with the great princes? [5] If he was like this, yet was not ruined, but became Lord Protector, why was it? Alas, Duke Huan of Ts'i had the greatest talents in the world; who could destroy him? In a glance he perceived that the ability of Kuan Chung was such that he could be entrusted with the state; this was the greatest wisdom in the world. So he (Huan) forgot his anger and forgot his enemies and there-

24 upon established Kuan as Chung Fu [6]; this was the greatest decision in the world. Huan established Kuan as Chung Fu and of his noble clan none dared to envy him.

Heaven ", since it comprised all of the then civilized world known to the Chinese, really all the world that they knew. I have translated these terms throughout by " state " and " empire " respectively.

[1] Hinting that he had incestuous relations with them.

[2] 邾 A principality in what is now Shantung.

[3] 莒 Not the same place as the preceding; a petty, short-lived state in present Shantung.

[4] The names of only five of them have come down to us.

[5] Yao, Shun, Yu, etc.

[6] Gave him a new name or style, " Father Chung," or explained as " to destroy for me and to serve as a father ".

Huan gave Kuan the position of Kao and Kuo,[1] but none of the officials of his court dared to hate him. Huan gave Kuan three hundred villages [2] on the register of families, but none of the rich dared to resist him. None of the noble, the base, the old, and the young, in their order, failed to follow Duke Huan and to honour and respect him. This is what the greatest talents in the world can do.[3] If a feudal noble has one talent like these, then no one can ruin him; Duke Huan had these several talents and had them to perfection; then who could ruin him? That he was Lord Protector was fitting; not by chance, but by destiny.

Then "The Confucians are only immature menials; their talk rarely mentions the five Lords Protector"—why is this? Because they did not have a just doctrine of government; they were not very successful; they were not very refined; they did not satisfy people's minds. Their course of action was approximately correct; they used judgment in employing and dismissing the people; they carefully accumulated their resources; they prepared implements of war; they were able to overturn their enemies. They conquered through a deceitful heart. They glossed over their contentiousness by an appearance of yielding the precedence to others; they relied on an appearance of benevolence (*Jen*) to enable them to tread the path of profit-seeking. They are heroes of the small-minded man. But how can they really be great enough to be placed in the same class with the great princes?

The Lords Protector were only apparently virtuous.

[1] Two nobles of high rank, entitled 上 卿.

[2] The term here used means a place of twenty-five families. The descendants of Kuan Chung held high feudal position for ten generations.

[3] Cf. a similar remark by Confucius, *An.* XIV, xx.

The Kings
were
virtuous.

But the Kings were different. They were most worthy, and could thereby save the degenerate; they were most powerful, and could thereby bear with the weak; in war they certainly could have imperilled the weak, but they rarely fought with them. They were refined and accom-
25 plished so as to manifest it to the whole empire. Then oppressive states became peaceful and developed of them-selves. They only punished by death the dangerous and violent. Hence capital punishment was used very rarely by the Sage-Kings. King Wen executed four people.[1] King Wu executed two people. Duke Chou finished this business, and when we come to King Ch'eng, there were no executions. Then how could it be possible that the right Way (*Tao*) was not carried out ? [2] King Wen carried it out in a state of one hundred *li*,[3] and the whole empire was united under him. Ch'ie and Chou violated it; they had the tremendous power of the empire, but they could not grow old like ordinary men.[4] Hence if a ruler can follow the Way, then a state of one hundred *li* is large enough to be independent; but if he cannot follow it, then Ts'u, six thousand *li* in size, would become the servant of its enemy.[5] Therefore, when a ruler does not exe himself to follow the Way (*Tao*), but instead enlarges his power, he puts himself in a dangerous position.

Named Mi, Yen, Kung, and Tsung.
Implying the answer, Of course it was.
[3] I.e., a small place.
They were killed in their prime.
[5] Referring to King Huai of Ts'u (328–299 B.C.) who died in Ts'in; his son, King Hsiang (298–263 B.C.) also served Ts'in.

THE METHOD OF MAINTAINING THE FAVOUR OF ONE'S LORD AND KEEPING IN OFFICE, AND OF NOT BEING DISLIKED TO THE END OF ONE'S DAYS

If your lord respects and honours you, then be reverent to him and observe rule and order, and thus restrain others. If your lord trusts and loves you, then be careful and humble. If your lord gives you the sole power, then hold it carefully and pay attention to your duties. If your lord is satisfied and familiar with you, then obey him and do not do wrong. If your lord is distant, then be completely honest and pure and be not faithless. If your lord injures or degrades you, then be fearful and do not harbour resentment ; if he honours you, do not brag ; if he trusts you, be not suspicious. **26** If your post is a great one, do not presume to keep its emoluments for yourself alone [1] ; if you receive office it is well to act as if you had not the ability for it ; you should first do everything possible in the way of declining it and offering it to others before accepting it. [2] When good fortune comes, be amicable and orderly ; when calamity comes, be quiet and orderly. If you become wealthy, then use it generously ; if you are poor, then economize. Be willing to accept a high or low station. Be willing to be rich or to be poor. Be willing to be killed, but never be willing to do wrong. This is the method of maintaining the favour of one's lord and keeping in office, and of not being disliked to the end of one's days. [3] Even though in circumstances

How to keep in office.

---

[1] Share with your family, clan, and dependents.
[2] Still the standard procedure for a recipient of office.
[3] Hsüntze found a patron in Prince Chüin-shen and was continued in office until old age and a change in government forced his retirement.

of poverty and retirement, the man who nevertheless makes this method his model may be called a fortunate man. The ode says :

"Men loved this One man [1]

Who carried on obediently the virtuous acts of his ancestors,

Ever talking and thinking how to be filial.

Illustriously the heir served his ancestors " [2]—

this expresses what I mean.[3]

THE METHOD OF SEEKING TO OCCUPY WELL A HIGH POSITION, AND TO DO GREAT THINGS, OF OBTAINING THE FAVOUR OF THE RULER OF A STATE OF TEN THOUSAND CHARIOTS,[4] AND OF SURELY AVOIDING ANY EVIL CONSEQUENCES

How to fill a high position.

There is nothing better than esteeming, associating with, and putting forward the worthy,[5] being gracious to all, doing away with all hatred, and not injuring others. If you are equal to your duties, then follow this method (*Tao*). 27 But if you are not equal to your duties, and fear to lose the ruler's favour, then there is nothing better than to

---

[1] A designation of the emperor or king.

[2] In continuing the work of his forefathers.

[3] *Book of Odes*, III, I, ix, 4. King Wen gives an example of right conduct in continuing the constructive work of his father and grandfather in strengthening his house and governing his state well.

[4] A large state.

[5] This term " Worthy " has a technical significance in Confucian ethics— it means those who have ability and virtue, especially ability in governing ; since *the* occupation, according to Chinese ideas, is governmental position. The Worthy is a degree lower than the Sage, who shows these qualities in a perfect degree. Micius advocated a similar view, that of advancing the worthy, but he did not use this term in a technical sense. Cf. *Micius*, ch. 8, 9, 10.

associate another with you quickly, to advance the worthy, to yield to the able, and be satisfied to follow in their train. In this way if you possess the ruler's favour, you will assuredly be glorious, and if you lose his favour you will assuredly be without fault.   This practice is valuable in serving princes and is assuredly the method of being certain of avoiding any evil consequences.[1]   For the wise man in his conduct of affairs, when he is sufficient, concerns himself with his inadequacy;   when he is safe, he concerns himself with his danger;   when he is contented, he concerns himself with his anxieties;   in difficulties he stresses previous preparation as if fearing a calamity greatly;   in this way, in all his affairs, he will not fail.   Confucius said :   " The skilled workman who values the measurement of his material will assuredly be economical;   the brave man who values humility will

---

[1] This paragraph shows the essentially practical nature of the Confucians. The Confucian philosophy was essentially a " legitimist " philosophy ;   they looked to the emperor as the great power in the country   whom the feudal princes must serve ;   in this respect Ts'in Shih Hwangti was but restoring the ancient Confucian ideal when he made himself the great power in the state.   During the latter part of the Chou period, the great feudal princes were usurping the imperial prerogatives and were condemned by the Confucians.   Cf. *Analects* III, i, ii.   But although Hsüntze accepted this idealistic Confucian doctrine,   he lived in the age of the Contending States, when the emperor's power was weak and the emperor had become merely the pontifex maximus ;   the real power was in the hands of the princes of the different states.   Hsüntze's pupils sought official position, as did all educated men of the day ;   hence he taught them how to seek preferment in the eyes of these very princes who illegitimately usurped power (cf. the last sentence of this book) ;   but he taught them to seek favour by righteousness, not artfulness, and therein expressed the Confucian spirit, in that his practical sense compelled him to make terms with the practical situation of the day, even though it was against the Confucian " legitimist " doctrine.

assuredly be a Worthy " [1]—this saying expresses what
I mean.

The stupid
man.

The stupid man does the opposite of this. When he
occupies a high position and wields authority, he likes to
do things alone and envies the worthy and the able ; he keeps
back the meritorious and heavily punishes those who are at
fault. His mind is proud and arrogant, and he thinks little
of old hatreds. On the one hand, he is stingy and not
generous ; on the other he seeks strenuously for authority
in order to injure others. Although he does not seek to be
insecure, will he succeed ? Therefore, though he be in an
honourable position, he is certainly insecure ; though he have
a high post, he will certainly lose it ; though he obtain the
ruler's favour, he will certainly be disgraced. You can
stand and wait for it to happen ; by a breath he will fall.
Why is that ? Because those who pull him down are many ;
but those who support him are few.

The Method of Governing the Empire

The correct
attitude of
the prime
minister.

28

By serving your prince you will certainly succeed ; by
looking after others you will assuredly become wise ;
establish the great mean and be not double-minded. Then
be respectful in putting this method first ; be loyal and
faithful in being controlled by it ; be careful in carrying
it out ; be honest and upright in keeping it ; in difficulties
follow it ; be diligent in repeating it. Although your lord
does not appreciate you, he will be without feelings of dislike
for you ; although your merit be very great, do not have the
appearance of boasting of your virtue. Seek for little, but

[1] This saying is not in the Classics.

merit much. Be not fatigued in love and respectfulness.
In this way you can never be other than agreeable. By
serving your prince, you are certain to succeed ; by looking
after others, you assuredly will become wise—this is what
I mean by the method of governing the empire

     *   *   *   *   *

The young serve the old ; the inferior serve the noble ; *The vicious serve the righteous—this is the rule of the universe.* the degenerate serve the worthy—this is the pervading rule of the universe. There are people whose circumstances are not below that of others, but who err and fall below others—the minds of evil men are like this. Their purposes do not escape their evil minds ; their actions do not escape their evil ways (*Tao*) ; yet they seek the reputation of being a superior man or Sage. For example, they are like a man who tries to bow down and lick heaven, or to save a person who is hanging himself by putting a halter around his feet—such a doctrine cannot be carried out ; the more it is done, the farther it will carry one from his goal. Hence if the occasion demands bending the superior man will bend ; if the occasion demands straightening up, he straightens up.[1]

[1] The superior man adapts himself to the situation.

BOOK VIII

THE MERIT OF THE CONFUCIAN [1]

The Model of the Great Confucians

When King Wu died, King Ch'eng [2] was a minor. Duke *Duke Chou's* Chou protected [3] King Ch'eng and succeeded King Wu in *virtue.* order to retain the country, because he did not want the country to rebel against the house of Chou. He took the throne of the Emperor; he acted as supreme judge of the national court; he took his ease as if his place were secure; yet the country did not consider him covetous of position. He killed Kuan-shou, [4] and dealt with the people of Hsü-yin [5]; yet the country did not consider him oppressive. He ruled

[1] A collection of essays on various subjects having general relation to the standard of moral life. While it contains undoubtedly genuine passages, yet we cannot be sure that all of this book is genuine. The second section, calling Hsüntze " Master ", may be compiled by his disciples.

[2] The son of King Wu. Cf. p. 21.

[3] He acted as regent, literally " acted as a screen for ". He was Regent for seven years.

[4] Kuan-shou was an older brother of Duke Chou, who circulated the rumour that Duke Chou wanted the throne for himself. He joined with Wu-ken in rebellion and was killed. Kuan was the name of the city which formed his appanage. He was the second son of King Wen. King Wu was the first, and Duke Chou the third. Kuan-shou with two younger brothers had been appointed as " Inspectors " in the territory of Yin, in which King Wu had continued Wu-ken, the son of Chou-sin; they assisted him in rebellion, and so Duke Chou had to fight one older and two younger brothers.

[5] The rebellious people of Yin were deported from Lo-yi, the old capital city of the empire under the Yin dynasty. Hsü-yin or Yin-hsü was a city ocated in the north of present Honan.

the whole country, and established seventy-one feudal states.
Of the Chi family [1] there were enfeoffed fifty-three [2]; yet
the country did not consider him partial. He educated
and trained King Ch'eng and had him instructed in the
Way, so he [3] was able to inherit the throne of King Wen.
Duke Chou turned over the rule to the legitimate scion of the
house of Chou. He turned back the throne to King Ch'eng;
so the country did not cease to serve the house of Chou.
Then Duke Chou faced north [4] and served the new King.
2 He could not for an instant make himself emperor, but
he could act for the emperor. [5] Because he was able to do
that, the country remained in the possession of his house;
if he had not been able to do so, the country would have left
his house. This is the way that Duke Chou protected King
Ch'eng and succeeded King Wu in order to retain the country,
because he did not want the country to depart from the house
of Chou.

When King Ch'eng was capped [6] and came of age, Duke Chou
turned over the rule to the legitimate scion of the house of
Chou and turned back the throne. It is plain that he did
not have the intention of destroying his master. [7] Duke Chou
then did not possess the rule; whereas formerly he had it,

[1] Chi was the family name of the Chou dynasty.

[2] Or 55 (?). Cf. *Spring and Autumn*, Chao Kan Hsi, eighth year.

[3] King Ch'eng.

[4] The emperor always faces south, and the courtiers face north. While
Duke Chou acted as Regent, he faced south; now he became only a courtier
and faced north.

[5] Omitting 不 to preserve the pentameter, and to complete the sense.

[6] A ceremony performed at maturity. King Ch'eng was capped at 14
years of age, at which time he took up the rule.

[7] King Ch'eng.

now he did not have it ; this was not abdication : King
Ch'eng formerly did not possess the rule, but now he had
it ; this was not taking it away from someone else : it was
the orderly passing over of the power in quite proper fashion.
Hence for a branch to take the place of the head of the house [1]
is not overstepping the bounds of what is right ; for a younger
brother to kill his older brother [2] is not oppression ; for a
prince and his minister to exchange positions [3] is not improper.
Because of the peacefulness of the country he [4] ascended the
throne of King Wen—this fact shows that the rights of a
branch and of the head of the house may also be exchanged.
The country was satisfied like one person and united.
Unless he were a Sage, he could not have done this—therefore 3
he is called the model of the great Confucians.

King [5] Chao of Ts'in [6] questioned the Master, Hsun
Ch'ing, saying : "Are Confucian literati of no use to a state ? "

The master, Hsun [7] Ch'ing, replied, "Confucian literati

Praise of the
Confucian
literatus.

[1] As Duke Chou took the place of his nephew, King Ch'eng, in ruling as
Regent.

[2] As Duke Chou condemned his older brother, Kuan-shou, to death for
treason.

[3] As Duke Chou ruled as Regent while King Ch'eng was a minor, and
became a vassal when King Ch'eng took the throne.

[4] King Ch'eng.

[5] This section is quoted in the 新 序 雜 事 篇.

[6] 306–251 B.C.

[7] In this section the character 孫 is used instead of 荀 for Hsüntze's
name, just as by Liu Hsiang in his Introduction. In ancient times these
two characters were pronounced alike, as in Cantonese and some other
dialects to-day, and so were interchanged. The supposition that the change
was made by Liu Hsiang because the personal name of King Hsuen of the
Han dynasty was 詢 seems to be without foundation ; had it been the
case, Liu Hsiang would have changed it throughout. I have indicated the
difference in the translation by omitting the umlaut from Hsün.

imitate the ancient Kings, and magnify the rulers of proper conduct (*Li*) and justice (*Yi*). They are diligent ministers or sons, and honour their superiors very highly. If the ruler would employ them, their place at your court would be most appropriate. When they are not employed, they retire, order the people, and are guileless—they are thoroughly obedient subjects. Although they be poor, harassed, freezing, or starving, they would certainly not follow evil methods (*Tao*) into avarice. Though they be without even a place to put down an awl,[1] yet they are clear as to the great principles of ruling a district.[2] They mourn and no one responds to them; yet they are familiar with the principles of ruling all things and of fostering the people. If their position is that of ruler, then they are material for a king or duke. If it is subordinate, then they are servants of society and the treasures of the prince. Although such an one should be retired in a poor rustic mean place, no one would fail to esteem him, because he sincerely holds to an honourable path (*Tao*).

4 When Confucius was about to be the Minister of Crime,[3] Mr. Shen-yu [4] did not dare to come to court to drink his mutton-broth; Mr. Kung-shen [5] divorced his wife; Mr. Shen-huei [6] crossed the border and fled. The traders of cattle and horses in Lu did not have false prices, but set them right and

---

[1] Landless or without rule.

[2] Lit., " The altars of the gods of the land and grains."

[3] In the state of Lu.

[4] These three were all men of Lu. The Family Sayings 家 語 speaks of this man as continually coming to court to drink his mutton-broth and impose upon the merchants. He was a glutton.

[5] His wife was adulterous, but he did not control her.

[6] He was extravagant beyond what the law allowed.

waited for a buyer. When he lived in a city or community, the boys of the city or community shared the produce of their nets, and those who had parents took more than the others ; the virtues of filial piety and reverence to elders so 5 influenced them. When Confucian literati are at your court, they adorn your rule ; when they are in inferior position, they beautify the customs. When a Confucian is in an inferior position, he is like what I have said."

The King said : " Yes. Then how is he when he is a ruler ? "

Hsun Ch'ing replied : " When he is a ruler, he is great. His purpose is fixed within him ; proper conduct (*Li*) is cultivated at his court ; the laws and correct measurements are rectified among the officials ; loyalty, faithfulness, love, and service-ableness are exhibited to the people. He would not do one unrighteous (not *Yi*) act nor kill one innocent man to get the Empire. Such rightness (*Yi*) is trusted by men. When it is known throughout the continent, the whole empire will respond to it like an echo. Why is this ? Because his name will be honoured and glorious, and the country will be willing to obey. Hence those who are near will sing and rejoice at him ; those who are distant will fall over themselves to hasten to him. All within the four seas will be as if one family ; none of the educated will fail to follow and obey him. There-fore he may be called a leader of men. The ode says : 6

'From the west, from the east,
From the south, from the north,
None thought but of obedience ' [1]

---

[1] *Book of Odes*, III, i, x, 6.

—this expresses my meaning. Then if, when the Confucian is in an inferior position, he is what I have said, and when he is a ruler he is what I have now indicated, how could he be said to be of no benefit to a state ? "

King Chao said, " Good."

*   *   *   *   *

The *Tao* is the Way the Superior Man acts.

The Way of the ancient Kings is the magnifying of benevolence (*Jen*). Follow the mean in acting it out. What is meant by the mean ? It is the rules of proper conduct (*Li*) and justice (*Yi*). The Way (*Tao*) is not primarily the Way of Heaven [1]; it is not the way (*Tao*) of Earth ; it is the way (*Tao*) man acts, the way (*Tao*) the superior man acts. The superior man is not called a Worthy because ne can do all that men of ability can do.[2] The superior man is not called wise because he knows all that wise men know. The superior man is not called a dialectician because he can dispute concerning all that dialecticians dispute about. The superior man is not called an investigator because he can investigate everything that investigators investigate into. He has his standard. In observing the high and low lands,[3] in determining whether they are arid or fertile, and in apportioning [4] the five grains,[5] the superior man is not as good as a farmer. In

[1] The *Tao* is not concerned with the mutations of the *Yin* and *Yang* or the peculiarities of mountains and rivers ; it is primarily ethical rather than metaphysical.

[2] But because he knows the rules of life—the rules of proper conduct and justice. Cf. p. 205.

[3] Plains and marshes.

[4] Fixing which grain is best for which kind of land. Rotation of crops was not practised.

The five grains are panicled millet, glutinous millet, beans, wheat and hemp.

knowing about wealth and goods, in determining their fineness or impurity, or in distinguishing their value or worthlessness, the superior man is not as good as a merchant. In using the compass and square, in applying the plumb line, or in being accustomed to the use of tools, the superior man is not as good as a workman. In not caring for the spirit of right or wrong, or of true or false, in getting each to modify the other so that both are shamed, the superior man is not as good as Huei Shih and Teng Si.[1] But if he is to estimate people's virtue and accordingly fix their rank, if he is to measure their ability and accordingly give them official position, if he is to cause the worthy and the unworthy both to get their proper rank, the man of ability and the man of no ability both to take their proper position; if all things are to be properly attended to ; if he is to respond to changes in the situation ; if Shentze and Micius are not to bring in their chatter ; if Huei Shih and Teng Sih are not to be allowed their investigations ; if speech must be in accordance with the right ; if business must be attended to, then in these matters the superior man will show his superiority.

*   *   *   *   *

If any piece of business or conduct is beneficial to the right, establish it ; but if it is of no benefit to the right, do away with it. For this is what is meant by a correct piece of business. If any doctrine is of benefit to the right, carry it out ; if it is of no benefit to the right, reject it. For this is what is meant by a correct doctrine. When a piece of business is incorrect, it is called a wicked piece of business. When a doctrine is incorrect, it is called a wicked doctrine (*Tao*).

Unorthodox doctrines.

[1] Leaders of the Neo-Micians ; great debaters and dialecticians.

A well-governed age rejects wicked business and wicked doctrines (*Tao*), but a disordered age follows after such. But as for making realities and unrealities interchange places, separations of whiteness and hardness, likenesses and 8 unlikenesses [1]—a cultivated ear will not hear such things; a cultivated eye will not see such things; a scholar practised in dialectic will not speak of such things; although he had the wisdom of a Sage, he would not be able to explain them briefly. Ignorance of them will not injure a superior man; knowing them will not prevent anyone from becoming a small-minded man. Ignorance of them will not prevent a workman or artisan from being skilled; ignorance of them will not prevent a prince from ruling well. If a king or duke prize them, it will confuse the laws; if the people prize them, it will confuse their business. But crazy, deluded, stupid, ignorant men from the first follow their [2] crowd of disciples; they discuss their [2] chatter and make plain their [2] illustrations; till they are old and their children are grown they do not see their [2] evil; therefore such are called first-class dolts. They are not even as good as those who physiognomize chickens or dogs to see if they will have fame [3]! The ode says :—

"Were you an imp or a water-bow,
Then you could be got at.

---

[1] Doctrines of the Neo-Micians. Cf., p. 49, notes 3 and 4.

[2] Referring to the teachers of these doctrines.

[3] Anciently domestic animals were prized as telling fortunes. But here it is not the cow or horse which tells the fortune, but the minor beasts. Hsüntze attacked fortune-telling and physiognomizing; he is saying that the disciples of these Neo-Micians are not as good as the most absurd of the fortune-tellers !

But when a person can be seen face to face and eye to eye,
  It does not take forever to see through him.
I am making this good song,
  To show how very shifty you are " [1]—
this expresses my meaning.

*   *   *   *   *

129382

I desire to be mean and yet noble, stupid yet wise, poor
yet right. Can I bring that about ? It is only accomplished
by study. That student who carries it [2] out is called a
scholar. [3] He who exerts himself and longs for it is a superior
man. [4] He who is versed in it is a Sage. Then what will
prevent me [5] from being on the one hand a Sage or on the other
hand a scholar or superior man ? Formerly I was undistin-
guished from the man on the street ; suddenly I am equal to
Yao and Shun ; is not this being mean and yet noble ?
Formerly in examining a door and house to determine their
difference I confused them and was unable to distinguish
them. [6] Suddenly I become the source of benevolence
(*Jen*) and justice (*Yi*), I distinguish right and wrong, I draw
a diagram of heaven and earth upon my palm like distinguishing black and white ; is not this being stupid yet
wise ? Formerly I was altogether a man without property ;

The benefits of study and self-develop-ment.

---

[1] *Book of Odes*, II, v, v, 8. Cf. p. 293 and notes for this passage.
[2] Study.
[3] One who has fixed his purpose to study—entered upon the Confucian
path. Scholar is a technical term here. The three grades of virtue are
scholar 士, superior man 君子, and Sage 聖人.
[4] The Chou-Li says : He who exerts himself to do good and is not indolent
therein is called a superior man.
[5] The first personal pronoun referring to an indefinite personal subject.
[6] So stupid.

suddenly I have the great ability of ruling the Empire; considered in this way, am I not poor yet rich? Now, if there were a man here who carefully hoarded a treasure of a thousand pieces of gold [1]; although he begged for food, people would call him rich. If he wished clothes, he could not wear that treasure; if he wished food, he could not eat it; if one wished to sell him something, he could not promptly pay for it. Then why do people call him rich? Is it not because the substance of great wealth is really in what he has? He is an extremely-rich man. Is he not poor and yet rich? Therefore the superior man is noble though he have no title; he is rich though he have no official emoluments; he is trusted though he does not advertise himself; he is 10 majestic though he does not rage; he is glorious though he be poor and retired; he is happy though he live alone: do not his circumstances of being most honourable, most wealthy, most important, and most dignified all increasingly show this to be true? Therefore it is said that a person cannot strive for an honourable name by forming cliques; he cannot gain it by bragging; he cannot coerce it by power; he must sincerely do this [2] and then only will it come to him. He who strives for it will lose it; if he yields it, it will come to him; if he is modest, his fame will accumulate; if he brags, it will be vain. Therefore the superior man pays attention to developing his inner capacities, but yields to others in external matters; he pays attention to cultivating virtue himself, and dwells in it by his modesty; in this way his fame arises like the sun and moon; the country responds like an echo to

[1] Lit., 鎰, a piece of gold of twenty taels (ounces) weight.
[2] Study.

the thunder.   Hence it is said : The superior man is retired
and yet manifest ; he is subtle and yet clear ; he yields to
others and yet conquers. The ode says :—

> " The crane cries in the middle of the marsh.
>
>   Its voice sounds to the sky "—

this expresses what I mean.[1]

Mean men are the opposite of this.   They form cliques, The small-
yet their associates are all the fewer ; they strive vulgarly, minded man.
and their reputation is all the more shameful ; they toil
hard to get peace and profit ; but they are in all the more
danger. The ode says :—

> " If people have no conscience ;
>
>   If they hate each other and are prejudiced,
>
>   When one receives position, but does not first yield to others,
>
>   He will himself come to ruin "—

this expresses what I mean.[2] Therefore a man whose ability
is small but who undertakes a large matter, is like a man
whose strength is small but who undertakes to carry a heavy
load ; he will let it go, be quite injured, and be unable to go
any distance with it.   He who is unworthy, but thinks 11
himself a Worthy, is like a hunchback who wants to
grow tall—the people who point at his hump would be all
the more numerous.[3]   Therefore the wise king is fixed in

---

[1] *Book of Odes*, II, III, x, 2.   The crane is unseen but yet is heard, so the
superior man's fame arises though he may not have official position.

[2] *Book of Odes*, II, VII, ix, 4. This is supposed to be part of a criticism
of King Yu by his relatives. In explaining this passage (as in many others,
as for instance, the quotation just above) Mao 毛 alludes to Hsüntze's
interpretation.

[3] His attempts to make himself tall only make his deformity more
prominent.

virtue and accordingly gives people rank ; what appointments
he makes are not contrary to the proper ranking [1] ; his faithful ministers are really able and then only dare they receive
office ; what they do does not overpass their ability. When
on the one hand the appointments are not contrary to
proper ranking, and on the other hand people's abilities
are not overpassed—that is the extreme of good government.
The ode says :—

> " There is peace on the right and left
>   Which also leads them to come "—

this speaks of the relationship of the superior and inferior
as not being disorderly.[2]

*   *   *   *   *

Four grades
of virtue.

The common people's [3] standard of virtue is that goodness
consists in following custom, that the great good [4] of life is
possessions and wealth, and that supporting one's parents is
to have already reached the right Way (*Tao*). When a person's
character is formed according to rule and his will is firm ; when
he does not allow his selfish desires to confuse what he has
learned—when a man is like that, he can be called a strong
scholar. When a person's character is formed according to
rule and his will is firm ; when he likes to correct himself

---

[1] The best men are always placed at the top.

[2] *Book of Odes*, II, VII, viii, 4.   Mao 毛 is misled by Hsüntze's comment
to interpret 平 平 by 治 辯. I have followed 箋. The ode is a description
of the feudal princes coming to pay homage to the Son of Heaven. Because
of his good government, resulting in peace among the feudal states, the
rulers are induced to come to his court.

[3] In contrast to that of the scholar, superior man, and sage, as below.

[4] Lit. 寶, treasure.

according to what he has learned, so as to force and to beautify his emotional nature ; when his speech is for the most part correct,[1] though he does not know everything ; when his actions are for the most part correct,[1] though not without effort [2] ; when his knowledge and reflection is for the most part correct, though not completely so ; when on the one hand he is able to magnify those whom he exalts,[3] and on the other hand he is able to instruct those who have not already attained to his achievements—when a man is like that, he can be called a solid superior man. When a person can adjust himself to the principles of all the Kings like distinguishing white from black [4] ; when he can respond to the changed situation of the moment like counting " one, two " ; when he can carry out the Rules of proper conduct (*Li*) and treat people according to ceremony, but yet be at ease in it like using his four limbs [5] ; when he can compel **12** the occasion to show his genius for producing achievements, like commanding the four seasons [6] ; when the goodness of his just government harmonizes his people so that though they be hundreds or tens of thousands in number he yet binds them together like one man—when a man is like that, he may be called a Sage.

---

[1] Lit., 當 apt.

[2] Lit. 安, the ease which comes from being naturally correct.

[3] The Sages.

[4] Easily.

[5] Naturally ; as the limbs are parts of the body, so proper and courteous actions are natural parts of his character.

[6] As easily as Heaven (the weather-producing Power) commands the four seasons to bring forth all vegetable life.

The Sage. How regular[1] his actions ! He is governed by principles. How dignified he is ! He is able to respect himself. How complete[2] his character ! He has an end and a beginning 13 to his actions. How contented he is ! He is able to prolong his days. How firm he is ! He steadily holds to the Way (*Tao*). How brilliant he is ! What he does is the essence of wisdom. How orderly he is ! His actions are according to fundamental principles. How luxuriant his character ! It is beautiful. How glorious he is ! His joy is the good of men. How mournful he is ! His fear is that men would do evil.

This Way (*Tao*) of his proceeds from one thing. What is this one thing ? It is that he grasps its spirit and holds it firmly. What is its spirit ? To be completely good and fully controlled is its spirit. That all things are insufficient to subvert him is to hold it firmly. To grasp its spirit firmly is to be a Sage.

The Classics. The Sage is the channel[3] of the Way (*Tao*). The Way (*Tao*) of the world pervades the Confucian doctrine ; the Way (*Tao*) of all the kings is united in it ; hence the Way (*Tao*) of the *Odes*, *History*, *Rites*, and the *Music* follows it. The *Odes* teach this as their purpose ; the *History* teaches this as its business ; the *Rites* (*Li*) teach this in their performances ; the *Music* teaches this in its harmony ; the *Spring and Autumn* teaches this in its subtleties. So the reason that the " Ballads

---

[1] Or " correct " ; 廉熙 explains it as 經端整貌 ; or " very easy ", 楊 explains it as 良易 ; both of which seem to be conjectural explanations based on this passage alone.

[2] The 說文 defines 分 as 文質備 ; or " resolute " 介.

[3] Lit., " pipe."

of the States "¹ do not countenance oppression is because they adopt it and restrain themselves; the reason that **14** the " Minor Odes "² are elegant is because they adopt it and beautify themselves; the reason that the " Major Odes "³ are the greater elegancies is because they adopt it and make themselves great; the reason that the " Praises "⁴ are the extreme of virtue is that they adopt it and permeate themselves with it. The Way (*Tao*) of the world culminates in it. He who follows it will be preserved; he who rebels at it will be ruined. From ancient to present times there has not been anyone who followed it, and was not preserved, or who rebelled against it and was not ruined.

*   *   *   *   *

A visitor said: " Confucius said, ' Was Duke Chou very virtuous? When he took high position,⁵ he was all the more respectful of others; when he became rich he was all the more stingy; when he had conquered his enemies he was all the more prepared for war.' " Rebuttal of criticism of Duke Chou.

In reply I said: " This is impertinent. It was not the conduct of Duke Chou and not the saying of Confucius. When ⁶ King Wu died, King Ch'eng was a minor; Duke

---

¹ The first division of the *Book of Odes*.

² The second division of the *Book of Odes*. The text contains a play on words: lit. " that the Minor Odes are the minor odes "—雅 means not only " the sound of wind instruments, hence an ode for singing ", but also " elegant, refined, and thoroughly correct ".

³ The third division of the *Odes*. There is here a similar play on words to that above. The Introduction to the *Odes* says that there were two kinds of states, small and large, hence the Minor and Major Odes.

⁴ The fourth division of the *Odes*.

⁵ Became Regent.

⁶ A partial repetition of p. 91.

Chou protected King Ch'eng and succeeded to King Wu; he took the throne of the Emperor. When he turned his back to the screen [1] and arose, the feudal nobles hastened to go below the hall.[2] At such a time who was respectful of others! [3]

"He ruled the whole country and established seventy-one feudal states; of the Chi family there were enfeoffed fifty-three. If a descendant of the Chou dynasty was not mad or deluded he certainly was made one of the glorious feudal nobles of the empire; who would say that Duke Chou was stingy!

"When King Wu put Chou to death, he did it on a day that the soldiers dreaded [4]; he faced east and resisted the great year [5]; then he got to the Fan,[6] it was overflowing; when he got to Huai,[7] the road was impassable; when he 15 got to Kung-t'ou,[8] the mountain fell. Ho-shou [9] was

[1] The silken screen in the audience chamber between the door and window. It was ornamented with hatchets or axe-heads.

[2] Audience ended.

[3] Meaning that Duke Chou, in thus ending the audience, maintained his own dignity.

[4] On the 甲 子 day, superstitiously avoided, King Wu joined battle with Chou-sin's forces. Cf. Book of History, V, II, 1.

[5] A cycle of twelve years, in which the same branch character returns. When King Wu was pursuing Chou, Yü-sin advised him not to go northward because the planet Jupiter was in the north; but King Wu did not heed this superstitious advice. Jupiter is called the 歲 星 because twelve of its courses through the zodiac make the great year 太 歲.

[6] A river in Shantung and Honan.

[7] A place of uncertain location, possibly 武 陟 縣 懷 慶 府, Honan, in the south of the state of 鄭, in the south of 襄 城 縣.

[8] A mountain in the principality of 共, situated in 耀 縣, 衛 耀 府, Honan.

[9] The eighth son of King Wen, a younger brother of Duke Chou.

afraid, and said : ' Is it not then quite probable that within three days the five calamities will visit us ? '

" Duke Chou said : ' He [1] disemboweled Pi-kan,[2] and imprisoned the Viscount of Chi [3] ; Fei-lien and Wu-lai [4] rule the government ; why is anything probable ?   Follow with the horse in ordered ranks and go forward ! '   In the morning they ate at Ts'i [5] ; in the evening they lodged at the Hundred Springs [6] ; at dawn they settled at the Wilderness of Moh.[7] They beat their drums,[8] and Chou's troops easily submitted [9] ; thereupon they overthrew the people of Yin [10] and killed Chou.   Then those who did the killing were not the people of Chou [11] but because of the people of Yin.   Hence there were no taking of heads or captives, no rewards for difficult

---

[1] Chou-sin.

[2] A worthy minister.

[3] A relative who remonstrated with Chou-sin.

[4] Two " favourites ", one a good runner and the other a strong man.

[5] A city in the state of Wei 衞, seven furlongs to the north of 開 州 大 名 府 Chihli.

[6] A place in the state of-Wei 衞, to the north-west of 輝 縣, 衞 輝 府, Honan.

[7] The battle-ground in 淇 縣 north of Honan, where the decisive battle was fought.

[8] The signal for the advance to the attack.

[9] Mencius did not believe the account of the pestles floating about in blood after the battle (*Book of History*, V, III, 9) and Hsüntze nowhere mentions that Chou's soldiers turned their spears upon each other as the *Book of History* declares.

[10] The people of Chou-sin of the dynasty of Yin.

[11] The retainers of the dynasty of Chou.   The Chinese distinguishes clearly between the dynasty of Chou 周 and Chou 紂 or Chou-sin, the last emperor of the dynasty of Yin, whereas in English it is impossible to distinguish them except by the context.

feats.[1]   On the contrary, they hung up the three kinds of
defensive armour [2] and put down the five kinds of weapons [3] ;
they united the country and established their music ; thereupon the Wu.[4] and Hsiang [5] arose and the Shao [6] and Hu [6]
ceased.   No one within the four seas [7] failed to change his
feelings and alter his reflections to be moved by them and
obey them.   Hence people did not close their outside doors [8] ;
16 in crossing the country there were no boundaries [9] ; in such
a situation who would be prepared for war ? "

*   *   *   *   *

The
evidences of
a great
Confucian.

Ts'ao-fu [10] was the best charioteer in the world, but without
a chariot and horses his ability could not have been seen.
Yi [11] was the best archer in the world, but without a bow
and arrows his skill could not have been seen.   The great
Confucian is the best harmonizer and unifier in the world,

[1] Of bravery in battle ; since there was no fighting.

[2] The cuirass, the helmet, and the shield ; or " the three kinds of hides "
(armour was made chiefly of hides) of the one-horned rhinoceros, of the
two-horned rhinoceros, and of the ox.

[3] The sword, the two-edged sword, the lance, the halberd, and the
arrow ; or, the lance, the halberd, the battle-axe, the shield, and the bow
and arrow.

[4] Wu's music.

[5] Also a piece of music of the Chou dynasty.

[6] Both are music of the dynasty of Yin.   The Shao was Shun's music.

[7] On the continent ; in the country of China.

[8] At night ; the people were so virtuous and obedient that there were
no thieves !   When we remember that the China of that day was entirely
a rural country, such a statement does not seem extravagant.

[9] It was like one family.

[10] The charioteer of King Mo 穆 of the Chou dynasty 1001–947 B.C.

[11] The Prince of Ch'iung ; a famous rebel who drove T'ai-k'ang of the
Hsia dynasty beyond the Yellow river to T'ai-k'ang Hsien in Honan about
2169 B.C., and kept the power until his death.

but without a place of a hundred *li*,[1] his merit cannot be seen.

If the chariot is good and the horses select, and yet a man cannot hereby travel far, a thousand *li* in one day, then he is not a Ts'ao-fu. If the bow is adjusted and the arrow is straight, and yet thereby a man cannot send it far and hit the bulls-eye, then he is not a *Yi*. If a man controls a place of a hundred *li*, but yet cannot harmonize and unify the whole country, and rule the strong and oppressive, then he is not a great Confucian.

Although such a great Confucian should be in retirement in a poor hamlet or a leaky hut, and though he be without even a place to put down an awl,[2] yet kings or dukes cannot contest with him in fame ; when he controls a place of a hundred *li*, a state of a thousand *li* cannot contest with him and conquer ; he will beat down an oppressive state and unify the whole country, yet no one will be able to overturn him—this is the evidence of a great Confucian. His speech is ordered and his actions are appropriate (*Li*) ; his conduct of affairs is without being dissatisfied with it ; in danger, his responses to changing situations are indirectly appropriate ; at the right time he moves his abode, at the right season he desists or takes up his business ; through a thousand affairs and ten thousand changes his way (*Tao*) is the same—this is the proof of a great Confucian. When he is out of office, the ordinary Confucian laughs at him[3] ; when he is in office heroes 17

---

[1] A small place to rule, in which to start his career and show his ability.

[2] Landless, poverty-stricken.

[3] At the great Confucian.

help him, paltry and insignificant fellows avoid him, evil [1]
teachings fear him, and the common people honour him.
When he is in office he unites the country ; when he is out of
office, by himself he establishes an honourable name. Heaven
could not kill them ; Earth could not bury them ; a time
like that of Ch'ie and Chih could not soil them ; unless they
had been great Confucians, they could not have been
established—such were Confucius and Tze Kung.[2]

Thus there are common men, there are common Confucians,
there are correct [3] Confucians, and there are great Confucians. They have no scholarship ; they are without correct
moral feeling ; and they consider riches and profit to be the
summum bonum—such are commom men.

They have large clothes, wide girdles, and high [4] hats ;
they sketchily follow the early Kings, but are satisfied with
the teaching of a confused age ; they have erroneous learning
and confused actions ; they do not know that they should
imitate the later Kings and unify their purposes ; they do
not know that they should exalt the rules of proper conduct
(*Li*) and justice (*Yi*) and regard the *Odes* and *History* as
important ; their clothes, hat, and deportment are quite
like that fashionable and common, yet they do not know
enough to dislike it ; their speech and talk has quite no
difference from that of Micius, yet they cannot clearly distinguish it ; they invoke the early Kings in order to cheat

Common
men.

Common
Confucians.

[1] Unorthodox.
[2] Probably Chung-kung. Cf. *Analects*, V, iv ; VI, i, iv ; XI, ii ; XII,
ii. Cf. Wang Hsien-ch'ien's Introduction 攷 證 f. 46 for discussion of this
name.
[3] Or " elegant ", developed in virtue.
[4] Or " narrow " ; or " like conch shells ", i.e. high and peaked.

stupid people and seek for a living [1] ;   if they get fed and accumulate enough to fill their mouths they are satisfied ; they follow their master, and they serve their talkative favourites and their upper class retainers, they are quite like life-long prisoners, not daring to have any other purposes— such are common Confucians.

He imitates the later Kings and unifies his purposes [2] ; he **18** exalts the rules of proper conduct (*Li*) and justice (*Yi*) and Correct regards the *Odes* and *History* as important ; his speech and and actions already accord with general principles ; yet there are things which his intelligence cannot deal with ; his following the doctrine has not attained to some things ; his learning has not come to some things, hence his intelligence cannot classify them.[3]   When he knows a thing he says he knows it ; when he does not know a thing he says he does not know it ; on the one hand he does not use the fact that he does not know that which he says that he knows and vice versa to deceive himself, and on the other hand, he does not use it to cheat others. Thereby he respects the Worthy, fears the law, and does not dare to be remiss or proud—such is a correct [4] Confucian.

He imitates the ancient Kings ; he is versed in the rules Great of proper conduct (*Li*) and justice (*Yi*); he unifies his purposes; Confucians. by the shallow he deals with the deep ; through the ancient he deals with the present ; through one example he deals with ten thousand ; if a matter has to do with benevolence (*Jen*)

[1] Lit., " clothes and food."

[2] Or " policies ", rules or ways of action.

[3] In a new situation he is unable to classify it and put it under an old rule and so be able to deal with it.

[4] Or " elegantly virtuous ".

and justice (*Yi*), although it is among the birds or beasts, it is like distinguishing white from black [1] for him ; in dealing with strange things and bizarre changes, which have not been previously heard of nor have been previously seen, he suddenly takes up one corner and then is able to state to what class it belongs and answer it [2] without any doubt or disconcertion ; he explains it and sees through it, and it corresponds to his explanation as two halves of a tally [3]—such is a great Confucian.

19   Consequently, if the ruler employs a common man, [4] a state of ten thousand chariots [5] will be destroyed [6] ; if he employs a common Confucian, a state of ten thousand chariots will be barely preserved ; if he employs a correct Confucian, a state of a thousand chariots will be at peace [7] ; if he employs a great Confucian. then from a place only a hundred *li* in size, after a while or after three years,[8] the country will be unified, the feudal princes will serve him ; if he [9] has a state of ten thousand chariots, he will appoint

[1] Easy.

[2] As for example in dealing with fallacies ; cf. p. 209.

[3] A piece of bamboo was split in two and half given to each of two men ; upon putting the two pieces ..ther, the genuineness of the token could be seen in that they fitted together exactly.

[4] As prime minister.

[5] A large state.

[6] Because of his exaltation of riches and profit instead of the benefit of the people.

[7] Undisturbed by enemies.

[8] Yang Liang says that T'ang of the Shang dynasty and Wen of the Chou dynasty ruled as King after three years of developing and influencing their states.

[9] The great Confucian.

or ·emove his officials, bring things to a proper state, and in one morning his fame will be great.[1]

Not having learned it [2] is not as good as having learned it ; having learned it is not as good as having seen it carried out ; having seen it is not as good as understanding it ; understanding it is not as good as doing it.   The development of scholarship is to the extreme of doing it, and that is its end and goal.   He who carries it out, knows it thoroughly.   He who knows it thoroughly becomes a Sage.   The Sage founds his conduct upon benevolence (*Jen*) and justice (*Yi*) ; he decides right and wrong accurately ; he makes his speech and action correspond to each other, not varying the least bit—there is no other reason for that than because he simply carries it [3] out.   Therefore he who has heard of it but has not seen it, will certainly err, even though he be widely learned. He who has seen it but does not understand it, will certainly be led astray, even though he have memorized it.[4]   He who understands it but does not carry it out will certainly stumble, even though he regard it as important.   If a man has not learned it nor seen it carried out, although his actions should be correct,[5] he would not be benevolent (*Jen*) ; every hundred of his actions would only be a hundred failures.

Therefore if a man is without a teacher or precepts,[6] then

(marginal note: The importance of the *Tao*.)

---

[1] Like T'ang or Wu in conquering their enemies in one battle.

[2] Right learning, the Confucian Way of life and knowledge.

[3] What he has learned—the Confucian Way.

[4] Like a certain Mr. Chih, spoken of in the 漢書禮樂志, who could tell all the ringing and drumming of the instruments and all the posturings of the dancers while performing each of the Odes, but could not state their meaning !

[5] By chance.

[6] Lit., " a Law " in the New Testament sense of the word.

if he is intelligent, he will certainly become a robber ; if he is brave, he will certainly become a murderer ; if he has ability 20 he will certainly cause disorder; if he is an investigator he will certainly become bizarre [1] ; if he is a dialectician, he will certainly go far from the truth. If he has a teacher and precepts, then if he is intelligent, he will quickly become learned ; if he is brave, he will quickly become awe-inspiring ; if he has ability, he will quickly become perfect ; if he is an investigator, he will quickly arrive at all truth ; if he is a dialectician, he will quickly be able to determine the truth or falsity of all things. Therefore the possession of a teacher and of precepts is the greatest treasure a man can have ; the lack of a teacher and of precepts is the greatest calamity a man can have.

If a man is without a teacher or precepts, he will exalt his original nature [2] ; if he has a teacher and precepts, he will exalt self-cultivation. Now a teacher and precepts are what is gained by self-cultivation, not what is obtained from original nature.

Original nature and acquired characteristics.

Original nature [3] is not good enough to set itself up as the ruler of a personality. Original nature is that which I cannot produce, yet which can be developed. Self-cultivation is that which I do not originally have, but which can be produced. Choices and rejections and habitual practice are the means of developing original nature. To concentrate on one

[1] Like Huei Shih and Teng Sih, the Neo-Micians.

[2] Which is evil, and so the man will be led into evil.

[3] Adding the character 性 after 性 ; the comment made by Yang Liang implies that there were two 性 characters in his text.

thing and not vary [1] is that whereby self-cultivation is **21**
perfected.   Practice alters a person's inclinations ; if kept
up for a long time it alters his inmost being.   If a person
concentrates on one thing, and does not vary, he will become
as wise as the gods and form a triad with Heaven and Earth.
For by collecting [2] earth a mountain is made, and by collecting
water the sea is made.[3]   If the common man on the street
cultivates [4] goodness and wholly completes its cultivation, he
will be called a Sage.   First he must seek, and then only
will he obtain ; he must do it, and then only will he reach
perfection ; he must cultivate [4] it, and then only can he
rise ; he must complete its cultivation, and then only can he
be a Sage.   For the Sage is the man who has cultivated [4]
himself.   A man who practises [5] hoeing and ploughing becomes
a farmer ; if he practises [5] chopping and shaving wood, he

---

[1] Study only orthodox teachings.

[2] The same character 積 above translated " self-cultivation " or
" practice " is here translated " collecting ".   The argument is that as by
積 (collecting) earth or water, mountains and seas are made, so by 積
(collecting or cultivating) goodness a great character is made.   Since in
English we have no word with the meaning of collecting both earth or
water and goodness, the translation cannot indicate the force of Hsüntze's
argument.

[3] Here follows the sentence : " The collection of mornings and evenings
is called a year ; the extreme of height is called Heaven ; the extreme of
lowness is called Earth ; the six directions (north, south, east, west, up,
and down) in the world are called the extremes (極, the word used for the
north pole)."   This sentence interrupts the thread of the discourse and
seems to be a gloss.

[4] 積.

[5] 積.

becomes an artisan [1] ; if he practises [2] trafficking in goods, he becomes a merchant ; if he practises [2] the rules of proper conduct (*Li*) and justice (*Yi*), he becomes a superior man. The son of an artisan always follows his father's trade, and the people of a city or state are satisfied to repeat its peculiarities. He who lives in Ts'u [3] becomes a man of Ts'u ; he who lives in Yueh [4] becomes a man of Yueh ; he who lives in central China [5] becomes a man of central China. This is not from the original human nature received from Nature, but attained by profuse cultivation. Hence, if a man knows how to pay attention to his choices and rejections, to be careful of his habits, and to magnify profuse cultivation, he will become a superior man. If he follows his nature and his emotions, and his scholarship is restricted, he will become a small-minded man. If a person is a superior man he is usually peaceful and honoured ; if he is a small-minded man he is usually in danger and disgrace. All men desire peace and honour and dislike danger and disgrace ; hence the superior man alone is able to obtain that which he likes ; the small-minded man daily invites that which he dislikes. The ode says :—

> " Now this good man
> 　　Is not sought after nor advances in office.

---

[1] 工 匠 in Hsüntze seems to mean " carpenter " throughout.

[2] 積.

[3] A partially civilized state to the south of ancient civilized China

[4] A still more barbaric state to the south-east of civilized China.

[5] Lit., 憂, the ancient part of China ruled over by the most ancient dynasty of Hsia, central and civilized China.

But that hard-hearted man
   Is thought of and promoted again and again.
So the people are avaricious and disorderly
   And prefer ways which are like poisonous weeds "
—this expresses my meaning.[1]

*   *   *   *   *

THE GRADES OF MEN

Their purposes are not free from crookedness and selfish- **Four Grades**
ness, yet they hope people will think them to be public- **of Men.**
spirited ; their actions are not free from foulness, yet they
hope people will think that they act correctly ; they **22**
are very stupid and ignorant, yet they hope people will
think them to be wise—such are ordinary men. In their
minds they restrain their selfishness and so they are able
to be public-spirited ; in action they restrain their emotional
nature, and so they are able to act correctly ; in knowledge
they like to inquire about things,[2] and so they are able to
have ability ; they who are public-spirited, who act correctly
and who have ability, can be called inferior Confucians.
In their purpose they are fixed in public-spiritedness ; in
action they are fixed in correct action ; in knowledge they

[1] *Book of Odes*, III, III, iii, 11.   A lament over the misgovernment of
King Li (878–842 B.C.)—he advanced the evil and neglected the worthy,
hence the people were led into evil. Such is the action of the small
minded man when in control of the State.

[2] Confucius, when he visited the ancestral temple, thought it proper to
inquire minutely about everything. *Analects*, III, xv.

comprehend all general principles ; men such as this can be called great Confucians. Great Confucians can be emperor, or the three dukes ; inferior Confucians can be feudal nobles, prefects, or officers ; ordinary men can be labourers, farmers, or merchants. The rules of proper conduct (*Li*) are the standards of all measurement [1] of ministers and officers by their ruler ; it includes all grades of men.

* * * * *

The Superior Man has his Standards. The speech of the Superior Man has limits [2] ; his actions have standards ; in his way of conduct (*Tao*) there is one thing which he emphasizes. In speaking of what should be sought for in government, he does not descend below the plane of the peace and care of the people [3] ; in speaking of what purposes should be set up, he does not descend below those of an officer [4] ; in speaking of what should be sought for in the Way of life (*Tao*) and virtue, he does not differ from those of the later kings. A way (*Tao*) which antedates that of the three dynasties is vague [5] ; a method which is different from that of the later kings is incorrect. If his speech is elevated or depressed, made small or made great, it does not go outside the foregoing. This is how the superior man

---

[1] Lit., "inch, foot, length between outstretched hands, and ten-foot length."

[2] Standards beyond which he will not go ; lit., " a boundary wall to its dwelling." Cf. *Analects* XVI, xxviii for a similar sentiment.

[3] To aggressive war and the absorption of other states.

[4] 士 ; to the purposes of ordinary people, money and wealth.

[5] The Hsia, Shang, and Chou dynasties—anything purporting to come from so ancient a date is too vague and uncertain to be believed or followed ; hence follow the later Kings.

keeps his purposes and ideas, even though they are animated, within the limits of its dwelling. Therefore if a feudal **23** noble in asking about government does not attain to the plane of the peace and care of the people, then do not answer him [1]; if a common man in asking to be taught does not rise to the plane of how an officer should act, then do not teach him.[2] If the doctrines of the hundred schools do not come up to the level of those of the later kings, then do not listen to them. For such a man is called a superior man; his speech has limits and his actions have standards.

[1] As Confucius did not reply when questioned about the art of war. *Analects* XV, i, 1. Or as Hsüntze replied when questioned about war as in Book XV.

[2] As Confucius replied when asked about husbandry—"Go to a farmer!" *Analects* XIII, iv, 1.

BOOK IX

KINGLY GOVERNMENT

PLEASE TELL ABOUT THE ART OF GOVERNMENT

Do not regard seniority but advance the worthy and able; **1**
dismiss the incompetent and incapable without delay; The art of
put incorrigible ringleaders to death without trying to reform Government.
them; develop the common people without waiting to compel
them by laws. When men's rank is uncertain, then there is
the order of seniority of their families.[1] Yet although a man
is the descendant of a king, duke, prefect or officer, if he
does not observe the rules of proper conduct (*Li*) and justice
(*Yi*), he must be relegated to the common ranks; although
he is the descendant of a commoner, if he have acquired learning, developed a good character, and is able to observe the
rules of proper conduct (*Li*) and justice (*Yi*), then elevate him
to be minister, prime minister, officer, or prefect. But lewd
people, scandal-mongers, evil-doers, people of perverted
abilities, shirkers, and unreliable people, should be trained,
given employment, and time for reformation. Stimulate them
by rewards; warn them by punishments; if they are satisfied
with employment, then keep them; if they are not satisfied
to work, then deport them. Defectives [2] should be received
and cared for; if they have ability, they should be given
positions. The authorities should employ them and clothe

[1] According to the order of their tablets in the ancestral temple.

[2] Lit., " the five kinds of defectives," the dumb, the deaf, the crippled,
the lame, and the disabled. Humpbacks, for example, were employed as
magicians and exorcists.

and feed them; they should all be cared for without exception. Those who are incorrigible should be put to death without 2 mercy. For this is what is called natural [1] virtue; this is the government of a king.

THE GREAT DISTINCTIONS TO BE MADE IN HOLDING COURT

Treat people according to *Li*.

Treat those who are good who come to you, according to what is right and proper (*Li*); treat those who are not good who come to you, with punishment. When those two kinds of people are distinguished, the worthy and the unworthy will not be mixed, right and wrong will not be confused. When the worthy and unworthy are not mixed, then heroes will come to you; when right and wrong are not confused, then the country will be well governed. If this is all done, your reputation will be great; the whole country will be willing to do your bidding, and desist from what you prohibit— the duties of a king will be completely performed.

Keep a mean between being distant and familiar.

Whenever in holding a court the ruler is severe and harsh, and does not like to treat the people pleasantly, then his subordinates are afraid and do not love him; they are all silent and do not tell him things. If this is the case, then great matters run the risk of being unfinished, and small matters run the risk of being ruined. If he is amicable and complaisant, and likes to treat people pleasantly, and does 3 not stop them, then malicious persons will approach him from all sides, and talk will bristle around him, which continually tires him out. If this is the case, he will have to listen to much and will be kept very busy; this will also

---

[1] Or " Heaven's ".

injure his government. For if he goes by law but does not look into things, then those cases to which the law is not applicable will certainly be done wrong. If he gives offices to men but does not keep acquainted with what they are doing, then those whose ability does not measure up to their duties will certainly fail. For unless he is a superior man he cannot follow law and yet investigate into things ; he cannot give office to men and yet know what they are doing ; he cannot be without secret plans ; he cannot leave any good man without office, and everything cannot be without some mistakes. For the man who is just is the standard [1] of how to hear cases [2] ; he who keeps to the mean [3] is the measure [4] of how to hold court. He who when there is a law, acts according to the law, but when there is no law, decides according to the analogies of the case, is doing the utmost possible in holding court. He who is prejudiced, shows a partisan spirit, and has no principles of action is the basest of all in holding court. For there has been bad government under good laws ; but from ancient times to the present there has never been known to be a bad government under a superior man.[5] It is said : " Good government springs from the superior man ; bad government springs from the small-minded man "—this expresses what I mean.

If the classes are equal, there will not be enough for every-

[1] Lit., the steelyard or balances.
[2] Hold court.
[3] Between harshness and overpleasantness.
[4] Lit., carpenter's inked string or plumb-line.
[5] Criticism of Shentze, who thought good laws were the essence of good government and depreciated the necessity of good men in the government.

Inequality. *Li* and *Yi* are necessary.

body [1]; when everyone's powers are equal, there is no unity in the state; when everyone is equal, there is no one to employ the people on public services. As soon as there was heaven and earth,[2] there was the distinction of above and below [3]; when the first wise king arose, the country he occupied had the division of classes. For two nobles cannot serve each other; two commoners cannot employ each other [4] —this is a law of nature. Were people's power and position equal, and their likes and dislikes the same, there would not be sufficient goods to satisfy everybody, and hence there would inevitably be strife. If there were strife, there would inevitably result general disorder; if general disorder, then general poverty. The ancient kings hated any disorder, and hence established the rules of proper conduct (*Li*) and justice (*Yi*) to divide the people, to cause them to have the classes of poor and rich, of noble and inferior, so that everyone would be under someone's control—this is the fundamental thing in 4 caring for the whole country. The *History* says: "They are only uniform in that they are not uniform"—this expresses what I mean.[5]

Follow the people's will.

When a horse hitched to a carriage is restless, a gentleman

[1] Cf. p. 65. Because everybody will seek the same goods (riches, etc.) and want just as much as those who have the most, and hence there will not be enough for all. This is criticism of the Mician doctrine of equality.

[2] Nature has its distinctions of superior and inferior.

[3] Lit., 上 下, elsewhere translated "superior and inferior", or "ruler and ruled".

[4] Only the superior can employ the inferior; we must remember that the simpler feudal civilization of Hsüntze's day made this a fact. "Employ" in ancient China was used of the employment of a government official by the ruler.

[5] *Book of History* V, xxxvii, 19.

is not secure in the carriage. When the common people are restless under the government, then a prince is not secure in his position. When a horse hitched to a carriage is restless, there is nothing better than quieting him ; when the people are restless under the government, there is nothing better than treating them generously. If he chooses the worthy and the good, advances the sincere and the reverent, stimulates filial piety and respectfulness for elders,[1] shelters the orphan and the widow, and helps the poor and the needy—if he does this, the common people will be satisfied with his government. When the common people are satisfied with his government, then only is a prince secure in his position. It is said : The prince is the boat ; the common people are the water. The water can support the boat, or the water can capsize the boat—this expresses my meaning.

For if a prince wishes to be secure, there is nothing so good as a just government and loving the people. If he wishes to have glory, then there is nothing as good as exalting the rules of proper conduct (*Li*) and reverencing the scholar.[2] If he wishes to establish a name for achievement there is nothing so good as esteeming the worthy and employing the able. These are the great virtues of a prince. When these three virtues are achieved, then all else will be achieved ; if these three virtues are not achieved, although he should indirectly achieve everything else, it would be of no avail. Confucius said [3] : He who is correct and right in great and

How to be truly successful.

---

[1] The virtue a younger brother should have for his older brother or a younger person for his elder, just as a son should show filial piety to his parents.

[2] The literary man, who is best fitted to hold office.

[3] This saying is not in the Classics.

small matters is a prince of the superior class ; he who is correct and right in great matters but sometimes right and sometimes wrong in minor matters is a prince of the middle class ; he who is wrong in great matters, although in small ones he should be right and correct—I have never seen that such an one left anything worth while to posterity.

Levying too heavy taxes leads to destruction.

Marquis Ch'eng [1] and Duke Sze [2] were experts at levying taxes and scheming extortion ; but their ability did not rise to the point of gaining the allegiance of their people. Tze Chang [3] was one who gained the allegiance of the people, but he did not rise to the point of exercising rule. Kuan Chung [4] exercised rule but did not rise to the point of 5 cultivating the rules of proper conduct (*Li*). He who only cultivates proper conduct (*Li*) can rule as a righteous king ; he who only exercises rule can be powerful ; he who only gains the allegiance of the people can be peaceful ; he who only levies taxes will be destroyed. For he who rules as righteous king [5] tries to enrich the people ; he who rules as lord protector [6] tries to enrich his retainers ; he who only preserves his state tries to enrich the nobles ; he who loses his state tries to enrich his coffers and fill his treasury. When the coffers are enriched and the treasury is full, yet the people are poor—this is what is meant by the saying : The nobles have superabundance but the masses are in want. If the enemy enters its territory, that state cannot defend itself ;

---

[1] Of Wei, 361–333 B.C.   [2] Also of Wei, 324–283 B.C.

[3] A disciple of Confucius ; often mentioned in the *Analects*. Chief Minister of the small state of Chen ; the ablest and most upright of statesmen among Confucius' contemporaries. Cf. *Analects* XIV, x ; V, xv.

[4] The famous prime minister of Duke Huan of Ts'i. Cf. *Analects* III, xxii.

[5] By right and virtue.   [6] By force.

if its army goes beyond its borders, it cannot attack ; hence
it will totter and fall.   One only needs to stand and wait for
it to happen.[1]   Hence, if I accumulate wealth, it will be for my
own destruction : the enemy will get it and become strong.
The man who only levies taxes is inviting marauders and
benefiting the enemy—this is the way (*Tao*) to destroy one's
country and endanger one's person.   Hence the wise prince
does not tread this path.

He who rules as righteous king [2] gains the allegiance of men ; he who rules as lord protector [3] gains the alliance of his equals ; he who rules by force [4] gains territory.   He who gains the allegiance of men can make the feudal nobles his ministers ; he who gains the alliance of his equals, makes friends of the feudal nobles ; he who gains territory makes enemies of the feudal nobles.   He who can make the feudal nobles his ministers can reign as king ; he who makes friends of the feudal nobles can rule as lord protector ; he who makes enemies of the feudal nobles is in danger.   Against the man who uses force, the cities of others are guarded and the military officers of others are belligerent ; but if I [5] by my strength overcome them, then I must inevitably injure the people of others greatly.   If I injure the people of another greatly, then they will certainly hate me greatly.   If they hate me greatly, then they will more and more seek to strive with me.   If the cities of another are guarded and his officers are

[sidenote: Force and warfare lead to destruction.]

---

[1] The destruction will come so soon that one need not wait long.

[2] Lawful government by truth, righteousness, and principle.

[3] The autocrat who works by force and diplomacy.

[4] The aggressor who works by force.

[5] The man who uses force ; a Chinese figure of speech, using the first
personal pronoun for a person hypothetically spoken of ; it partakes of the
Chinese grace of modesty.

belligerent, but I by my strength overcome them, then I must unavoidably injure my own people greatly. If I injure my people greatly, then they will certainly hate me greatly. If my people hate me greatly, then they will continually be less willing to strive for me. If the people of another more and more seek to strive with me, and my own people are continually less willing to strive for me—this is the way that a strong ruler becomes weak. If territory comes to me but my people leave me—I shall have much trouble but little gain. If that which I need to guard [1] is increased, yet that whereby it should be guarded [2] be reduced—this is the way that a great country becomes small. Then the feudal nobles will certainly

6 form alliances, nurse their hatred, and not forget their enmity. They will wait for the weaknesses of the ruler who is strong through force to show themselves; they will take advantage of his defeat—this will be the time of danger for the ruler who is great through force.

The true policy of the strong ruler is to conserve his strength and not strive.

The true policy (*Tao*) of the man who knows how to rule by force is not to be anxious to use force. He ponders over the edicts of the emperor; he conserves his strength; he consolidates his power. When his strength is conserved, the feudal nobles cannot weaken him; when his power is consolidated, they cannot despoil him. If the empire is without a righteous king or lord protector in control, such a man will always prevail. This is the true policy (*Tao*) of the man who knows how to rule by force.

The policy of the lord protector

But the lord protector acts differently. He opens up new lands; he fills granaries and storehouses; he provides good

---

[1] My territory.   [2] My loyal people.

implements ; he carefully prepares officers of ability and talent. Then he gives them rewards in order to encourage them to progress ; he severely punishes in order to restrain them. He preserves those who have lost their country and sustains those whose line of succession has run out ; he protects the weak and restrains the oppressive. Yet he has no intention of acquiring territory ; then the feudal nobles will be friends with him. His way is to treat enemies as friends [1] ; he respectfully meets the feudal nobles,[2] and then the feudal nobles will be pleased with him. They make friends with him because he does not seek territory ; if he appears to want territory, the feudal princes would be distant to him. They are pleased with him because he treats enemies as friends ; if he appears to want to make them his subordinates, then the feudal nobles will leave him. Hence he makes it plain that his motives are not to gain territory ; he makes them believe in his way (*Tao*) of treating enemies as friends. If the empire is without a righteous King in control, such a man will always prevail. This is the true policy (*Tao*) of the man who knows how to be a Lord Protector.

King Min was ruined by the five states [3] ; Duke Huan [4]

should be to make friends and not to gain territory.

---

[1] He treats everyone, enemy as well as friend, courteously and respectfully.

[2] In calling a convocation of the nobles to determine important matters, as did Duke Huan.

[3] In 284 B.C. this king of Ts'i was defeated by the combined forces of the states of Yen, Chao, Ts'u, and Ts'in, and he was compelled to abdicate and flee to Chü (formerly an independent state, but then absorbed by Ts'u).

[4] Of Ts'i. 685–643 B.C. Chuang threatened to kill Huan if he did not return some territory. Huan was Lord Protector, Chief of the feudal princes of the empire·

was captured by Chuang [1] of Lu—it was for no other reason than that they did not follow this policy, but sought to be king. [2]

The policy of
the King is to
rule by virtue.

But the righteous king acts differently.   His benevolence (*Jen*) fills the empire ; his justice (*Yi*) permeates the land ; **8** his majesty pervades the country.   His benevolence (*Jen*) fills the empire, hence there is no one in the empire who does not cherish regard for him ; his justice (*Yi*) permeates the land, hence no one in the empire fails to honour him ; his majesty pervades the country, hence no one in the empire cares to oppose him.   His unassailable majesty assists in his method (*Tao*) of winning the people, [3] hence he conquers without fighting, he captures cities without attacking them ; the whole empire submits without moving a soldier.   This is he who knows the true policy (*Tao*) of the righteous king. He who knows these three means, [4] if he wishes to be King, he can become King ; if he wishes to become Lord Protector, he can become Lord Protector ; if he wishes to become strong, he can become strong.

THE ASSISTANTS OF A KING

They should beautify their actions by proper conduct (*Li*) and justice (*Yi*) ; in listening to reports and attending to business, it should be according to rule ; they should pay attention to minutiæ and detail.   In their actions they

---

[1] Duke Chuang, 693–662 B.C.

[2] Emperor.

[3] By humanity, righteousness, and justice.

[4] Benevolence, justice, and majesty.

should adapt themselves to changes in circumstances and never be at a loss. Such people can be the assistants of a king.

THE GOVERNMENT OF A KING

Its principles (*Tao*) should not depart from those of the three dynasties [1] ; its methods should not differ from those of the later Kings.[2] Principles (*Tao*) which differ from those of the three dynasties are loose ; methods which differ from those of the later Kings are incorrect. There are models for garments [3] ; there are rules for buildings [4] ; there is an established way of grading officials and soldiers. Mourning rites, sacrifices, and their appropriate utensils all have their gradations.[5] All music which is not correct [6] should be totally abandoned. All colours which are not subdued [7] should be totally dispensed with. All utensils which are not of the ancient sort should be destroyed. This is what is meant by returning to the ancient. This is the government of a king.

It should follow the Way of the Kings.

THE PRINCIPLES OF A RIGHTEOUS KING

He does not honour those who are without virtue ; he does not make those who have no ability officials ; he does not reward those who have no merit ; he does not punish those

Fairness and Justice.

[1] Of Hsia, Shang, and Chou, i.e., it should be founded on the principles established by the ancient and great rulers.

[2] The details of the administration of past dynasties are so ancient that they are obscure ; hence follow the recent precedents and laws, established by the great Kings of the present dynasty, and so be sure to be right.

[3] Ceremonial garments and ordinary clothes.

[4] Palaces and houses.

[5] I.e., classical and ancient.

[6] Appropriate to the rank of the deceased.

[7] Garments dyed gaudily or brilliantly embroidered not to be used ; probably because in ancient times there were no brilliant dyes.

who have no guilt. In his court there are no positions for
favourites ; among the people there are none who live off the
country.[1] He advances the worthy and employs the able,
9 and does not neglect any grade.[2] He represses the
unprincipled and restrains the overbearing ; yet his punishments are not extreme. The people are observant, and all
know that he who is virtuous in his home will receive reward
at the court; he who is evil in secret will receive punishment in public. This is what is meant by fixing the principle
of action. These are the principles of a righteous king.

THE METHODS OF A RIGHTEOUS KING

He only
tithes the
land ; no
customs dues.

He grades taxation and rectifies the amount of service to
be given[3] ; he regulates everything in order to nourish all
his people. He levies a tithe on the land. At the customs
houses and market places[4] he inspects travellers[5] but does
not levy duties.[6] He prohibits or permits forestry and fishing,
according to the season ; but he does not tax it. He appraises
the land[7] and assesses its tax. He regulates tribute[8]
according to the distance of the place. There should
be a circulation of valuables[9] and grain[10] without restriction

[1] Idle favourites ; grafters.
[2] He honors virtue, even in the lowest grade of officialdom.
[3] In lieu of taxation.
[4] Every road, river, and market in China is still dotted with customs
houses and barriers which levy duty upon all commerce.
[5] To prevent evil characters from entering.
[6] Free trade within the empire ; still one of China's desiderata.
[7] According to how much it can produce.
[8] Sent by the more distant parts of the empire.
[9] In that time, trade was still by barter.
[10] Millet and rice.

or hindrance, enabling foodstuffs [1] to be freely transported, and all within the four seas [2] to be like one family. Then those who are near will not hide their ability, and those who are distant will not grumble at their toil. [3] There will be no unenlightened or secluded country which will fail to fly to serve him and be satisfied and rejoice in him. This is **10** what is called being a leader and teacher of men. These are the methods of a righteous King.

On the north sea [4] there are swift horses and great dogs; **Benefits of free trade.** if this policy were carried out, then China could obtain, raise, and use them. On the south sea there are fine feathers, ivory, rhinoceros hides, copper, cinnabar, and cornelian; then China could get them, and be enriched thereby. On the eastern sea there is purple,[5] coarse linen, fish, and salt; then China could get them and wear and eat them. On the western sea [6] there are felt rugs, furs, dyed yåk-tails; then China could get them and use them. Then people who live on the borders of the sea would have a sufficiency of wood; people who live in the mountains would have plenty of fish; farmers would have a sufficiency of implements without chopping, scraping, making pottery, or smelting; the workman and

[1] A rice-producing province will still prohibit the export of rice to keep down the price of food within the province.

[2] A famous saying. The continent of China was supposed to be surrounded by four seas.

[3] In public service.

[4] To the north of China towards the great sea supposed to bound the land at the north.

[5] A dye plant.

[6] This expression merely means to a great distance in the west. This passage is a remarkable indication of the extent of early commerce. All these goods went by land, and only a peaceful country and developed civilization could enable traders to travel such distances.

the merchant would have sufficient pulse and millet without ploughing the fields. For the tiger and leopard are fierce, yet the gentleman could have them skinned and use them. For nothing which heaven covers or the earth sustains would fail to yield up all its goodness and be brought for his use. On the one hand they would adorn the worthy and good, and on the other they would nourish the people and give them happiness. This is what it means to be a great ruler.

11 The ode says :

> " Heaven made the high hill,[1]
>
>   King T'ai brought it under cultivation.
>
> He began the work ;
>
>   King Wen tranquillized it "—

this expresses my meaning.[2]

The Way of the Kings can deal with everything. It [3] is able to deal with the confused through its classifications ; it is able to deal with the myriad [4] through the one.[5] What is begun can be brought to completion ; when a thing is brought to completion, another can be begun, like a ring without end. Whoever departs from it, his empire decays.

Heaven and Earth ; Li and Yi, and the superior man. Heaven and Earth are the source of life. The rules of proper conduct (*Li*) and justice (*Yi*) are the source of good government ; the superior man is the source of the rules of proper conduct (*Li*) and justice (*Yi*).[6] To carry them [7] out,

---

[1] The original home of the Chou dynasty in Shensi.

[2] *Book of Odes,* IV, I, v. Also quoted on p. 178. The meaning is that the great king can utilize the opportunity given by nature to bring forth great results.

[3] The kingly method of government.

[4] Everything.

[5] One principle.

[6] They issue from him ; here it refers to the King-Sage.

[7] *Li* and *Yi.*

to practise them, to study them much, and to love them greatly
is the source of being a superior man. For Heaven and
Earth give birth to the superior man ; the superior man
brings Heaven and Earth into order; the superior man
forms a triad with Heaven and Earth ; he is the controller
of all things, the father and mother of the people. Without
the superior man Heaven and Earth are not ordered, the
rules of proper conduct (*Li*) and justice (*Yi*) have no control.
When on the one hand there is no prince and leader, on the
other hand there cannot be the distinction of father and son [1]—
this is what is called extreme disorder. The prince and minister,
the father and son, the older and younger brother, husband
and wife [2]—here we have a beginning and end, an end and
a beginning ; this social structure exhibits the same principles
as Heaven and Earth ; it is of equal permanence with the
universe [3]—this is called the great foundation. [4] Hence
mourning rites, sacrificial rites, court ceremonies, and methods
of courtesy are governed by one principle. Promotion, degrada-
tion, condemnation to death, permission to live, [5] giving and
taking away [6] are governed by the same principle. That

[1] No social order.

[2] Four out of the five Confucian social relations ; the fifth is the relation
of friend to friend ; omitted because it shows no distinction of superior
and inferior, and hence is not fundamental to the social order.

[3] Lit., " the ten thousand things."

[4] Of life. The kingly government is founded on the distinctions of
ordered society.

[5] The opposite of condemnation to death, i.e., acquitting an accused
man and allowing him to live. We must remember that in Hsüntze's
time government was not by law, but by the ruler, who was and is yet
the law-maker, prosecutor, and judge. The acquittal of an accused man
was solely dependent upon his word.

[6] Of wealth and office.

the prince should be treated as prince, the minister should be treated as minister, the father should be treated as father, the son as son, the older brother as older brother, the younger brother as younger brother, is following the same principle. That the farmer should be treated as farmer, the
12 scholar as scholar, the labourer as labourer and the merchant as merchant is the same principle.

The essence of humanity is social organization. Water and fire have essences,[1] but not life; herbs and trees have life, but no knowledge; birds and beasts have knowledge but no sense of what are rights (*Yi*). Man has an essence, life, knowledge, and in addition has a sense of human rights (*Yi*); hence he is the highest being on earth. His strength is not equal to that of the bull [2]; his running is not equal to that of the horse; yet the bull and horse are used by him. How is that? Men are able to form social organizations, the former [3] are not able to form social organizations. How is it that men are able to form social organizations? Because of their distinctions.[4] How is it that distinctions can be carried out? Through rights (*Yi*).[5] For class rights (*Yi*) are harmonized through social distinctions. When people are harmonious, they can unite; when united, they have greater strength; when they have great strength, they

---

[1] 氣, a mobile term for explaining and denoting whatever is supposed to be the source of primary agent in producing and modifying motion, as if it were animated air. It is akin to the concept of form. In Mencius, Legge has translated it " the passion-nature ".

[2] The Chinese use the buffalo cow, a great, bulky, ferocious-looking beast.

[3] Beasts; bulls or horses.

[4] Social distinctions, high and low.

[5] Rights, rights-ness, the personal rights of each class, what is right and just.

become strong; when strong, they can dominate nature
Hence they can have palaces and houses for habitation.
Hence they can order their actions according to the four
seasons and control all things. Hence they can enjoy the
goodness of the whole world. They gain this for no other
reason than that they have social distinctions and class
rights (Yi). Hence, if men are to live, they cannot get along
without forming a social organization. If they form a social
organization, but have no social distinctions, then they will
quarrel; if they quarrel, there will be disorder; if there is
disorder, people will fail to co-operate; if they fail to co-
operate, then they will be weak; if they are weak, then
they will not be able to dominate nature. Hence they could
not have palaces or houses for habitation. All of which means
that people cannot abandon the rules of proper conduct
(Li) or class rights (Yi) for an instant. He who is able
thereby [1] to serve his parents, is said to have filial piety; he
who is able thereby to serve his older brother is said to have
brotherly respect; he who is able thereby to serve his superior
is said to be obedient; he who is able thereby to utilize his
inferiors is said to have the virtues of a prince. A prince
is one who is good at social organization.[2]

If this doctrine (Tao) of forming a social organization is Conservation
carried out as it should be, then all things will fulfil their of resources.
appropriate function; the six kinds of domestic animals will
all thrive; all living beings will fulfil their destiny.[3] For if

---

[1] By Li and Yi.

[2] The character for " forming a social organization " 羣 contains the
character for " prince ", 君, as one of its component parts.

[3] Obtain their proper development and fulfil their true function in life.

their nourishment and growth is at the proper season, then the six kinds of domestic animals will develop and increase ; if killing [1] and saving alive are at the proper season, then grass and trees will flourish. If government decrees are timely,[2] the people will be united, the worthy and the good will serve the ruler ; it will be the rule of a Sage-King. When shrubs and trees are in bloom and leaf, the axe must not enter the forest, people must not cut short the life of the trees or shrubs when young, nor stop their growth ; when sea tortoises,[3] water lizards,[4] fish, turtles, eels, and sturgeons,[5] are full of roe or have spawned, nets or poison must not enter the marshes or pools, people must not cut short the life of these water creatures when young nor stop their growth. The springtime ploughing, the summertime weeding, the fall harvesting, and the winter storing away of the grain—these four things must not be out of season.[6] Hence the five cereals will not fail, and the people will have an abundance

13 of food. Ponds, pools, streams, and marshes should

[1] Harvesting grain at the right season ; cutting trees only when fully grown ; there may also be implied that " closed seasons " should be observed in hunting, and that war should be carried on only when it will not interfere with the cultivation of the crops.

[2] The same word as above translated, " at the proper season."

[3] Said to be twenty feet around, supposed to be the original scaly animal. Hsüntze has used (with the exception of the last two) almost the same list of water animals as enumerated in the *Doctrine of the Mean,* XXVI, 9.

[4] A large triton or gavial, ten feet long, found in South China, prized for its skin (used for drum heads) and flesh (served at weddings).

[5] Described as a large sea-monster, 20 to 30 feet long.

[6] Hence the Chinese government still, through its almanac, informs the farmer of the exact day when each of these seasons and times for particular agricultural activity begins ; though the calendar is lunar, yet these dates are determined on the basis of a solar calculation.

be strictly closed [1] at the proper time ; hence fish and turtles will be very plentiful, and the people will have a surplus for use.[2] The cutting down and growth of timber should not be at the wrong season ; then the mountains and forests will not be bare,[3] and the people will have a surplus of timber. This is the way the Sage-King uses the country's resources. On the one hand, he observes the heavens,[4] and on the other he applies it [5] to the earth. He fills up what is lacking in heaven and earth,[6] and diffuses it upon all things.[7] He makes plain that which was obscure ; he makes long that which was too short ; he enlarges that which was too narrow. Although he is as wise and great as the gods, yet he is very simple. Hence it is said : By one principle [8] he unifies the whole. The man who acts in this way is called a Sage.

THE ARRANGEMENT OF OFFICIALS [9]

The Master of Ceremonies should know the number of stables for sacrificial animals for preparing delicacies for guests of state and for sacrifices. The Minister of the Interior should know the number of all the clans, of inner and outer city walls, and of the established utensils.[10] The Minister

The Master of Ceremonies. The Minister of the Interior. The Minister of War.

[1] To fishing.

[2] For barter, over and above what is needed for food.

[3] Evidently deforestation of the mountains had already begun. This word " bare " means literally, " bald and bare like the head of an infant."

[4] To determine the seasons and times.

[5] His knowledge of the seasons.

[6] He orders the natural resources of the country, especially husbandry.

[7] Lit., " the ten-thousand things." Heaven, earth, and the ten-thousand things make up the universe.

[8] *Li* and *Yi.*

[9] On this section cf. *Book of History*, V, xx, 7–12.

[10] Standards of measurement and weight.

of War[1] should know the number of regiments,[2] battalions,[3]
14 armour, soldiers, chariots, and companies.[4] The prepara-

The Chief Instructor. tion of the laws and edicts, the examination of odes
and essays, the elimination of licentious[5] music, and
obediently to do each at its proper time so that barbarian
or popular ditties should not confuse the odes[6]—such should

The Minister of Works. be the business of the Chief Instructor. To build embank-
ments and bridges, to keep the ditches and canals clean; to
drain off overflow water; to keep the reservoirs from overflowing[7]; in the right season to lead water in[8] or to stop it,[9]
so that although the year be bad and afflicted with floods or
drought, the people will have something to weed and mow—

The Bailiff. such should be the business of the Minister of Works. To
inspect the high and low lands,[10] to examine fertile and poor
soils, to regulate the planting of the five grains,[11] to examine
into the merit of the farmers,[12] carefully to attend to storing
the grain, and obediently to do each at its proper time, so

---

[1] Lit., " cavalry." Cavalry was the most important arm of military
service.

[2] Lit., 師, 2,500 men. For the sizes of these divisions of the
army also cf. Legge, *Book of History*, vol. ii, p. 302.

[3] Lit., 旅, 500 men.

[4] Lit., 伯, 100 men. Each chariot had a company of men, also given
as 75 men, accompanying it.

[5] Unorthodox.

[6] Orthodox music to be kept uncorrupted and alone performed.

[7] Irrigation has always been an important part of Chinese agriculture.

[8] To the reservoirs.

[9] The water from entering the reservoir.

[10] The plain and the marsh.

[11] Glutinous milled, panicled millet, beans, hemp, and wheat; to
apportion each to its proper soil.

[12] See whether they are lazy or industrious, and to encourage industry.

that the farmers simplify and make few their activities [1]— such should be the business of the Bailiff.[2] To regulate the The Warden of Parks and laws about fire,[3] to care for the hills and forests, the marshes, Ponds. herbs, trees, fish, turtles and all vegetables, at the 15 right time to close or open the season,[4] so that the country shall have abundant supplies of things to use and its wealth never be exhausted—such should be the duties of the Warden of Parks and Ponds. To make the countryside obey, to control The Local Official. the market-squares and residential quarters of cities, to get people to rear the six domestic animals, to superintend arboriculture, to encourage morality, to urge filial piety and brotherly reverence, obediently to do each at the proper time, so that the people obey the ruler's edicts and are satisfied to live in the country—such should be the duties of the Local Official. To supervise all the artisans, to examine into the The Super- intendent of seasons and activities of the men,[5] to separate fine and rough Artisans. articles, to encourage well-made and useful goods, so that goods which are carved and coloured are not made at home [6]— such should be the duties of the Superintendent of Artisans. To observe the *Yin* and *Yang*,[7] to prognosticate by the The Witch and Wizard. action and reaction of these powers of nature,[8] and by the

[1] Concentrate on agriculture and do not waste time on other activities, such as carpenter-work, pottery, etc.

[2] An officer who had oversight of the fields.

[3] Burning the hillsides and marshes for fertilizer.

[4] For cutting trees, fishing, etc.

[5] I.e., to decide the time for different works. There should be a harmony between the seasons, the earth-exhalation (formative element), the materials, and the skill of the workman.

[6] Possibly an old guild or patent law to encourage fine craftsmanship.

[7] Negative and positive principles of Chinese cosmology and geomancy.

[8] Foretell the weather (?).

looks of the sky, to scorch the tortoise-shell,[1] to arrange divining stalks,[2] to preside at the prayer for averting evil, to observe the five omens,[3] to know their good and bad fortune, auspiciousness and inauspiciousness—such should be the duties of the hunchback witch and the lame wizard.[4]

The Mayor. To care for the disposal of refuse from graveyards and privies,[5] to repair the roads, to repress robbers and thieves, to tranquillize hotels and shops, obediently to do each at the proper time in order that travelling merchants may be undisturbed 16 and commerce may be unobstructed—such should be the

The Minister of Crimes. duties of the Mayor of a market-town. To repress the unprincipled, and restrain the overbearing, to guard against the wicked and remove the evil-doers, to execute them according to the five punishments, so that the oppressive and overbearing change their actions and wicked deeds are not performed—such should be the duties of the Minister of Crimes.

The Prime Minister. To make the admonition of the people the foundation of his policy, to correct the laws, both to hold court and at times to inspect the officials, to measure their merit and consider

---

[1] A form of divination.

[2] Divination by the milfoil. These systems of divination are found in the *Book of Changes* and were commonly used. They are mentioned in many places besides the *Book of Changes*, so this is not necessarily a reference to that book.

[3] Rain, sky clearing, overcast sky, want of sequence, or baleful.

[4] Cripples, male and female, were given the official post of witch or wizard ; lame men were made soothsayers ; these had charge of divination.

[5] Every hill is made into a graveyard, and used for pasture ; hence it is a source of fertilizer, which is gathered by the farmers, especially the women and children. Nightsoil is used for fertilizer and has a

their rewards, and carefully to do each at the proper time, so that all the government servants spur themselves to the greatest efficiency and all the common people do not become negligent—such should be the duties of the Prime Minister. To consider the rules of proper conduct (*Li*) and music, to correct morals, to extend culture, to ennoble customs, both to inquire into and judge them and to harmonize them—such should be the duties of a Prince or Duke.[1] To bring morals to perfection, to be an example of extreme greatness, and of utmost refinement, to unify the empire, to stimulate even the lowest, so that no one in the empire will fail to obey and acknowledge him—such should be the duties of the Emperor.[2] Then if the government is evil, it is the crime of the Prime Minister ; if the morals of a state deteriorate, it is the fault of the Prince or Duke. If the empire is not unified and the

The Prince or Duke.

The Emperor.

---

[1] The head of a feudal state. They were at first enfeoffed as only Duke or Marquis at the most ; but by Hsüntze's time most of them had arrogated to themselves the title of King, and so Hsüntze has to use this term " prince ", 辟, to be understood ; however, he disapproved of their arrogating to themselves the title of King, which properly belonged only to the Emperor, so he does not use that title, but another term, 辟, meaning " prince " or " sovereign ", at which no one could take offence, but which was a rebuke to these self-styled kings, inasmuch as that word was not used in their titles. This is an example of a typically Confucian rebuke to constituted authority. In a highly cultured country such as ancient China, it would be patent to every educated reader. Confucius used this method of praising or blaming kings and lords frequently in his *Spring and Autumn*, and it is such remarks as this one that are meant by the phrase, " the subtleties of the *Spring and Autumn*."

[2] Here the term " King ", 王, misappropriated by the feudal rulers, is used for the Emperor, to make the point unmistakable. He is styled the 天 王, on the analogy of 天 子.

feudal princes are commonly disloyal,[1] then that man should not be Emperor.

* * * * *

Good government and prosperity depends on the ruler. With [2] all these officers, some have reigned as righteous King; with all these, some have become Lords Protector; with all of them, thrones have been preserved; with all of them, thrones have been lost. The rule of a kingdom of ten thousand chariots [3] is that whereby majesty and strength is established, whereby fame is beautified, whereby enemies are subjected, and whereby the country is made peaceful or unquiet, good or bad. But the government depends entirely on the ruler, not on others. Whether the rule of a king or lord protector will be stable, in danger, or destroyed depends wholly on the ruler himself, not on others.

Therefore when a country's majesty and strength is insufficient to imperil a neighbouring enemy; and its fame is insufficient to control the whole empire; such a country could not be independent. How could it avoid 17 becoming suddenly embarrassed? When the whole

[1] The state of affairs in Hsüntze's day is that described in this sentence. This is one of the few places in Hsüntze where the Emperor is criticized. Hsüntze and the Confucians probably expected the overthrow of the Chou dynasty, but not that of the feudal system itself.

[2] From this point on to the end of this book, Yang Liang has made no comment. Possibly these pages were lost in his copy. The idiom of vocabulary is simpler than the preceding, but thoroughly in Hsüntze's manner.

[3] Originally only the Emperor had 10,000 chariots; but later it came to mean a large state.

empire is coerced by one aggressive state and I [1] wake up to find that I am doing what I really do not want to do, and that I am daily assisting a Ch'ie [2]; this fact will not prevent me from becoming a Yao [3]; yet this is not the way that merit or fame will come, nor does it follow from this fact alone that my rule will either be permanent or destroyed, peaceful or dangerous. The establishment of fame and the conditions determining the permanence or destruction, the peace or danger of a prince will certainly depend on the ruler's sincere purpose in the time when he is self-satisfied and flourishing. He who is a real king is in earnest [4] about his state, and he will rule his country righteously. He who endangers or destroys his state also endangers or destroys his state in the days when it is flourishing. Accordingly, I should be neutral and impartial, and when there are various alliances of states, [5] I should be quiet, curb my troops, and not move them, and so watch the aggressive states clinch with each other. Therefore I should make my official admonitions peaceful; I should restrain my ardour and mark time; I should exercise oversight over the people and polish them; while I do that, my troops will become the strongest in the empire. Accordingly I should cultivate

(margin note: How a dependent state can become supreme through virtue.)

---

[1] The ruler of a particular state who wishes to be righteous. The Chinese language uses the first personal pronoun in a hypothetical example, where we use the third person.

[2] An abandoned, wicked emperor; we should say " a Nero ".

[3] A famous, good emperor.

[4] Sincerity, one of the Confucian virtues.

[5] When the number of important feudal states was reduced by fighting to seven, there were alliances of six against a powerful seventh and of a weak state with the seventh against the five—this is what is referred to here.

benevolence (*Jen*) and justice (*Yi*) ; I should sincerely elevate my country to prosperity ; I should rectify the laws ; I should choose the worthy and good for my officials ; I should nourish the people ; while I do that, my fame will become the greatest in the country. My authority will make me important ; my army will make me powerful ; my fame will make me great. Then Yao and Shun, who unified the country, could not be one iota [1] greater than I should be. Those who seek to gain power and to subvert others will retire ; and as a result the worthy and the good, officials who recognize a Sage, will of themselves come forward to offer their services. Punishments and government will be fair ; the people will be harmonious ; the customs of the state will be regulated ; and as a result the army will be powerful, cities will be impregnable, and enemy states will accordingly submit of their own volition. I should pay attention to the essentials of life,[2] I should accumulate wealth and not recklessly procrastinate and waste ; this will cause all the numberless officials and people to act according to the laws and usages ; as a result wealth will accumulate, and the country will therefore become rich of its own accord. When these three things [3] are realized in this fashion, the **18** empire will submit and the prince of an aggressive state will accordingly himself not be able to use his army against me. How is that ? He will have no one to send against me. Those whom he would send

---

[1] Lit., " one-ten-thousandth of an ounce," or " a grain of dust."

[2] Agriculture and sericulture.

[3] Righteous authority, a loyal army, and great fame (reputation for virtue).

must be his people. But his people would be attached
to me ; they would rejoice in me as in their father
and mother [1] ; they would love me as the fragrance of an
epidendrum ; then they would turn and regard their own
superior as a branding iron or tattooing needle, as an enemy
to themselves. That is human nature. Although a man
were a Ch'ie or a Chih,[2] how could he be willing to do what
he hates or to injure him whom he loves ? For that man [3]
would have gained his allegiance.

Through these principles it was possible in ancient times
for a man who originally had only one state to gain the
empire ; not by invading it, but because he was so very
willing to cultivate his government. Thus he could punish
the aggressive and curb the fierce. Thus while Duke Chou [4]
was subjugating the south, the northern states grumbled,
saying, "Why does he fail to come to us alone ? "
When he was subjugating the east, the western states
grumbled, saying "Why does he come to us only last
of all ? " [5] Who could strive with such a ruler ?
Therefore a ruler who acted in that fashion could
advance from his own state to be Emperor. In times
of prosperity he strives for peace in order to give quiet
to his army and rest to his people. He shows loving

---

[1] Cf. *Mencius* II, i, v, 6 for an argument similar to this one, but less
developed in detail.

[2] A notorious robber.

[3] Whom he loves.

[4] Regent in the time of King Ch'eng and consolidator of the Chou
Empire.

[5] *Book of History*, VI, ii, iii, 6 ; quoted by Mencius three times.

affection to his people [1]; he selects an officer who is conversant with affairs to manage everything. This man in peace gathers in the harvest and develops the country, and so there is an abundance of everything.

The militarist.

The militarist [2] will continually expose and destroy the heart of his country. Now I [3] shall develop my state, soothe it, and protect it. [4] The wealth and the grain in his treasury he [5] will daily procrastinate and waste in the midst of a wilderness. [6] Now I shall accumulate wealth and gather it in granaries and storehouses. He will daily injure and exhaust before his enemies those officers who are his skilled limbs and brave emissaries. [7] Now I would inspirit them, inspect them, and polish them at my court. In this manner he would daily accumulate defeat, and I should daily accumulate ease. In the relation of prince and minister, ruler and ruled, he would be greatly disliked, and the relations of the two would daily become more distant and hateful; I should be greatly revered, and the relations of the two would daily become

---

[1] The present text adds: " He opens up new land; he fills his granaries and storehouses; he provides good implements; then he gives them rewards in order to encourage them to progress; he severely punishes in order to warn them "; which is a doublet of what is said of the lord protector, p. 128 f. These sentences are probably a later addition, as they seem to interrupt the progress of thought here as well as to be quoted from the earlier part of this book.

[2] Lit., " the man of soldiers, armour, and weapons."

[3] The same " I " as two paragraphs above.

[4] Lit., " cover it over ", the opposite of " expose it ".

[5] The militarist.

[6] His country will become a wilderness from being fought over and neglected; or his battles will be not in his country, but outside of it—he will use his treasures outside of his country.

[7] Lit., " claws and teeth."

more respectful and loving. In this way I should await his collapse, and would be sure of gaining his territory. The man who acts in this fashion [1] would become a lord protector.

The man who follows the ordinary customs when he is established in authority ; who, when he does things, follows the ordinary precedent ; who, in making appointments to office or in cashiering officials, advances ordinary officials ; who, in dealing with his inferiors and his subjects, is generous and kindly ; such a ruler will be merely secure in his office.[2] He who, when he is established in authority, is disrespectful and unpleasant ; who, in doing things, likes to keep his plans to himself, and keeps others in doubt ; who, in making appointments and in cashiering officials, advances the flattering and cunning ; who, in dealing with his inferiors and his subjects, likes to encroach upon and plunder them ; such a ruler will be insecure and in danger. He who, when he is established in authority, is proud and overbearing ; who, in doing things, spoils them ; who, in making appointments and cashiering officials, advances the ignorant and the false ; who, in dealing with his inferiors and his subjects, likes to exhibit his power to the extreme and is heedless of his reputation ; who likes to use his power of collecting taxes, but forgets his fundamental duties,[3] such a ruler will be destroyed.

Of these five classes, a ruler should not fail to make a good choice. He who makes a good choice of the means of being a King, Lord Protector, merely secure, insecure, or destroyed,

The man who is merely secure,

19

insecure,

or   ruined.

---

[1] As " I " would act.
[2] Merely escapes overthrowal.
[3] Of stimulating and caring for agriculture and sericulture.

will rule others; he who does not choose well will be ruled
by others. He who makes a good choice will rule as King [1];
he who does not make a good choice will lose his throne.[2]
The difference between the man who is King [3] and him who
is destroyed [4] is the difference between ruling others and being
ruled by others. This difference is very great.

[1] Lit., " Wang," 王.

[2] Lit., " Wang," 亡, pronounced the same as the preceding " rule
as righteous King ".

[3] Lit., " Wang," 王.

[4] Lit., " Wang," 亡, the extreme of loss; not only the individual
himself loses his throne and life, but his family too, and a strange
surname succeeds to power, thus cutting off the sacrifices and service
to the spirits of the family, which is the greatest of misfortunes.

BOOK X

A RICH COUNTRY

All things are present together in the world, but have **1**
different forms. Of themselves they are not appropriate [1]; The importance of social divisions.
but they are used by men—this is art. Different grades of
men live together with similar likings, but different moral
standards (*Tao*), with similar desires but different amounts
of knowledge—this is nature. Their original capabilities
are alike in wisdom and stupidity. But their developed
abilities are different and they are distinguished by their
wisdom and stupidity. If their ability could be alike yet their
wisdom be different; if they could act selfishly without
incurring trouble; if they could give reign to their desires
and not be limited; then the people's hearts would be
aroused to strife and there could be no satisfaction. If this
were the situation,[2] a wise man could not get to rule; if a
wise man did not get to rule, he could not gain merit or fame.
If he could not gain merit or fame, the multitude would
not be separated into their proper classes. If the multitude
were not separated into their proper ranks, the positions of
prince and subject would not be established. If there were
no prince to rule the subjects, if there were no superior to
rule the inferiors, the country would be injured and people
would give rein to their desires.

---

[1] No natural teleology.
[2] Because of the resulting disorder.

People desire and hate the same things. Their desires are many but things are few. Since they are few, there will inevitably be strife. For what a hundred workmen accomplish goes for the nourishment of one individual; yet an able person cannot be skilled in more than one line; one man cannot govern two departments.[1] If people leave their positions and do not serve each other, there will be poverty; 2 if the masses are without social divisions, there will be strife. He who is impoverished is in trouble; he who strives will suffer calamity. For the purpose of rescuing people from trouble and eliminating calamity there is no method as good as that of making social distinctions plain, and forming a social organization. If the strong coerce the weak and the wise terrorize the stupid and the people who should be subjects rebel against their rulers and the young insult the aged and the government is not guided by virtue,[2] if these are the circumstances, then the aged and the weak will suffer the trouble of losing their support and the strong will suffer the calamity of division and strife.

Work is what people dislike; gain and profit is what they like. If there is no distinction of occupation, then people will have difficulty in getting work done and the calamity of striving in order to obtain any desired result. If the union of male and female, the separation from other males and females inherent in the relation of husband and wife, the

[1] Each man can be skilled in only one direction, as K'uei (Shun's Director of Music) specialized on the standards of music and Ts'i (Shun's Minister of Agriculture) specialized in agriculture.

[2] The government should make the strong and wise respect the rights of others—that is Yi.

making of engagements by the relatives of the groom and bride to be, the sending of betrothal presents and the going to get the bride, are not according to the rules of proper conduct (*Li*); if this is the case, then men will have the trouble of losing their mates and the calamity of having to struggle to gain any sex relation. Hence for this reason wise men have introduced social distinctions.[1]

[1] The remainder of the book contains nothing of interest which is not a repetition of what is elsewhere stated. There are paragraphs on the importance of enriching the people and storing the surplus, as the fundamental thing in enriching a state ; the importance of social organization and class divisions ; the importance of making class divisions plain in making the country prosperous ; the importance of caring for the people ; the advantage of benefiting the people but not seeking benefit for oneself and of loving the people but not imposing public service upon them ; the moral character of a state can be seen in the prosperity or lack of it among the people, in the character of the court and officialdom and ruler ; war is caused by desire for fame or territory or by anger, but the benevolent man gains his fame and territory without fighting and no one can be angry with him ; and government consists in the cultivation of morality.

A PARAGRAPH FROM BOOK XI
KINGS AND LORDS PROTECTOR

For the superior there is nothing as good as loving [1] his
inferior and ruling according to the rules of proper conduct The
(*Li*). The relation of the superior to the inferior should be importance of loving the
that of protecting infants. In treating people who are inferior people.
to oneself, if a subject has committed a petty wrong, although
he be an orphan, childless, a widower, or widow,[2] do not
apply the government regulations to him. Then the inferiors
will love [3] their superior, and rejoice in him as in a father
and mother; they can be killed rather than disobey him;
the prince and the ministers, the rulers and the ruled, the
noble and the base, the old and the young, even to the
common people, all will make this their greatest standard of
conduct. Then they will all examine themselves within,
and be careful of their duties. In this respect all the Kings
were alike, and it is the central and indispensable thing in
the rules of proper conduct (*Li*) and laws.[4]

---

[1] 愛

[2] The most helpless of people.

[3] 親; the love of a superior to inferior is 愛; that of inferior to
superior is 親.

[4] In thus making love the essential thing in *Li* and law, Hsüntze reaches
his highest insight and comes close to breaking through the crust of tradition-
alism. But we find only this isolated utterance. He goes on to apply this
statement to government and thereby introduces the element of precept
and rule again.

BOOK XV

A DEBATE ON MILITARY AFFAIRS [1]

Lin-wu-chuin [2] debated military affairs with the master, 1
Hsun Ch'ing, [3] before King Hsiao-ch'en [4] of Chao.

The King said, " I should like to ask what are the important points of military art."

Lin-wu-chuin replied : " On the one hand observe the seasons, [5] on the other take an advantageous position ; observe the movements of the enemy ; when following the enemy attack them ; when preceding them, reach the goal first. These are the important points in managing an army."

The master, Hsun Ch'ing, said, " No. What I have heard of the ancient methods (*Tao*) is that in managing an army or a war, everything depends on uniting the people. If the bow and arrow did not fit each other, Yi [6] could not hit the bulls-eye with it. If the six horses did not team together,

The important thing in military art is uniting the people.

---

[1] This book is probably an expansion of a possibly historical disputation by Hsüntze, made by his disciples.

[2] Said to be a general of the state of Ts'u. " Chuin " is literally a term of respect, equivalent to " sir ", but not necessarily indicating the individual to whom it is applied belongs to the nobility. Lin-wu was this man's appellation ; his name and surname are unknown. To avoid the English connotation f " Sir ", I have left " Chuin " untranslated.

[3] Hsüntze. The character used for his surname here is 孫.

[4] 265–245 B.C.

[5] Soldiers were levies, not mercenaries, and had to return home to work the crops ; otherwise the country would suffer.

[6] A legendary mighty archer.

Ts'ao-fu [1] could not go far with them. If the officers and
people had not been attached and accordant with their prince,
T'ang and Wu could not have conquered. Hence the man
who can get the accord of the people is the best man at
managing an army. Hence the only important point in
military affairs is in getting the accord of the people."

Lin-wu-chuin said, " No. What is valuable in military
affairs is strength and advantage; what is done is sudden
alteration of troop movements and deceitful stratagems.
He who knows best how to manage an army is sudden in
his movements; his plans are very deep laid; and no one
2 knows whence he may attack. When Hsun [2] and Wu [3]
led armies, they had no enemies in the whole country;
why should it be necessary to wait for the accord of the
people ? "

The master, Hsun Ch'ing, said, " No. What I am speaking
of (Tao) are the armies of the benevolent (Jen) man, the
purposes of righteous Kings. What you value is planning
on the instant, strength and advantage; what you do is
attacking, capturing, sudden alteration of troop movements,
and deceit [4]—the deeds of the nobles.[5] The armies of the

---

[1] A famous legendary driver.

[2] Hsun-wu, general of King Ho-lü of Wu, 514–496 B.C.

[3] Wu-chi, general of Duke Wu of Wei, 812–758 B.C.

[4] Stratagems.

[5] In contrast to the Kings, such as T'ang, Wen, Wu, etc., who were, or
ought to have been, perfectly righteous. The contrast between the theory
of morals and the conduct of men forced the Confucians into this dualistic
system of ethics—the kingly morality, which was truly righteous, and
the morality of the nobles, which was inferior and broke over the theoretical
standard. But this dualism was merely that of the ideal and the actual;
it was not a theoretical dualism.

benevolent (*Jen*) man cannot use deceit. The former [1] can
be deceitful, disrespectful, and exhaust the people. Between
the prince and the subject, the ruler and the ruled, there is
a separation, since there are deviations from virtue. For a
Ch'ie to deceive a Ch'ie, is like the wise deceiving the stupid—
some success may be looked for. For a Ch'ie to deceive a
Yao, is like using an egg instead of a stone in throwing, or
using a finger to stir boiling water, or like going into water
or fire; if you go into it you will be burned or drowned.
For with the benevolent (*Jen*) man, the commanders and
commanded, all the generals, are of one mind; the three
armies [2] are of like strength; the subject serves his prince,
and the inferior serves his superior as the son serves his
father or the younger brother serves his older brother, or as
the hand and arm defend the head and eyes and cover the
breast and abdomen. To deceive and surprise the enemy
has just the same effect as first to alarm and then attack him.
Moreover when a benevolent (*Jen*) man controls a state of
tc_i *li*,[3] he will have intelligence from a hundred *li* [4]; when
he controls a state of a hundred *li* he will have intelligence
from a thousand *li*; when he controls a country of a thousand
li, he will have intelligence from the whole continent. [5] His
wisdom and his admonitions will certainly strike the people

[1] The armies of the nobles.

[2] The centre and the two wings of what we should call one army. Or,
" army " is a brigade of 12,500 men; a large state had three brigades.

[3] A very small place. A " *li* " is a third of a mile.

[4] People from a distance of their own accord give him news. Confucian
ethics does not stress loyalty to one's own particular leader so much as
loyalty to the larger good; the first has been exalted, but leaving an
unworthy leader to go over to a better one has been encouraged.

[5] Lit., " from the four seas."

harmoniously and unite them. For when the soldiers of a
benevolent (*Jen*) man are gathered together, they form files ;
when scattered, they form ranks.[1] His army reaches as far
as the long blade of Mo-hsie [2]; whoever runs against it is
cut in two. It is as keen as the sharp point of Mo-hsie ; whoever meets it is destroyed. When inactive it is like a rock ;
whoever butts against it will be gored and broken like a
drooping deer, dripping and wet, and will retreat. Moreover,
whom would the prince of an aggressive country send against
me ? [3] Those [4] whom he would send must be his people.
But his people would be attached to me ; and they would
rejoice in me as in their father and mother ; they would love
4 me as the fragrance of an epidendrum. On the other
hand, they would regard their superior as a branding iron or
a tattooing needle, as an enemy. Although a man's passions
be those of Ch'ie or Chih, how could he be willing to do what
he hates and injure him whom he loves ? [5] This would be
like trying to get a man's sons and grandsons to injure their
own father and mother ; instead they would certainly come
and inform him ; then how could he be deceived ? Hence
the country which a benevolent (*Jen*) man controls is daily
more illustrious. Those of the nobles who obey him before he
attacks will be safe ; those who do not obey until after he
attacks will be in a dangerous position. Those who think of

[1] They are well-drilled.

[2] Name of a famous sword.

[3] " Me " represents the man of perfect virtue ; a figure of speech—" if
I were a man of perfect virtue."

[4] [5] The sentences enclosed by these figures are a doublet of those on
p. 146 f.

opposing him will lose territory, and those who resist him will
be destroyed. The ode says :—

> " The martial King [1] displayed his banner.
>
> Reverently he grasped his battle-axe.
>
> He was like a blazing fire,
>
> Which no one can stop "—

this expresses my meaning." [2]

King Hsiao-ch'en and Lin-wu-chuin said, " Good. I should
like to ask, What methods (*Tao*) do a king's [3] armies use ?
What movements are permitted them ? " [4]

The master, Hsun Ch'ing, said, " Among all the things
in the minds of the great kings, generals and leaders were
the least important matters. [5] I should like to be permitted
next to speak (*Tao*) of the reasons for the strength or weakness,
preservation or ruin of those who are kings [6] and nobles, [7]
and of the circumstances which bring safety or danger. If
the prince is a worthy person, his country is well-governed
and prosperous ; if the prince is without ability, his country
is ill-governed and decadent. The country which magnifies
the rules of proper conduct (*Li*) and honours justice (*Yi*) is
well-governed and prosperous ; the country which treats

[Sidenote: Sources of strength and weakness.]

---

[1] King T'ang.

[2] *Book of Odes*, IV, III, iv, 6. This is the next to the last of the odes.
The meaning is that T'ang won because his character impressed men's minds ;
although he used military power, his character preceded him and won the
battle for him.

[3] The king, as the embodiment of virtue.

[4] Sarcastic ; if a king conquers by virtue, what can his armies do ?

[5] This sentence does not seem to connect up with the King's question.
Is there a hiatus here, or is Hsüntze merely avoiding the King's question ?

[6] As exemplifying the ideal.

[7] Exemplifying the actual standard.

M

negligently the rules of proper conduct (*Li*) and which esteems justice (*Yi*) lightly is ill-governed and decadent. The one which is well-governed and prosperous is strong; the one which is ill-governed and decadent is weak. These are the sources of strength and weakness. If the ruler can be relied upon, he is able to use his subjects for his purposes; if the ruler cannot be relied upon, then he is unable to use his subjects. He who is able to use his subjects is strong; he who is unable to use his subjects is weak—this is the abiding principle of strength and weakness. He who magnifies the rules of proper conduct (*Li*) and investigates merit is of the first class; he who stresses official emoluments and honours self-restraint is of the second class; he who values military merit most of all and esteems self-restraint lightly is of the lower class. These are the general ranks of strength and weakness." [1]

*　　　*　　　*　　　*　　　*

[1] At this point there is inserted a mass of material that is unrelated to the subject. First there are a series of antithetical sentences on the weakness and strength of states, including " He whose weapons and defensive armour is strong and complete, convenient and efficient, is strong; he whose weapons and defensive armour is weak, inferior, not convenient, nor efficient is weak ", which sentence would seem more appropriate to Lin-wu-chuin than to Hsüntze; next comes a comparison of the military systems of Wei and Ts'in, in favour of the latter, but exalting Duke Huan, King T'ang, and King Wu above them, and condemning the two former states for using mercenary troops. It is the cultural influence of the rules of proper conduct (*Li*) and justice (*Yi*) that unites the people. This is the reason it was so easy for T'ang and Wu to overcome Ch'ie and Chou, and to kill Chou like a solitary common man. Four generals of the Contending States are mentioned (all of them of then recent times) whose armies were not unified but were rather robber soldiers (an appellation which well fits most of China's

King Hsiao-ch'en and Lin-wu-chuin said, "Good. 9 I should like to ask what are the qualities that make a general ? "

The master, Hsun Ch'ing, said, " In wisdom there is nothing better than getting rid of doubts ; in action there is nothing better than being without mistakes ; in performing my [1] duties there is nothing better than doing them in such a way that I can have no regrets. Performance of my duties can improve only to the stage where there is no chance for regret. Perfection cannot necessarily come from any öne element. Hence my orders and edicts should be severe and awe-inspiring ; my rewards and punishments should seek to be certain and believed in ; my camps and storehouses should seek to be well-arranged and secure ; my shiftings, advances, and retreats should seek to be safe and stable ; they should seek to be quick and speedy. In spying upon the enemy and watching their movements, I should seek to be hidden and deep ; I should seek to have my spies associate and mix with the enemy's groups. In meeting the enemy and in a decisive battle I should do (*Tao*) what I am certain of, not what I am uncertain about. This is what is meant by the six arts.[2] To be without doing what I desire because I desire it, and setting aside what I hate because I hate it ; to be without impatience for a victory and forgetfulness of a

The Qualities that make a General.

soldiers to-day !) and five princes of the states of more ancient times, as having unified their armies, but not as T'ang and Wu—all of which material is probably spurious and introduced subsequent to the composition of this book.

[1] A figure of speech ; Hsüntze identifies himself with the general here spoken of.

[2] Enumerated in the sentences beginning : " Hence my orders and edicts."

defeat ; not to try to make myself awesome in my own realm, but despised outside it ; not to think only of seeing the gain and disregarding the loss [1] ; in all planning to seek to do it thoroughly and in using wealth to be generous—this is what is meant by the five powers. There are three things in which I would not obey my master's orders ; I can be killed rather than be made to rest from completing that which is not finished ; I can be killed rather than be made to attack with no intention of winning ; I can be killed rather than be made to cheat the people—this is what is meant by the three extreme attainments.[2] Whenever a general has received his orders from his master to command the three armies, when the three armies are properly disposed, all the military officers have assumed their proper order, and all things are in their proper places, and when the master cannot then move them to joy [3] nor the enemy move them to anger [3]—this is what is meant by a minister of extremely great attainments.[4] Thought must precede action, be stressed and be attentive. To be careful of the end as of the beginning, to have the end and beginning alike [5]—this is what I call great happiness. Success in all things comes from being attentive ; defeat in being careless. Hence when attention overcomes careless-ness, there is happiness ; when carelessness overcomes attention, there is complete failure. When reflexion over-comes desire, there is obedience ; when desire overcomes

---

[1] In a plan of action.

[2] Attain to these points and never vary from them.

[3] Against orders.

[4] The general was also a minister. His attainments are such that he can establish this discipline in his army.

[5] Both full of promise.

reflexion, there is calamity. Fighting should be like guarding a post [1]; marching should be like fighting; if a general gains glory, he should act as though it were luck. To 10 pay attention to one's plans without relaxation; to pay attention to business without relaxation; to pay attention to the officers without relaxation; to pay attention to the people without relaxation; to pay attention to the enemy without relaxation—these are what are called the five things to be done without relaxation. If a man carefully performs these six arts, five powers, and three extreme attainments, and observes them by the aid of respectfully paying attention without relaxation—this is what I mean by the greatest general in the world, who would be as wise as the gods."

Lin-wu-chuin said, "Good. I should like to ask what are the King's military regulations?"

The master, Hsun Ch'ing, replied, "They are: to beat the drum for an advance to the death; to drive forward to the death; to have all officers devoted [2] to their posts; to have the officers and prefects [3] hold the ranks to the death. When the drum sounds, to advance; when the gong sounds, to retreat. To obey orders is the most important thing; to gain glory is secondary. The crime of advancing when there is no order to advance and of retreating when there is no command to retreat, is equally great. Do not kill the aged or the weak; do not march over the crops. Do not seize those who submit; do not let those go who are obstinate; do not arrest those who haste to obey. Whomever you kill, do not kill his subjects; kill those who cause the people to

The King's military regulations.

---

[1] Avoid over eager pursuit.

[2] In the Latin sense of this word; devoted to death.

[3] Here high military officials, mail-clad warriors fighting from chariots.

rebel ; but if among the people there are those who defend these injurious individuals, they too are injurious. Hence those who yield to the sword shall live ; those who resist the sword shall die ; those who haste to obey shall bring tribute.

The people welcomed King Wu.

"Wei Tze-k'ai [1] was invested with the fief of Sung. Tsao Cheh-lung [2] was killed in the presence of the army. The people of Yin [3] who submitted were saved alive and were treated the same as the people of Chou. [4] Hence those who were near sang and rejoiced ; those who were distant fell prostrate and hastened to submit. There was no darkened or rustic state which did not hasten to send envoys and joyfully seek peace. Within the four seas [5] it was as if there was one family. No enlightened people failed to comply and submit. The foregoing is what is meant by a leader of men. The ode says :—

"From the west, from the east,

From the south, from the north,

None thought but of submitting "—

this expresses what I mean. [6]

[1] This man was the half-brother of Chou-sin, the last monarch of the Chang dynasty Wei Tze-k'i had opposed the course of Chou-sin, and submitted to the new dynasty ; so was given a fief and ordered to continue the ancestral sacrifices to the deceased emperors of the Shang dynasty. He ruled 1112–1079 B.C. His name was Wei Tze-k'i ; because the character K'i was also that of the Emperor Chin of the Han dynasty, it was changed to K'ai, probably by Liu Hsiang.

[2] A general of the state of Chao who slandered the empress. Or, a flattering courtier of Chou-sin.

[3] The dynasty of Shang or Yin : Hsüntze is referring to the conquest of the Yin dynasty by King Wu.

[4] The dynasty of which King Wu was the first emperor.

[5] The whole continent This sentence is a popular proverb.

[6] *Book of Odes*, III, 1, x, 6. Also quoted by Mencius, II, 1, iii, 2.

"The Kings[1] had executions, but no battles. If a city[2] was held, they did not attack[3]; if the army[4] was obstinate, they did not attack it.[5] If the ruler and ruled were satisfied with each other, then they congratulated them. They did not massacre cities; they did not ambush armies; they did not hold down the people; they did not keep the army over the season.[6] Hence the people of countries which were ill-ruled rejoiced at their[7] government, and were not satisfied with their own rulers, but wished them[8] to come."

The Kings had executions, but no battles.

11

Lin-wu-chuin said, "Good."

*　　*　　*　　*　　*

Chen-hsiao[9] asked a question of the master, Hsun Ch'ing, saying, "When you discuss military affairs, you always speak of benevolence (*Jen*) and justice (*Yi*) as the roots of action. The benevolent (*Jen*) man loves others; the just (*Yi*) man follows principle; then why do you speak of military actions? All that armies are good for is to contend and take things from others."

How can war ever be consistent with virtuous rule?

[1] The ideal Kings.
[2] An enemy city.
[3] For fear of injuring their own army.
[4] The enemy's army.
[5] They won by virtue, overcoming the enemy's hearts, not by physical strength.
[6] The militia should only be called up when their absence would not injure the crops; they should not be kept in arms at harvest-time—thus showing the proper subservience of military to agricultural and peaceful matters.
[7] That of the Kings.
[8] Wished the Kings to come and take them over. Cf. *Book of History*, IV, ii, 6.
[9] A disciple of Hsüntze.

The master, Hsun Ch'ing, said, " It is not as you think. This benevolent (*Jen*) man loves others. He loves others, hence he hates what injures others. This just (*Yi*) man follows principle. He follows principle, hence he hates those that lead others astray. These armies are for the purpose of stopping tyranny and getting rid of injury, not to contend and take things from others. Hence when the armies of the benevolent (*Jen*) man remain in a place, it is like a god being there [1] ; when they have passed, civilization develops. It was like the falling of a timely rain ; no one failed to rejoice—this was when Yao punished Huan-tou [2] or Shun punished the ruler of the Miao [3] or Yu punished the Minister of Works,[4] or T'ang punished the lord of Hsia,[5] or King Wen punished Ch'ung, or King Wu punished Chou ; these four Emperors [6] and two Kings all used benevolent (*Jen*) and

[1] I.e., marvellous. Hsüntze did not believe in the existence of gods or spirits, but he uses the term " god " or " godlike " regularly to express the idea of the marvellous or the superhuman—" like what a god would do if there were gods."

[2] Cf. *Book of History*, II, I, iii, 12, and this page, note 4.

[3] Aboriginal tribes. Cf. ibid.

[4] This event is otherwise unknown ; the *Book of History* II, I, iii, 12, states hat Yao " banished the Minister of Works to Yu-chou ; confined Huan-ou on Mt. Tsung ; drove the ruler of the Miao into San-Wei ; and held Kun a prisoner till death on Mt. Yu. When these four criminals were dealt with the whole empire submitted." Elsewhere (p. 219) Hsüntze states that Yao dealt with Kun, Huan-tou, and the Minister of Works—here he states that three different emperors punished these three men.

[5] Ch'ie, the last of the Hsia dynasty.

[6] The Son of Heaven (emperor) does not seem to have been called " King " during his life until the Chou dynasty ; (but Yang Liang says : " The Hsia and Yin rulers were called Kings, 王, or Emperors, 帝 indifferently.") Previous to the Chou dynasty they were called Emperor, 帝, only after death. The Chou-Li says, " When their tablets are placed in the ancestral temple

just (*Yi*) armies to gain the empire. Therefore those who
were near were attached by their goodness ; those who were
far loved their justice (*Yi*). Their armies did not ensanguine
their swords, yet distant regions came to submit to them ;
their virtue was so great that it reached to the four ends
of the world. The Ode says :—

> " The virtuous man, my prince,
> His justice (*Yi*) is without blot "—

this expresses what I mean.[1]

*　　　*　　　*　　　*　　　*

Li Sze[2] questioned the master, Hsun Ch'ing, saying, *Ts'in's*
" Ts'in's[3] armies for four generations have been victorious ; *advance.*
it is the strongest state in the country ; it has overawed the
feudal princes ; this has not been done by benevolence (*Jen*)
and justice (*Yi*) but merely by taking advantage of the
course of events."[4]

The master, Hsun Ch'ing, replied, " It is not as you think. *It is by an*
What you call advantage is an unadvantageous advantage. *evil method.*
What I call benevolence (*Jen*) and justice (*Yi*) is the most
advantageous advantage. This benevolence (*Jen*) and justice

---

they are styled " Emperor, 帝." This term for Emperor, 帝, is not that
used now, 皇 帝, which only began with the Ts'in dynasty. Hence the
" Four Emperors " refers to those preceding the Chou dynasty and the
" two Kings " refers to those of the Chou dynasty.

[1] *Book of Odes*, I, xiv, iii, 3.

[2] A disciple of Hsüntze, later the famous prime minister of Ts'in Shih
Hwangti, who ordered the burning of the Confucian Classics. Hsüntze
has received a good deal of odium because Li Sze was his disciple. Here
Hsüntze shows his disagreement with Li Sze. Cf. *H.*, 239 ff.

[3] The state which was shortly to conquer all the others.

[4] His estimate of the situation was quite correct.

(*Yi*) is that wherewith I reform my government. When the government is reformed, the people are attached to their ruler; they rejoice in their prince, and easily die for him; hence it was said, 'Of all military affairs, generals and leaders are the least important matters.'[1] Ts'in for four generations has been victorious, but it has been fearful, continually fearing that the whole country would unite and crush it. This is what I call armies of recent days; their power did not have the right beginning. Hence when T'ang exiled Ch'ie, he did not pursue him when he reached Min-t'iao.[2] When King Wu killed Chou, it was not until the morning of Chia-tze[3] that he conquered—this was all because of their previous cultivation—this is what I mean by armies governed by benevolence (*Jen*) and justice (*Yi*). Now you do not seek for it at the source, but search for it at the end—this is wherein the present generation is misled."[4]

---

[1] Cf. p. 161.

[2] The ancestral home of Ch'ie, to which he fled, and where he was allowed to live a prisoner until his death.

[3] 甲子, the first day of the cycle.

[4] The next section is quoted in Sze-ma Ch'ien's *Historical Record* between two sections of Book XIX, and seems to have been originally part of that book, so is transcribed there. Cf. p. 216 f.

The rest of the book seems spurious (if this part is not so). The conversational form does not reappear, and the various speakers disappear. The subject matter is chiefly an elaboration of the preceding—rewards and punishments are not enough to support a state, virtue must also be cultivated, together with faithfulness and justice, to make the people attached to the ruler and willing to die for him. The three ways of ruling men—by virtue, by force, and by wealth, being respectively righteous rule, weakness and poverty. It is easy to capture a country, but the important thing is to consolidate the conquest.

A PARAGRAPH FROM BOOK XVI
A STRONG COUNTRY

All wicked men arise because the rulers do not honour justice [1] (*Yi*) nor reverence it. Now justice (*Yi*) is for the purpose of restraining men from evilly associating with wicked men. Now the rulers do not honour justice (*Yi*) nor reverence it, and so the people under them all discard their will to justice (*Yi*) and hasten to make their hearts evil. This is how wicked men arise. Moreover, the ruler should be the teacher of the ruled, and the ruled should keep in tune with the ruler like an echo responds to a sound or like a shadow resembles its object. Hence those who are the rulers of others must follow this principle.[2] The just (*Yi*) man within accords with men, and without he accords with things ; above he is at peace with his lord, and below he is in harmony with the people. To accord within and without, above and below, is the nature of justice (*Yi*). Then of all important things in the world, justice (*Yi*) is the fundamental thing and faithfulness is next to it. Among the ancients, Yu and T'ang founded themselves on justice (*Yi*) and practised faithfulness, and so the empire was well-governed ; Ch'ie and Chou discarded justice (*Yi*) and rebelled against faithfulness and the empire was ill-governed. Hence he who is over men must be careful of the rules of proper conduct (*Li*) and justice (*Yi*), and also practise loyalty and faithfulness ; and then only will he fit for his position. This is the greatest fundamental thing for princes.

Evil is from the rulers neglecting Yi.

The people should accord with their rulers.

Yi,

faithfulness,

Li, and loyalty

[1] *Yi* may be translated justice or righteousness ; it means rightness. observance of rights proper to that class of people.

[2] *Yi.*

BOOK XVII

CONCERNING HEAVEN

Heaven [1] has a constant regularity of action. Yao [2] was not necessary to support its order, nor could Ch'ie [3] destroy its
order. Respond to it in governing a country and success
will result ; follow it in misgovernment, and calamity will
result. If the fundamentals for life [4] are plentiful and are
economically used, then Heaven cannot impoverish the
country ; if the essentials of life are sufficient and the activities
of man in preparing them are well timed, then Heaven cannot
afflict the country. If the right Way of Life (*Tao*) is cultivated and not opposed, then Heaven cannot send misfortune ;
flood or drought cannot cause a famine ; extreme cold or
heat cannot cause suffering ; supernatural powers cannot
cause calamity. But if the fundamentals for life are neglected
and used extravagantly, then Heaven cannot cause the
country to be rich ; if the essentials of life are scarce and

12

Do not
depend on
Heaven for
prosperity,
but depend on
your virtue.

---

[1] The word for Heaven, 天, may mean a personal God or the materia
sky. Hsüntze uses it in an impersonal sense, so that it very nearly corresponds to the English " Nature", and in places in this book it has been so
translated. But when this is the case, the Chinese equivalent, " T'ien,"
has been added to clarify what is meant. Hsüntze is attacking the popular
superstitious conception of Heaven, and so it has seemed better to translate
天 by " Heaven " to show the connexion between the two concepts of
" Heaven " and " Nature ". In the Classics and the popular conception,
Heaven was an anthropomorphic Deity, while for Hsüntze, Heaven is
Nature, or Law.

[2] A great and good Emperor.

[3] An evil tyrant, a " Nero ".

[4] Agriculture and sericulture, which give food and clothing.

the activities of men in preparing them are inopportune,
13 then Heaven cannot make that country prosperous.
If a person rebels against the right Way of life (*Tao*), and
acts unseemly, then Heaven cannot make him fortunate.
Therefore even if flood or drought do not come, there will
be famine ; even if cold or heat do not approach, there will
be suffering ; even if supernatural powers do not act, there
will be calamity. Observing the proper time for action and a
good government and prosperity are contemporaneous ;
calamities and good government are not contemporaneous.
One ought not to grumble at Heaven that things happen
according to its Way (*Tao*). Hence to know the Way of
Heaven is man's duty [1] ; he who does this is a great Sage. [2]
To produce without acting and to obtain without seeking, [3]
this is what is meant by the office of Heaven. Therefore
although the Way of Heaven is deep, this man will not put
deep thought on it ; although it is great, he will not use his
ability for its investigation ; although it is mysterious, he
will not scrutinize it—this is what is meant by refraining from
contesting with Heaven. Heaven has its seasons, Earth has
its wealth, Man has his government. The foregoing is what
is meant by being able to form a triad with Heaven and
Earth. [4] To give up that wherewith one can form such a triad

[1] The *Book of Changes* says : " To know about men, but not about
Heaven, this is to be a Sage."

[2] He who has all wisdom.

[3] These sentences show the influence of Laotze. Hsüntze's doctrine of
Heaven as impersonal law is taken from Laotze.

[4] Cf. *Doctrine of the Mean*, XXII. Man is able to utilize the seasons
(Heaven), gain the earth's wealth through the efforts of his rulers (in
China the state controlled agriculture, appointed times for sowing, reaping,

and to desire to know those with whom he forms a triad is
to be led into error.[1]

The fixed stars make their round ; the sun and moon   No spiritual
alternately shine ; the four seasons come in succession ; principle in the universe.
the *Yin* and *Yang*[2] go through their great mutations ; the
wind and rain widely affect things ; all things[3] acquire
their germinating principle, and are brought into existence ;
each gets its nourishing principle[4] and develops to its completed state. We do not see the cause of these occurrences,
but we do see their effects—this is what is meant by the
influence of the spirits.[5] The results of all these changes are
known, but we do not know the invisible source—this is,
what is meant by the work of Heaven. Only the Sage does;
not seek to know Heaven. When the office of Heaven has
been established, and the work of Heaven has been perfected,
the human body is prepared and the human spirit is born ;
love, hatred, joy, anger, sorrow, and pleasure are embodied—
these are what are meant by the natural (*T'ien*) emotions.
The ear, the eye, the nose, the mouth, the body, and the
limbs, each receive stimuli and cannot be interchanged—

etc.), and so he is able to form a triad or trinity with Heaven and Earth.
Heaven and Earth were great deities ; they now become expressions of
universal Law, and man becomes equal with them.

[1] Give up agriculture and sericulture, and instead seek to know the
secrets of Heaven and Earth—speculation. This is an attack on Chuangtze
and similar speculators.

[2] The negative and positive cosmic principles.

[3] Lit., 萬 物 " the ten-thousand things ", here particularly referring
to vegetable life.

[4] Wind and rain.

[5] Effects, the causes of which are unknown, are attributed to the spirits ;
spirits do not really cause anything ; what are called the actions of spirits
are natural occurrences.

these are what are meant by the natural (*T'ien*) senses.

14 The heart [1] is established in the central cavity [2] to control the five senses—this is what is meant by the natural (*T'ien*) ruler.

Knowing Heaven consists in the fulfilment of human duties.

To use what is not of one's kind to nourish one's kind [3]— this is what is meant by the natural (*T'ien*) nourishing. To act according to one's station is what is called happiness ; to act contrary to one's station is called calamity—this is what is meant by the natural (*T'ien*) government. To darken one's natural (*T'ien*) ruler, [4] to confuse the natural (*T'ien*) senses, to throw away the natural (*T'ien*) nourishing, to act contrary to the natural (*T'ien*) government, to violate the natural (*T'ien*) emotions so as to destroy the work of Nature (*T'ien*) [5]—this is what is called the great calamity. The Sage purifies his natural (*T'ien*) ruler, rectifies his natural (*T'ien*) senses, makes the natural (*T'ien*) nourishment sufficient, [6] obeys the natural (*T'ien*) government, nourishes his natural (*T'ien*) emotions, in order to develop to perfection his natural usefulness. [7] When he acts thus, he knows what he can do and what he cannot do. Then heaven and earth fulfil their proper function, and he can employ the material world. When his actions are completely governed, the nourishment for the people is completely obtained, and in his life he injures none—this is what is meant by knowing Heaven (*T'ien*).

---

[1] It is the seat of psychic life, and " mind ".

[2] The thorax.

[3] E.g., animal flesh to nourish mankind.

[4] The mind.

[5] The same as the " work of Heaven " above.

[6] Cultivates agriculture and sericulture.

[7] The same as " the work of Nature (*T'ien*) ", above.

For great skill consists in knowing how to do a thing without striving; and great wisdom consists in not needing to reflect about things.[1] What is known about Heaven is that we see its phenomena have their regular sequences; what is known about Earth is that it is seen that it meets the conditions of life and can produce; what is known about the four seasons is that it is seen that they have a definite number, **15** and can be used to serve humanity; what is known about the *Yin* and *Yang* is that it is seen that they interact and can be used in ruling a country. If the man who has a responsible post attends to what belongs to Nature (*T'ien*), the people of themselves will keep to the right Way of life (*Tao*).

Are good and bad government, prosperity and calamity, from Heaven (*T'ien*)? I reply: The sun, the moon, the heavenly bodies, the auspicious times, the astrological calculations of the calendar were the same in the time of Yu as in that of Ch'ie. In the time of Yu there was good government and prosperity; in the time of Ch'ie there was ill-government and calamity; prosperity and calamity do not come from Heaven.

Good and bad action, prosperity and calamity, are from man.

Do they come from the seasons? I answer: The myriad plants spring up, flourish, and grow in spring and summer; they are nourished, the grain develops, is reaped and gathered in in the fall and winter. In this also the times of Yu and Ch'ie were the same. Yu had prosperity and Ch'ie had disaster; prosperity and disaster do not come from the seasons.

Do they come from the Earth? I answer: When

---

[1] This sentence shows the influence of Laotze.

a plant or a state obtains a place on the earth, it lives ; when
its place on the earth is lost, it dies ; in this too Yu and
Ch'ie were the same. Yu had prosperity, Ch'ie had misfortune.
Prosperity and misfortune, good and bad government, are
not from the Earth.

The ode says :—

> "Heaven made the high hill :
>
> > King T'ai brought it under cultivation ;
>
> He began the work :
>
> > King Wen tranquillized it "

this is the answer to the problem.[1]

The Superior Man imitates Heaven and Earth in their constancy.
Nature (*T'ien*) does not suspend the winter because men
dislike cold ; the Earth does not suspend its spaciousness
because men dislike distances ; the superior man does not
suspend his good actions because of the railings of little-
minded men.

Heaven (*T'ien*) has a constant way of action ; Earth has
a constant numerical size ; the superior man has a constant
decorous demeanour. The superior man talks of what is
constant with him, but the little-minded man counts his
accomplishments. The ode says :—

> "If a person acts according to the rules of proper conduct
> (*Li*) and justice (*Yi*),
>
> > And does not overpass their bounds,
>
> > Why should he be anxious about people's talk ? "—

this expresses what I mean.[2]

---

[1] *Book of Odes*, IV, i, v. This Ode implies that the success of the Chou
dynasty was due to its founders, especially King T'ai and King Wen ;
Nature provided the opportunity, but it was man who worked out his
success.

[2] This ode is not now preserved.

The King of Ts'u [1] has a thousand chariots following him— **16** this is not wisdom. The superior man eats pulse and drinks water—this is not foolishness. It is what is fitting to the circumstances.

If a person's will is cultivated, his virtuous acts are many, his knowledge and thoughts are clear, then his reputation will spring forth in the present, and be recorded with the worthies of ancient times. It springs forth from what is within one's power. Therefore the superior man is anxious about what is within his power, and does not seek for what is from Heaven. The little-minded man does not concern himself with what is within his power, and desires what comes from Heaven.[2] The superior man is anxious about what is within his power, and does not seek for what comes from Heaven—this causes daily progress. The little-minded man does not concern himself with what is within his power and seeks for what comes from Heaven—this causes daily retrogression. Therefore the reason why the superior man progresses daily and the reason why the little-minded man retrogresses daily is the same.[3] The reason for the difference between the superior man and the little-minded man consists in what we have just said.

Fame and character development are from one-self, not Heaven.

When stars fall or the sacred tree groans,[4] the people of the whole state are afraid. We ask, " Why is it ? " I answer : There is no reason. This is due to a modification of Heaven and

Ominous signs— heavenly and human.

[1] A large feudal state in what was then southern China, but now the Yangtze valley.

[2] Good luck.

[3] It depends on what he puts his mind on.

[4] The sacred tree by the local altar to the *lares rustici.*

Earth, to the mutation of the *Yin* and *Yang*.[1] These are
rare events. We may marvel at them, but we should not
fear them. For there is no age that has not experienced
eclipses of the sun and moon, unseasonable rain or wind, or
17 strange stars seen in groups. If the ruler is illustrious
and the government tranquil, although these events should
all come together in one age, it would do no harm. If the
ruler is unintelligent and his government is bent on evil,
although not one of these strange events should occur, their
non-occurrence would be without avail to prevent his fall.
Hence the falling of stars and the groaning of the sacred tree
are from the modification of Heaven and Earth, the mutation
of the *Yin* and *Yang*. These are rare events. We may marvel
at them, but we should not fear them. When human ominous
signs come, then we should be really afraid.

What is a human ominous sign ? Using a poor plough [2] and
thereby injuring the grain ; the losing of the effect of the
fertilizer in hoeing and weeding ; the losing of the allegiance
of the people by a government bent on evil; when the fields are
uncultivated and the harvest is bad ; when the price of grain
is high and the people are starving ; when there are dead
bodies on the roads—these are what I mean by human ominous
signs. When the government is not wise ; when appointments
to office and degradations from office are not opportune ;
when the fundamental matters [3] are not attended to—these
are what I mean by human ominous signs. When the rules

---

[1] Cf. the commentary of Tso on the *Spring and Autumn*, Duke Hsi,
16th year (Legge's trans. I, 170), for an echo of this passage.

[2] Made of poor wood.

[3] Agriculture and sericulture.

of proper conduct (*Li*) and justice (*Yi*) are not cultivated; when the inhabitants of the inner and outer apartments [1] do not keep apart; when men and women are immoral; when parents and children distrust each other; when the ruler and ruled are at cross purposes and separate; when distress from robbers becomes common—these are what I mean by human ominous signs. These ominous signs are born of disorder. When all three kinds of ominous signs come together, the country cannot be peaceful. To speak of things in this way, is to come very much nearer the truth; these misfortunes are the most grievous ones.[2] It is said: The **18** *History* does not speak of supernatural events. To set aside discussions and investigations which are not pressing, and not to engage in them—this is the right things for princes and their vassals to do. The love of father and son, the proprieties separating husband and wife, should be daily cultivated like the cutting and polishing of a precious stone, and they will not be lost.

If people pray for rain and get rain, why is that? I answer: There is no reason for it. If people do not pray for rain, it will nevertheless rain. When people save the sun or moon from being eaten,[3] or when they pray for rain in a drought, or when they decide an important affair only after divination— this is not because they think in this way they will get what

Prayer for rain.

---

[1] Females and males, respectively.

[2] The present text here contains the following spurious sentences: "If unopportunely you compel the people to forced labour, then cows and horses will breed together and the six domestic animals become an ominous sign. We can marvel at these events, but we should not fear them."

[3] In an eclipse.

they seek, but only to gloss over the matter.[1]   Hence the
prince thinks it is glossing over the matter, but the people
think it supernatural. He who thinks it is glossing over the
matter is fortunate ; he who thinks it is supernatural is
unfortunate.

Li and *Yi* are the true principles of life.

Of the things that are in heaven there are none brighter
than the sun and moon ; of the things that are on earth,
there are none brighter than water and fire ; of goods there
are none brighter than pearls and jade ; of the things that are
human there are none brighter than the rules of proper
conduct (*Li*) and justice (*Yi*). For if the sun and moon were
not high, their brightness would not be great ; if water
and fire is not gathered together,[2] their sheen would not be
great ; if pearls and jade were not gleaming on the outside,
19 kings and nobles would not think them precious ; when
the observance of proper conduct (*Li*) and justice (*Yi*)
are not added to the wealth of a country, its merit and fame
do not shine. Hence the destiny [3] of men is from Heaven ;
the destiny of a country is from observing the rules of proper
conduct (*Li*). The prince who exalts the rules of proper
conduct (*Li*) and gives office to the worthy can rule as king ;
he who makes law important and loves the people can rule
as lord protector ; he who loves his own profit and multiplies
deceit is in dangerous circumstances ; he who strives for
power and seeks to overturn others, he whose ways are
dark and bent on evil will be overthrown.

---

[1] Hsüntze's reinterpretation of divination.
[2] Much in one place.
[3] Non-deterministic fate.

How can exalting Heaven and wishing for its gifts be as Rely on self, good as heaping up wealth and using it advantageously ? not Heaven. How can obeying Heaven and praising it be as good as adapting oneself to the appointments of Heaven and using them ? How can hoping for the proper time and waiting for it be as good as seizing the opportunity and acting ? How can relying on things increasing of themselves be as good as putting forth one's energy and developing things ? How can thinking of things and comparing them be as good as looking after things and not losing them ? How can wishing that things may come to pass be as good as taking what one has and bringing things to pass ? Therefore if a person neglects what men can do and seeks for what Heaven does, he fails to understand the nature of things.

*   *   *   *   *

The principles of proper conduct [1] have remained unchanged *Li*. through the time of all the Kings. They are sufficient to permeate [2] the Way of life (*Tao*). One king fell and another rose ; that which conformed to these principles permeated them all. When these principles permeate a government, there can be no misgovernment or disorder. He who does not know how to make them permeate his actions does not know how to alter his actions to suit changing conditions. When they permeate the whole of a person's conduct, he can never fail. Ill-government and calamity is born of their lack ; good government comes from exhausting their minutiæ.

[1] This term is supplied from the context. Probably we should prefix " *Li* " to this section as a title.

[2] The figure is that of a string that runs through a " string " of cash, and holds them together.

For when that which the Way of life (*Tao*) stresses is the golden mean, it can be followed ; when it is an extreme, it
20 should not be done ; when it is evil, a person is greatly misled. One who walks in the water tests its depth. If he does not test it rightly, then he is likely to fall into the water. The one who governs the people tests their virtue. If he does not test rightly there is likely to be disorder. What he tests by is the rules of proper conduct (*Li*). If there is no proper conduct (*Li*) the age is dark. When the age is dark there will be great disorder. For the right Way of life (*Tao*) is never unclear. Conduct relating to what is without and within the family circle is tested differently. Conduct which refers to these inner and outer circles has its uniform principles. Thus we can remove the causes which would make the people sink into trouble.

*   *   *   *   *

Criticism of the philosophers.

All things are one section of the Way (*Tao*) ; one thing is a section of all things ; the stupid man sees only one section of one thing, and thinks that he knows the Way (*Tao*) ; but he has no such knowledge. Shentze [1] has insight about what is behind but none about what is before. Laotze [2] has insight about what is bent, but not about what is straight. Micius [3] has insight about what is universal, but not about

---

[1] Shen Tao 慎 到 said that the worthy should not be rewarded nor should the able be given office, i.e., he did not advocate stimulating the people to improve by advancing them in office. His writings were collected in forty-two books, which are now lost.

[2] 老 子 Reputed author of the Tao Teh Ching. He spoke of the bent being better than the straight, and the weak overcoming the strong.

[3] Or Mo Ti 墨 翟. Advocated the equality of all in the sight of Heaven, and universal love ; he is criticized for neglecting the place of the individual in society in favour of universal love.

the individual. Sungtze [1] has insight about the few, but
not about the many. If one considers what is behind, but
not what is before, then the common people cannot enter
into the gate of progress. If one considers the bent but
not the straight, then the noble and base are not distinguished.
If one considers the universal, but not the particular, then
the government cannot operate.[2] If one considers the few **21**
but not the many, then the common people will not
progress. The *History* says :—

> " Without any selfish likings,
>> Reverence the Way (*Tao*) of the Kings ;
> Without any selfish dislikes
>> Reverence the path of the Kings "—

this expresses what I mean.[3]

---

[1] Sung Hsin 宋 鈃 or Sung K'en 宋 牼, a native of the state of Sung, a
contemporary of Mencius and mentioned by him. He held that men's desires
tend to become simple and few, whereas each person thinks that they tend
to become greater and more complex. His writings were collected in
eighteen books, now lost. The criticism is that his doctrine was only true
in some instances, but not in the majority of instances. Hsüntze spends
a good deal of time rebutting his theory of desire. Cf. p. 206 ff.

[2] Because the government is founded on the subordination of some
individuals to others.

[3] *Book of History*, V, IV, 14.

BOOK XVIII

ON THE CORRECTION OF ERRORS

The sophists common to-day say: "It is best for a lord to be secretive." This is not so. The lord is the singing-leader of the people; the ruler is the model of the subject. When they hear the singing-leader, they respond; when they see the model, they act accordingly. But when the singing-leader is silent, the people are without response; when the model is inaccessible, then the subjects do not act according to it. If they do not respond nor act according to the model, then the ruler and ruled cannot help each other. If things are thus, then it is the same as if there were no ruler, than which no misfortune is greater. For the ruler is the foundation of the subjects. When the ruler makes known clearly what is to be done, then the subjects are governed well. When the ruler is upright and sincere, then the subjects are honest and guileless; when the ruler is just and right, then the subjects are easily straight. When they are governed well, then they are easily united; when they are honest and guileless, they are easily employed.[1] When they are easily straight, then they are easily understood. When they are easily united, then the state is strong; when they are easily employed, then the ruler gains glory; when they are easily understood, then the ruler is illustrious. This is the source of good government.

But when the ruler is secretive, then the subjects are

1
Secretiveness
and openness.

---

[1] On public works; this was a levy, not paid work.

confused ; when the ruler is inaccessible and difficult to fathom, then the subjects are embued with falseness ; when the ruler is partial and crooked, then the subjects form cliques. When the subjects are confused, they are united with difficulty ; when they are imbued with falseness, then they are difficult to employ ; when they form cliques, they are difficult to understand. When they are united with difficulty, the state is not strong ; when they are difficult to employ, the ruler has no glory ; when they are difficult to understand, then the ruler is not illustrious. This is the source of bad government.

Hence it is best for a lord to be open, and not to be hidden. It is best to make things known and not to be secretive. For when the custom (*Tao*) of a lord is to be open, then his subordinates are calm ; when the custom (*Tao*) of a lord is to be inaccessible, then his subordinates are uneasy. For when 2 the subjects are calm, then they honour their ruler ; when the subordinates are uneasy, then they despise their ruler. For when the ruler is easy to know, then his subjects love their superior ; when the ruler is difficult to know, then his subjects fear their ruler. When the subjects love their ruler, the ruler is at rest ; when the subjects fear their ruler, the ruler is in danger. Hence there is nothing in his practices (*Tao*) that a lord should hate more than being difficult to know, nothing more dangerous than to cause his subjects to fear him. It is said : When those who hate a person are many, he is in danger. The *History* says : " He was able to make his illustrious virtue show clearly." The ode says : [1]

" Below he was illustrious."

---

[1] *Book of Odes*, III, I, ii, 1. For explanation, cf. p. 279, note 4.

Hence the ancient Kings made themselves open ; how could they be especially inaccessible ?

*   *   *   *   *

The sophists common to-day say : " Ch'ie and Chou were the legal rulers of the empire ; T'ang and Wu rebelled and took it by force." [1] This is not so. If by being Emperor is meant that Ch'ie and Chou possessed the registers and census records of the empire at that time, then yes. If it means that they themselves possessed the empire, then no. If it means that the empire could be said to be in the hands of Ch'ie and Chou, then no. In ancient times the Emperor had a thousand [2] officials, and the feudal princes a hundred officials. By being king [3] is meant to have his command performed through the states of China [4] through these thousand officials. By being prince is meant to have his command performed throughout his borders through those hundred officials, and although his state be not at peace, yet not to be cast aside, displaced and ruined. The descendants of the Sage-Kings [5] inherited the empire ; the authority and the registers were in their hands. But if the Imperial Clan of the Empire had not a man of ability,[6] it was unfit for its position. On the one hand his subjects hated him, and on the other the

[margin: Were T'ang and Wu rebels ? The right to revolt.]

[1] Cf. pp. 19, 20, *A Sketch of Chinese History.* Cf. also *Mencius*, I, II, viii, where he was asked the same question. This teaching is found in Chuangtze, Book XVII.

[2] Round numbers ; other records say Shun had fifty officials, and Yu 100 ; in the Chou dynasty the emperor had 300 officials.

[3] The Chou dynasty emperors called themselves Kings.

[4] The term is 諸 夏 " all the Hsia ", Hsia being the name for the first Chinese dynasty. The dynastic name was taken as a geographical name.

[5] Yu and T'ang ; by implication Wu is included here too.

[6] To rule the empire.

feudal princes revolted. Near the capital, those within his own borders [1] were not united ; at a distance, the feudal princes did not obey. His commands were not performed within his own borders. The feudal princes even invaded and sliced off some of his territory [2] ; they attacked and chastised him. When such was the situation, although he had not yet fallen, I say that he did not truly possess the empire. When the Sage-Kings died, those who possessed the authority and registers became weak, and became unable to control the empire.

3   When the country has no real prince,[3] if there is a feudal noble who has ability, and if his virtue is illustrious and his majesty is great, none of the people of the country will be unwilling to take him for prince and leader ; then if he should seek out and kill this isolated and wasteful tyrant, he would not injure anyone, he would be a blameless [4] subject. If he put to death the prince of a tyrannous state, it would be the same as killing an ordinary individual.[5] A person like this can be said to be able to wield the empire. He who is able to wield the empire can be called a King. T'ang and Wu did not capture the empire ; they cultivated their ways

[1] The peculiar domain of the emperor, not held in fief by another.

[2] This was the situation in the time of Hsüntze himself ; but politeness prevented him from expressing the conclusion that the Chou emperors were doomed. Confucius, Mencius, and Hsüntze all sought employment at the important states, but never even attempted to enter the service of the Chou emperors.

[3] A prince who really governs ; in the sense that a weak ruler is no ruler.

[4] Lit., " without a crime."

[5] He would not be committing the crime of " parricide " (the ruler was regarded as a father). Cf. *H.*, p. 258 f.

(*Tao*); they carried out the principle of justice (*Yi*); they exalted the common benefit of the Empire; they did away with the common sources of injury to the empire; and so the empire turned to them. Ch'ie and Chou did not resign the empire; they perverted the virtue of Yu and T'ang; they confused the distinctions of the rules of proper conduct (*Li*) and justice (*Yi*); their bestial actions heaped up misfortune for them, completed their evil destiny, and the empire dismissed them. He to whom the empire turns is called King [1]; he whom the empire dismisses, is ruined.[1] Hence the fact that Ch'ie and Chou did not possess the empire and that T'ang and Wu did not murder their prince is clear from this argument.

T'ang and Wu were the father and mother of the people.[2] Ch'ie and Chou were the hated murderers of the people. The sophists to-day say that Ch'ie and Chou were princes, T'ang and Wu were murderers; then their argument is for killing the father and mother of the people and making a leader of their hated murderers—there is no calamity greater than this. If we understand that he who can unite the people is their prince then the empire was never united under Ch'ie and Chou.[3] But there never has been the doctrine that T'ang and Wu were murderers—that is directly slandering them.

For the empire is the weightiest thing there is. Unless the emperor himself is extremely strong, he will not be able to bear its weight. It is the largest of all. Unless he is

---

[1] " To be King " is " Wang ", 王 ; " to be ruined " is " Wang ", 亡. This play on words is also found at the end of Book IX.

[2] They were so called.

[3] I.e., they were not really emperors.

most discriminating, he will not be able to divide it properly.
It is the greatest of all. Unless he is most wise, he will not
be able to harmonize it. Unless he is a Sage, he will not
be able to fulfil these three extreme requirements. Hence
unless he is a Sage, he will not be able to rule as lawful King.
The Sage is he who has completely followed the Way (*Tao*)
4 and is wholly correct therein. He holds the balances [1]
in the empire. Ch'ie's and Chou's thoughts were extremely
dangerous; their purposes were extremely dark; their
actions were extremely evil. Their relatives kept distant
from them; worthy people despised them; their own people
hated them. They were the descendants of Yu and T'ang,
but they did not gain the following of one person. They
disemboweled Pi-kan and imprisoned the Viscount of Chi. [2]
They were killed, their dynasty fell, and they became the
great scorn of the empire. He whom later generations call
evil should study their histories. This is the way of the
man who is not able to resist his wife. [3] For an extremely
worthy man protects the whole country—such were T'ang
and Wu. An extremely weak man cannot resist his wife—
such were Ch'ie and Chou.

The sophists common to-day say that Ch'ie and Chou
possessed the empire, and that T'ang and Wu were their
feudatories—how could there be a greater error! It is like
a hunchback witch or a lame cripple [4] exalting himself and
thinking that he had knowledge! For a state can be captured

---

[1] Discerns right and wrong.

[2] Cf. note 13, p. 217, and note 1, p. 218.

[3] Chou was led on by Ta-ki, his concubine; and Ch'ie by his concubine.

[4] Cf. note 4, p. 142.

by force, but the empire cannot be captured by force.[1] A state can be captured by craft, but the empire cannot be captured by craft. The man who captures by force may possess a state, but he cannot possess the empire. Why is this ? I answer : A state is a small thing. A small-minded man can possess it. Small methods can gain it. Small power can control it. The empire is a large thing. A small man cannot possess it. Small methods (*Tao*) cannot gain it. Small power cannot control it.[2] The Empire is extremely large ; unless a man is a Sage, he cannot possess it.

*   *   *   *   *

The sophists of the day say : " The ancient beneficent rulers [3] had no corporal punishments, but instead had punishments by altering the clothing. Instead of kneeling on a line, there was wearing an inky turban ; instead of cutting off the nose, there was wearing straw fringes [4] ; instead of castration, there was cutting off the leather knee-pads ; instead of cutting off the feet, there was wearing hemp sandals ; instead of execution, there was wearing ochre coloured clothes without any hems—the ancient beneficent government was like this."

Should corporal punishment be abolished ?

This is not so. Do you think that that government was

---

[1] This is a legitimate deduction from the Confucian teaching. A similar statement is found in *Mencius*, VII, ii, xiii. It is the essence of the Confucian philosophy of history. The victory of Ts'in showed its falsity. Cf. *H.*, chap. XVI, especially p. 286 f.

[2] At this point there is inserted the following sentence, which is probably an interpolation after the time of Ts'in Shih Hwangti, as it expresses the final form of the Confucian philosophy of history which did not appear until the Ts'in dynasty's violent rise and dramatic fall gave this interpretation : " A small man can possess a state, but he would inevitably fall."

[3] Yao and Shun.

[4] On the cap worn by adults.

beneficent ? If so, men certainly did commit crime, and not only did they not use corporal punishments, but also they did not use punishments by altering the clothing. There is no greater confusion than thinking that if a man has committed a crime, his punishments should be directly lightened, so that a murderer should not die, a man who has assaulted another should not be punished, so that for an extremely great crime the punishment should be extremely light—the ordinary man does not know that there is anything to dislike in such punishment !

6 The origin of all punishment is the restraint of violence, the hatred of evil, and the warning against its future occurrence.[1] That a murderer should not die, or a man who injures another should not be punished, is favouring violence and being liberal to robbers, not hatred of evil. For punishments by altering the clothing are dangerous ; they are not born of the ancient beneficent government, but come from the confused and evil present.

The ancient beneficent government was not thus. All the ranks of nobility, and the different grades of officials have rewards and punishments to repay them for their deeds ; as their deeds, so their reward. That one thing should lose its appropriate recompense is the beginning of confusion. That a man's virtue should not correspond to his rank ; that his ability should not correspond to his official grade ; that rewards should not fit merit ; that punishments should not fit the crime—there is no misfortune greater than this ! In ancient times King Wu chastised the monarch of the Shang

---

[1] This is the Confucian penal theory. Cf. *H.*, p. 265 f.

dynasty [1] ; he killed Chou ; he cut off his head and hung it
on a crimson banner. Now chastising the violent and punish-
ing the overbearing is the summit of good government. All
the Kings agreed that a murderer should die, and that whoever
injures another should be punished. We do not know the
origin of this idea. When punishment fits the crime there
is good government ; when it does not fit the crime, there is
bad government. Hence in good government the punishments are severe ; in bad government the punishments are
light. Therefore the crimes committed against a good
government are severe ; the crimes committed against a bad
government are light. The *History* says : " Punishments
at times are light and at times are severe " [2]—this expresses
what I mean.

* * * * *

The sophists of the day say : " T'ang and Wu could not
make people obey their orders." [3] Why is this ? They say :
" Ts'u [4] and Yueh [5] would not admit their government."
This is not so. T'ang and Wu were the best people in the world
at making prohibitions and commands. T'ang lived in Po, [6]

Were T'ang and Wu really powerful ?

[1] Lit., " the possessor of Shang," 有 商, i.e., Chou.
[2] *Book of History*, V, xxvii, par. 19.
[3] Hence were not perfect.
[4] An important s.   to the south of what was then China.
[5] A state south-east of what was then China. Both of these states
were semi-barbarous, and on the edge of the civilized country, hence
less amenable to the Emperor. The fact probably was that these two
states never did acknowledge T'ang and Wu for the reason that in their
days Ts'u and Yueh were barbarous, beyond the confines of the then
known world, and were unable to acknowledge any Emperor.
[6] A place in what is now eastern Honan.

King Wu lived in Hao,[1] both places of a hundred *li*.[2] The empire was united, the feudal princes became their vassals, enlightened people all were moved to follow them and yield to their influence. How is it that Ts'u and Yueh alone would not admit their government ? In governing, those Kings[3] observed the situation and regulated the service of vassals accordingly ; according to their distance they graded their tribute and offerings. Why should it be necessary that they should all be alike ? Hence the people of Lu[4] offered bowls ; the people of Wei[5] offered tubs ; the people of Ts'i[6] offered 7 wine-skins.   If the soil and the situation of peoples are different, their utensils and adornments cannot but be different. Hence the states of China are alike in clothing and in institutions. The Mang, Yi, Rung, and Ti[7] are alike in dress, but different in institutions. Nobles granted fiefs within the royal domain do royal service ; those granted fiefs outside the royal domain do feudal service ; on the feudal marches they do voluntary service ; the Mang and Yi[8] do forced service ; the Rung and Ti[9] do intermittent service. Those who do royal service offer slaughtered victims[10] ;

[1] A place in what is now south-west Chihli.

[2] I.e., very small centres.

[3] T'ang and Wu.

[4] A central state ; it was Confucius' home.

[5] An important feudal state occupying southern Chihli and eastern Honan.

[6] An important state occupying northern Shantung and southern Chihli. In each case these are articles in which that state excelled.

[7] Aboriginal tribes on the different borders of civilized China.

[8] Aboriginal tribes on the south and east.

[9] Aboriginal tribes on the north-west and west.

[10] To the father and grandfather of the Emperor.

those who do feudal service offer sacrifices [1]; those who do voluntary service make offerings of thanks [2]; those who do forced service offer tribute; those who do intermittent service acknowledge the king. The offering of slaughtered victims is daily; the offering of sacrifice is monthly; the offering of thanks is seasonal; the tribute is yearly; the acknowledgment of the king is once a generation. [3] This is what is meant by considering their circumstances and regulating their service, grading their tribute and offerings according to their distance—this is the extreme of kingly government.

Moreover, T'su and Yueh were of the class that made a seasonal offering of thanks, or yearly tribute, or acknowledgment of the king once a generation. Must they necessarily have been like the others, and put in the class which made daily offerings of slaughtered victims or monthly sacrifices, before it could be said that they admitted the Emperor's government? This is a doctrine like using the compasses on a grindstone. [4] The saying goes: Shallow, not able **8** to fathom the deep; stupid, not able to be acquainted with wisdom; a frog in a pit or well, with whom one cannot speak of the happiness of the eastern sea [5]; lean men of the

[1] To the great-grandfather and great-great-grandfather of the Emperor.
[2] To the two founders of the race.
[3] Upon his accession.
[4] Inappropriate; grindstones were never round and hence compasses could not be used on them.
[5] An allusion to Chuangtze's famous allegory. A well-frog boasted of his greatness to the turtle of the eastern sea; but when the turtle described the immensity of the ocean, and that it is not affected by the duration of time nor by the volume of water, and hence had great happiness, the frog was dumbfounded.

ditches,[1] with whom one is not able to reach up to the heights of the government of the Kings—this expresses what I mean.

* * * * *

Did Yao and Shun abdicate?

The sophists of the day say : " Yao and Shun abdicated and yielded the throne." [2] This is not so. The emperor's authority and position are the most honourable : he has no enemies in the country ; then to whom would he yield ? [3] His virtue was pure and complete ; his wisdom and kindness was most illustrious. When he faced the south [4] and judged the country, all living people were moved, obeyed, and yielded to his influence. The country had no retired officers [5] nor any neglected good men. What was like his acts was right ; what was unlike them was wrong. Then why should he have yielded [6] the empire ?

The sophists reply : " At death they yielded to another dynasty." This also is not so. When the Sage-Kings were on

---

[1] Beggars, i.e., shallow thinking.

[2] Because Yao passed over his own son, Tan-chu, and selected Shun as his successor and gave him the reins of office before he (Yao) died. Similarly Shun passed over his son, Shang-chuin, and selected Yu, and gave him the throne. Yao and Shun alleged old age as a reason for thus retiring from the government before death. Yu's son succeeded him after his death, and the Hsia dynasty then began its long reign. This criticism is found in Chuangtze, xvii.

[3] Taking yield in the sense of yielding to another stronger than he. Abdication seems to have come to mean being forced to give up the rule to someone else, and be a term of reproach. Cf. p. 92 f.

[4] On his throne.

[5] Retired, because they could not conscientiously obey the dictates of the Emperor.

[6] Because he was not able to rule the empire, and had to call in another to rule instead. Hsüntze is combating two current definitions of the word " yield " sophistically included in this statement, which would make Yao and Shun inferior rulers.

the throne, they passed decisions on people's virtue and
thereby decided their rank; they measured their ability
and accordingly gave them official position. They did everything to enable the people to do their duty, and each one to
gain his appropriate reward. They caused those who were
unable to do this to control their desire for gain by justice
(*Yi*), and to beautify their nature by artificial culture; then
they united them as their people. When the Sage-Kings had
died, and there was no Sage in the country, then certainly
there was no one with sufficient virtue to whom the empire
could be abdicated. If there is a Sage in the country, and he
is among the Emperor's descendants, then the empire does
not leave that family; the dynasty does not change, **9**
the states do not alter their fealty; the empire is submissive and turn to him [1] without any difference. What
change is there if a Yao [2] succeeds Yao? If there is no
Sage among his descendants, but if there is one among the
three Dukes,[3] then it is best that the empire should go to
them; they will revive and restore it.[4] Then the empire is
submissive; it turns to him without any difference. If a
Yao [5] succeeds Yao, what change is there? Only a change
of dynasty, an alteration of government, is difficult. Hence
when the Emperor lives, the country all exults; it is most
obedient and well-governed; according to people's virtue is

---

[1] The new emperor.

[2] A member of the same family; no change in dynasty.

[3] The Grand Tutor, the Grand Assistant, and the Grand Guardian. Cf.
Book of History, V, xx, 5.

[4] The figure is that the empire decays at the death of a Sage-King; but
another Sage-King, coming after, revives it.

[5] A man of the same qualities and ability, a Sage-King.

their rank determined. The man who is able to carry the responsibility of the empire must nevertheless die. He has completely carried out the distinctions of the rules of proper conduct (*Li*) and justice (*Yi*); what need is there in adding the virtue of abdication?

The sophists answer: "He abdicates from old age and decay." This also is not so. His body and vital force, his sinews and strength may decay, but his wisdom, his power of thought, his power of acceptance and rejection [1] does not decay.

They answer: "He is old and not adequate to the labour of government and rests from it." This is also the idea of one who is afraid to work. The emperor's authority is extremely great, but his person is extremely luxurious; his heart is most joyful. He is in nowise forced to act against his will, and he does not toil; in honour he has no superior. His clothes and coverings are coloured and variegated, with much embroidery; pearls and jade are added to it as ornamentation. His food and drink includes much meat and all delicacies, with very fragrant flavours. His feasts are prolonged [2]; 10 the drum is beaten to invite him to eat; the 'Yung' [3] is played when removing the five sacrifices.[4] A hundred servants hold the sacrifices [5]; they wait in the western anterooms. When he holds audience, there is erected a curtain of feather screen; when he turns his back to the silken screen between the door and window and rises, the nobles hasten

---

[1] His power of choice, his will.

[2] Many courses and delicacies.

[3] An ode, IV, ii, vii, only used by the Emperor.

[4] The food of the Emperor is offered as if it were a sacrificial offering to him; this is the extreme of respectfulness.

[5] The food.

to go below the hall.[1] When he goes out of the inner door,
the witches and wizards busy themselves.[2] When he goes
out,[3] the Master of Ceremonies and his assistants busy themselves. When he rides in the Imperial Chariot, there **11**
is a fine rush mat to care for his comfort ; by each side is
a fragrant flower to care for his sense of smell ; in front
there are ornamented yokes to care for his sense of sight.
There is the harmonious sound of little bells [4] ; when going
slow there are the Wu and Hsiang [5] ; when going fast there
are the Shao and Hu [6] to care for his sense of hearing. The
three dukes respectfully hold the shaft ends and grasp the
inner reins.[7] The nobles grasp the wheels or steady the
chariot or lead the horses. The marquises of great states [8]
arrange themselves behind ; the prefects follow them. The
marquises of small states [9] and officers of the first class
follow them. The soldiers wear their armour and line the
streets. The common people run off and hide ; none of them
dare to look. At rest the Emperor is like a great god [10] ; in
action he is like the Ruler of Heaven.[11]

[1] Audience closed.
[2] To remove any evil influences from his path.
[3] Of the palace.
[4] On yoke or arm rest.
[5] Names of two pieces of music.
[6] Names of two pieces of music ; the Shao was Shun's music.
[7] Ornamental reins from the inner side of the team of four horses
abreast.
[8] Rulers of important fiefs.
[9] Rulers of smaller fiefs.
[10] Lit., " spirit."
[11] The Chief of the gods, God. This sentence does not imply that Hsüntze
believes in gods and God ; he is merely using the popular conception as an
analogy.

Is there any support for old age and care for decay as fine as this ? If an old man would rest, would he have peace and joy like this ? Hence I say : The nobles get old, but the Emperor does not get old ; there is abdication of a state, but no abdication of the empire—the ancient and the present 12 are the same in this respect. Hence to say that Yao and Shun abdicated and yielded the throne is a lie ; it is the tradition of shallow minds ; it is the doctrine of low minds ; it is an ignorant and erroneous principle ; it is changing the small to the big ; the appropriate to the inappropriate ; it cannot reach up to the great principles of the empire.

*　　　*　　　*　　　*　　　*

Were Yao and Shun all that is claimed of them ?

The sophists of the day say : " Yao and Shun were not able to instruct and transform others. Why is this ? Chu [1] and Hsiang [2] were not transformed by their influence." [3] This is not so. When Yao and Shun came to the throne, they were excellent at instructing and transforming others. When they faced south [4] and judged the empire, all living people were moved, obeyed, and yielded to their influence. Then if Chu and Hsiang alone were not influenced, this was not the fault of Yao and Shun, but the crime of Chu and Hsiang. Yao and Shun were the most virtuous men of the empire ; Chu and Hsiang were the most paltry men in the empire, insignificant fellows of an hour. The sophists of the day do

[1] The son of Yao.

[2] The younger brother of Shun.

[3] A Sage should be able to influence all about him, the whole country in fact ; how much more should he be able to influence and transform those who stood in the relation of filial subservience to him—his son or younger brother.

[4] On the throne.

not blame Chu and Hsiang, but attack Yao and Shun. Is not this extremely erroneous? Yi [1] and Feng-men were the best archers the country has known, but they could not hit the bulls-eye with a bent bow and crooked arrow. Wang-liang and Ts'ao-fu were the best drivers the country has known, but they could not go far with lame horses and a broken chariot. Yao and Shun were the best at instructing and transforming that the country has known, but they could not cause paltry insignificant fellows to be transformed. What age has not had paltry fellows? What time has not had insignificant fellows? From the time of Ta'i-hao [2] and Sui-jen [3] there have always been such. Hence those who originate such teachings are unfortunate; those who study them suffer their calamities. He who demolishes them gains congratulations. The ode says:—

" The ills of the people under us

    Are not sent from Heaven;

They speak fair words and then backbite each other;

    Their numerous quarrels are from men "—

this expresses what I mean. [4]

*   *   *   *   *

[1] A legendary archer.

[2] Another designation of Fu-hsi, who is the first emperor of Chinese historians, placed about the beginning of the third millennium B.C.

[3] The alleged first producer of fire, which he did by rubbing two sticks together. He is supposed to have preceded T'ai-hao; another theory is that he followed T'ai-hao—which seems to be what Hsüntze implies here. By his use of these two names, Hsüntze means, " From the beginning of the race."

[4] *Book of Odes*, II, IV, ix. 7.

Were
ancient
burials
mean ?

13   The sophists of the day [1] say : " In ancient times they gave princes mean burials ; coffins were only three inches thick ; there were only three thicknesses of grave-clothes and coverings over the corpse ; when buried in the field the grave did not disturb the field, for they did not raise a mound. The decadent present gives sumptuous burials and ornaments the coffin, so it raises a mound." This teaching does not rise to the state of knowing the methods (*Tao*) of good government, and it is ignorant of the reasons for raising a mound or doing the opposite.

All those who rob men must have a reason. If it is not because they do not have enough, then it is because the wealthy have too much. But the Sages caused their people all to be rich and thoroughly satisfied, and did not allow anyone to have too much above what was right. Hence robbers did not rob, and thieves did not take things. Dogs and pigs vomited beans and millet [2] ; farmers and merchants all could give away from their stored up wealth. The customs were beautiful ; men and women did not take things on the roads, and the people were ashamed to pick up anything that had been dropped. Hence Confucius said : If the empire has the right way (*Tao*), the robbers will be the first to change. Although a body were covered with pearls and jade, although embroidery filled the inner coffin and yellow gold filled the outer coffin, although cinnabar were added to it, and it was made heavy with copper, although rhinoceros horn and ivory were like trees,[3] although cornelian and the

---

[1] Here probably referring to Micius ; this was his doctrine.

[2] There was such abundance.

[3] In the grave ; numerous.

dragon's moustache [1] were like their glittering fruit, **14**
yet men would not dig into the grave.[2] Why was that ?
Because the idea of seeking for gain was suppressed, and the
shame of transgressing one's duty was great.

But the present is evil and is the opposite of that. The
ruler does not keep the law, causing the ruled to act lawlessly ;
the man of wisdom does not get to think deeply, the man
of ability does not get to rule, the worthy man does not get
position. When things are like this, on the one hand the
natural endowment of man is lost, on the other hand the
benefits of the earth are lost, and in addition the harmony
of men is lost. Hence all things fail, riches are hid, and
calamity arises. Kings and dukes suffer because they do
not have enough, and the common people freeze, are hungry,
and starve. Then Ch'ies and Chous are everywhere and
robbers and thieves rob so as to endanger even the rulers.
Accordingly there will be bestial actions and the avarice
of tigers and wolves. In order to pay the salary [3] of great
men they will have little children roasted.[4] When this is
the situation, what more is it to dig up men's graves and
snatch the jewels out of their mouths and seek for gain ?
If a man were thus mean and he were buried, he would
certainly be dug up. How could he get a peaceful burial ?
They [5] will eat his flesh and gnaw his bones.[6]

[1] Probably the name of a gem.
[2] To rob it.
[3] Lit., " dried meat," which was the ancient salary of a teacher.
[4] Avariciousness.
[5] Those whom he has oppressed.
[6] From hatred.

Then to say that in very ancient times burials were mean, and hence graves were never dug up; but in the evil present burials are sumptuous, hence graves are robbed,[1] is the mistake of an especially wicked man who is confused by wrong doctrines, so that he cheats stupid people and causes them to sink into the mire, so that they illicitly gain profit [2]— this is what is called great wickedness. It is said: He endangers others but himself is safe; he injures others but himself gains profit—this expresses what I mean.

* * * * *

Will the doctrine that insult is no disgrace prevent quarrels ?

Your teacher [3] Sungtze [4] says: "To see clearly that to meet with insult is no disgrace will prevent people from quarreling. Men all consider it a disgrace to meet with insult, hence they quarrel. When they know that it is no disgrace to be insulted, they will not fight."

In answer I say: Then is it also according to men's feelings not to hate insult? They [5] replied: "Hate it but do not consider it a disgrace." I answered: If that is the case, you will certainly not gain what you desire. All men's quarrels must be explained because of what they hate, not 15 because of what they consider a disgrace. Now can it be that the actor [6] or dwarf or familiar servant who is cursed and insulted and yet does not retaliate, does so because he knows

[1] A reference to Micius' advocacy of simple burials.

[2] By saving on burials.

[3] A discussion with two or three of Sungtze's disciples. Detached and added to this chapter, but plainly by Hsüntze.

[4] Cf. p. 185, note 1. Sungtze's younger contemporary, Yin-wen-tze, also had this teaching.

[5] The disciples of Sungtze.

[6] Actors were considered the dregs of society.

that being insulted is no disgrace ? The man who does not retaliate, does so because he does not mind insult. Now suppose a man should come in through the sewer and steal another man's pigs : then the owner would draw his sword and halberd and drive him out, and the thief could not escape death or wounds. How could this be because the owner understood the loss of his pigs as an insult ? If this man does not shrink from a fight, it is because he hates to lose his pigs. Although he should consider insult no disgrace, if he does not fight, it is because he does not mind losing his pigs. Although he should know that insult is no disgrace, if he hates to lose his pigs, he will certainly fight. Then whether he fights or not does not depend on whether he is disgraced or not, but whether he hates to lose his pigs or not.

Now your master Sungtze cannot understand that people hate insult and wants to persuade people that it is no disgrace. Is not this extremely erroneous ! Although he had a mouth and tongue like a bell and clapper, it would be of no use. If he does not know it is of no use, then he is not wise.. If he does know it is of no use, then he is consciously cheating people. Then he is not benevolent (*Jen*). There is no shame greater than not to be benevolent (*Jen*) or unwise. If he thinks it is beneficial to people and is really of no benefit to people, then he suffers a great disgrace and has to retire [1]— there is no doctrine more defective than this !

Your teacher Sungtze says : To receive insult is no disgrace.[2] In reply to him I say : All discussions must establish

The only criterion of right is the Way of the Kings.

---

[1] Because his doctrine forbids fighting.

[2] The same Chinese word, 辱, translated " disgrace " in the preceding paragraphs is translated " shame " in this paragraph.

a point of reference, and then only can they be worth anything. Without a point of reference, right and wrong cannot be discriminated, and the argument cannot be settled. For what we have heard called, " The greatest point of reference 16 in the world," whence the boundaries of right and wrong, rank and title, terms and resemblances, arise, is the government of the Kings. All talking and discussions about realities and terms have the Sage-Kings for a model. Then the discrimination between glory and shame made by the Sage-Kings is right. This distinction has two criteria. There is just (Yi) glory and there is the glory of circumstances. There is just (Yi) shame and there is the shame of circumstances. A cultivated will, many virtuous actions, and brilliant thoughts—this is the glory which comes from within oneself; this is called just (Yi) glory. High noble rank, great tribute,[1] or emoluments,[2] and surpassing power—above there are the emperor andthe feudal nobles, ànd below there are the cabinet ministers, the prime minister, the officers and the prefects—this is the glory which comes from without; this is called the glory of circumstances. Licentiousness, filthiness, transgression of duty, evil principles, pride, oppression, and avarice—this is the shame which comes from within oneself; this is called just (Yi) shame. Revilings, insults, pullings of the hair, beatings with the hand, beatings by heavy or light rods, cuttings off of the knee cap, decapitations, quarterings, being led in chains, splittings of the tongue—this is shame which comes from without; this is called the shame of circumstances. These are the two criteria

---

[1] Referring to the Emperor or feudal nobles.
[2] Referring to the high officials.

of glory and shame. Hence the superior man can have the
shame of circumstances, but cannot have just (*Yi*) shame.
The mean-minded man can have the glory of circumstances
but cannot have just (*Yi*) glory. There is nothing to hinder
him who has the shame of circumstances from being a Yao ;
there is nothing to hinder him who has the glory of circumstances from being a Ch'ie. Only a superior man can have
both just (*Yi*) glory and the glory of circumstances ; only a
mean-minded man can have both just (*Yi*) shame and the
shame of circumstances. This is the discrimination of glory
and shame. The Sage-Kings had this for their method ;
officers and prefects had this for their way (*Tao*) ; the officials
kept it ; among the people it became custom ; all ages
cannot change it.

Now, according to your teacher Sungtze, this is not so. 17
He alone wrests the facts to suit himself, and seeks in one
day to alter them. His doctrine certainly cannot be carried
out. It is like rolling mud into balls to stop a river or the sea,
or to uphold Mount T'ai [1] by pigmies. It will fall down and
break to pieces without waiting an instant. If the two or
three disciples who admire your master Sungtze, do not stop
it, you will perhaps injure yourselves.

*   *   *   *   *

Your master, Sungtze, says : " Men's passions seek little, Do men's
but everyone thinks that his own passions seek much." [2] This passions seek
is an error. Hence he leads all his disciples, splits hairs in his little ?
discussions, makes clear his examples and terms, and wants
to make men understand that their passions seek little. In

---

[1] On the five great mountains of China.
[2] Cf. p. 293 f.

reply to him I say : Then is it so that in men's passions their
eyes do not desire very much colour, their ears do not desire
very much sound, their mouths do not desire very much
taste, their noses do not desire very much smell, their bodies
do not desire very much idleness [1] ; is it that men's emotions
do not desire these five extremes ?   The disciples replied :
Men's passions are really like that.

I answer : If this is so, then his doctrine is certainly not
true.   To say that men's passions do desire things, but in
these five extremes they do not desire much is like saying that
men's passions desire wealth and position, but do not desire
goods ; or that they love beauty, but dislike Si-shih.[2]   The
ancients thought otherwise, i.e. that men's passions desire
much, and do not desire little.   Hence they rewarded men by
18 riches and   plenty, and punished them by reduction or
taking away their goods.   In this respect all the Kings were
alike.   Hence the first class of " worthies " enjoyed the
emolument of the empire,[3] the next class of " worthies "
enjoyed the emoluments of one state,[4] the lowest class of
" worthies " enjoyed the emoluments of fields and cities,[5] and
honest and upright people had plenty of clothing and food.
Now your master, Sungtze, thinks that their passions desire
little and do not desire much.   Then did the early Kings
reward men by what they did not desire, and punish them by

[1] Evidently Sungtze's argument was that men do not like the extremes
of bright colour, loudness, etc., hence their passions seek moderation, not
much, simplicity not multiplicity.

[2] A beautiful concubine of the King of Wu, sent him by Yueh.

[3] Became emperor.

[4] Became dukes or marquises.

[5] Became officers or prefects.

what they did desire ?   There is no confusion greater than
this !   Now your master, Sungtze, has a commanding
presence and loves to persuade people ;   he gathers disciples,
establishes a school, and writes essays.   So his persuasion
cannot avoid making the best of governments the worst
of governments.[1]   Is not this extremely erroneous !

[1] The goal of philosophy is good government.

BOOK XIX

ON THE RULES OF PROPER CONDUCT (*LI*)

Whence do the rules of proper conduct (*Li*) arise? Man [1] by birth has desire. When desire is not satisfied, then he cannot be without a seeking for satisfaction. When this seeking for satisfaction is without measure or of limits, then there cannot but be contention. When there is contention, there will be disorder [2]; when there is disorder, then there will be poverty. The former Kings [3] hated this confusion hence they established the rules of proper conduct (*Li*) and justice (*Yi*) in order to set limits to this confusion, to educate, and nourish men's desires, to give opportunity for this seeking for satisfaction, in order that desire should never be extinguished by things, nor should things be used up by desire; that these two should support each other and should continue to exist. This is whence the rules of proper conduct (*Li*) arise.

Thus the rules of proper conduct (*Li*) are to educate and nourish. Meat, grain, the blending of the five flavours, are

1 Li arises from the necessity of regulating human desires.

Li is to educate and nourish.

---

[1] Beginning here, Sze-ma Ch'ien quotes this passage in his *Historical Record*, Chapter on Rites. He quotes almost verbally, omitting a clause here and there, and making just enough changes and improvements on this text to make it plain that it was original with Hsüntze.

[2] This word, 亂, includes the ideas of a confused social state, bad government, and lack of prosperity.

[3] The ancient monarchs who were supposed to have established China's social order and civilization.

that whereby the mouth is educated and nourished. The pepper, the orchid, fragrance and perfume are that whereby the nose is educated and nourished. Engraving, cut gems, engraved metal, elegant compositions are that whereby the eye is educated and nourished. Bells, drums, pipes, stone chimes, lutes, lyres, reed organs are that whereby the ear is educated and nourished. Large houses, deep temples, fine rush mats, elevated beds, bedrooms, low tables and bamboo mats[1] are that whereby the body is nourished. Hence the rules of proper conduct (*Li*) are to educate and nourish. When the superior man has gotten its education and nourishment, he also esteems its distinctions.

The social distinctions of *Li*.

What are meant by its distinctions? There are the classes of the noble and the base; there are the inequalities of the senior and the younger; there is what is appropriate to those who are poor and those who are rich, to those who are unimportant and those who are important. Hence the imperial chariot[2] has a fine rush mat wherewith to take care of the emperor's body; by his side is carried a fragrant flower wherewith to take care of his sense of smell; in front it has ornamented yokes to care for his sense of sight; the harmonious sound of little bells,[3] when going slow the Wu and Hsiang,[4] when going fast the Shao[5] and Hu[6] are to care for his sense of hearing; the dragon flag with nine scallops

[1] Like those used by the Japanese to-day.
[2] Used in going to the sacrifice to Heaven—the chariot of state.
[3] On yoke or arm-rest.
[4] King Wu's music.
[5] The music of Shun; it captivated Confucius so much that he forgot the taste of meat for three months.
[6] The music of T'ang.

on the lower border to refresh his spirits; a sleeping rhinoceros,[1] a male tiger,[2] alligator adorned harness, a silken canopy,[3] dragon yoke-ends, to care for his majesty. Hence the horses of the imperial chariot must be very trustworthy and well trained, and then only driven—thus caring for his safety. He has very capable braves, willing to die, who have agreed to be temperate, in order to care for his life. Very prudent men expend his money and use it in order to care for his wealth. He has very sagacious men who are respectful and courteous in order to preserve his calmness. He has very discreet men who observe the rules of proper conduct (*Li*), justice (*Yi*), and all principles of refinement, in order to care for his emotions. Hence if it appears that a man is only seeking for a livelihood,[4] he shall certainly die. If it appears that he is only seeking gain,[5] he shall certainly meet with injury. If he is a lazy careless scholar, seeking only a quiet life,[6] he shall certainly be in danger. If he thinks that emotional pleasure is joy,[7] he shall certainly be destroyed. For if a man concentrates on the rules of proper conduct (*Li*) and justice (*Yi*), then he will gain both[8]; if he concentrates on satisfying the emotional nature, then he will lose both. Hence the Confucian doctrine causes men to

---

[1] Ornaments on the chariot.

[2] Another ornament on the chariot.

[3] The description in Sze-ma Ch'ien's *Historical Record* omits this item.

[4] Soldiering as a means of livelihood, unwilling to die or be temperate among the bodyguard of the emperor.

[5] Unable to use money prudently.

[6] Unwilling to be respectful and courteous.

[7] True enjoyment, not knowing the rules of proper conduct.

[8] Both the rules of proper conduct and justice, and also the emotional nature.

gain both ; the Mician doctrine [1] causes men to lose both—this is the difference between the Confucian and Mician doctrines.

XV, 12 [2]

Li is the greatest thing in government.

The rules of proper conduct (*Li*) are the greatest thing in government and in making social distinctions ; they are the foundation of strength and security : they are the way (*Tao*) of being majestic : they are the focus of honour. Kings and dukes gained the empire by following them. By not following them, they lost their territory.[3] Hence strong armour and trained armies were insufficient to gain virtue ; high city walls and deep moats were insufficient to make those rules feared. If they followed this principle (*Tao*) [4] they were successful ; if they did not follow this principle (*Tao*), then they failed.

XV, 13

Ts'u failed because it did not cultivate Li.

The people of Ts'u [5] use shark skin and rhinoceros hide for armour, as hard as metal or stone, spears of steel from Wan,[6] sharp as a bee's sting ; they are quick and active, as fast as the whirlwind ; yet its army was almost

---

[1] Doctrine of Mo Ti ; this attack on Micius, which is so characteristic of Hsüntze, is omitted in the *Historical Record*.

[2] At this point the *Historical Record*, 史 記, inserts a section from Book XV of Hsüntze, and then goes on quoting Book XIX. This section seems to have been displaced from this point in our present text of Hsüntze, and consequently I have inserted it here. There are variations in the text of the *Historical Record* and Hsüntze which show that the *Historical Record* tried to polish up Hsüntze's text, and that this passage is original with Hsüntze.

[3] Lit., " fell from the local shrines of the deities of the land and grains."

[4] The principle of *Li*.

[5] The state under which Hsüntze held office during the latter part of his life.

[6] The district of Nan Yang, in southern Honan.

destroyed at Ch'ui-sha [1] and T'ang Mieh [2] was killed. Chuang Ch'iao [3] arose and Ts'u was divided into three or four. How could it be said not to have strong armour and trained troops ? The reason for its defeat was that it did not unite the people by this principle (*Tao*).[4] The Ju [5] and the Ying [6] were thought to be obstructions very difficult to surmount ; the Yangtze and Han [7] were thought to be moats : the state was bounded by the Teng [8] forest and bordered by the Fang Ch'eng mountains [9] ; yet the army of Ts'in came and captured Yen [10] and Ying [11] like shaking a rotten stick. How could it be said not to have any firm ramparts, narrow passes, or mountain defiles to hinder the army ? The reason for its defeat was that it did not unite the people by this principle (*Tao*).[12]

Chou disemboweled Pi-kan,[13] imprisoned the Viscount of **The failure of Chou.**

[1] Location uncertain. Possibly Ch'ui Hsiang 垂 卿 in P'ei Chuin 沛 郡, present Hsiu Chou, northern Anhuei. In this battle, which occurred in 301 B.C., the armies of Ts'i, Han, and Wei together attacked Ts'u and killed the T'su general. It is said that over a thousand men were killed in the battle.

[2] The Ts'u general.

[3] At first a robber chieftain, then the general of Ts'u.

[4] That of the rules of proper conduct.

[5] A river in Honan, tributary of the Huai.

[6] A river in Honan.

[7] A tributary of the Yangtze, joining it at Hankow.

[8] In the south of Honan.

[9] On the north boundary of Ts'u, literally " square city walls ".

[10] A principality in what is now northern Hupeh, south of I-Ch'eng-hsien.

[11] The ancient capital of Ts'u, just north of the present Chiang-ling-hsien, Ching-chou-fu, in southern Hupeh.

[12] That of the rules of proper conduct.

[13] A relative of Chou. He is said to have remonstrated with Chou upon his excesses ; whereupon the latter cried, " They say that a Sage has seven orifices in his heart (the seat of the understanding). Let us see if this is the case with you." He then caused Pi-kan to be disemboweled before him.

Chi,[1] and invented the torture of the roasting pillar [2] ; he
incessantly commanded executions ; his ministers and
subordinates trembled—none of them were sure of their lives.
Yet when the army of Chou [3] came, his orders were not obeyed
by his subordinates ; and he could not make use of his own
people. How could it be said that his commands were not
stern or his punishments were infrequent ? The reason for
his fall was that he did not unite his country by this principle
(Tao).[4]

The Kings conquered because they cultivated Li.

The soldiers of ancient times had only spears, shields, bows,
and arrows ; yet enemy states submitted without attempting
a battle. They did not build inner or outer city walls ;
XV, **14** they did not dig moats. They did not establish outposts ;
they did not make much of strategems. Yet states were
peaceful, unafraid of outside enemies, and secure. There
was no other reason but that they knew the right way of
action (Tao) [5] and were fair to the people ; at the right season
they employed the people,[6] and sincerely loved them ; the
subject accorded with his ruler like a shadow to its object
or an echo to its source. If anyone did not obey the law, then

---

[1] One of the foremost nobles. For protesting against the evil courses of
his master, he was thrown into prison. King Wu released him, and raised
a tumulus to Pi-kan. The Viscount of Chi retired to Corea, on the ground
that he could not serve a sovereign who was a usurper. The authorship
of part of the *Book of History* is attributed to him.

[2] A copper pillar was greased and placed over hot coals ; the culprit had
to walk across the pillar and fell into the coals. This phrase may also be
translated " the punishment of the cupboard ".

[3] Of the new dynasty of Chou.

[4] That of Li.

[5] According to Li.

[6] On public works or in the army.

only did they visit him with punishment. Hence they only needed to punish one man and the whole country obeyed. The criminal did not blame his superior, for he knew that the fault was his own. For this reason punishments were few, yet the ruler's majesty and the fear of him went everywhere. There was no other reason than that they followed this principle (*Tao*).[1] In ancient times the emperor Yao in governing the whole country killed one man[2] and punished two men,[3] and then the whole country was well ruled. It is said : The majesty and fearfulness of the ruler should be great, but it should not be tried out ; punishments should be established, but not used—this expresses my meaning.[4]

The[5] code of proper conduct (*Li*) has three sources ; Heaven and Earth gave birth to it—this is a source ; our ancestors made it fit the situation—this is a source ; the princes and teachers formed it—this is a source. Without Heaven and Earth, how could it be born ? Without our

The three sources of *Li*

---

[1] That of *Li*.

[2] He imprisoned Kun, the father of Yu, for life on Mt. Yu. Cf. *Book of History*, II, I, iii, 12, for Yao's treatment of these three criminals. Kun was disobedient and failed to restrain the floods. The passage in the *Book of History* may also be interpreted that Kun was executed ; this seems to have been Hsüntze's interpretation. Legge prefers to take the former interpretation that Kun was merely imprisoned, because it would be unlikely that Yao should kill the father of Yu.

[3] He banished the Minister of Works to a place in the northern extreme of his kingdom, Yu-chow, and confined Huan-tou on Mt. Tsung. Cf. the *Book of History*, loc. cit.

[4] This is the end of the section from Book XV ; I have followed the *Historical Record*, in continuing from Book XIX.

[5] From here on this section is quoted by the *Ritual of the Senior Tai* as well as the *Historical Record*.

ancestors, how could it be produced ? Without princes and
teachers, how could it be given form ? If one of these were
lacking, men would be without peace. Hence the Code of
proper conduct (*Li*) on the one hand serves Heaven [1] and on
the other Earth [1] ; it honours our ancestors and magnifies
the princes and teachers—this is how it serves the three
sources of the code of proper conduct (*Li*). Hence the Kings [2]
have Heaven for their first ancestor [3] ; the feudal nobles
dare not move or replace the family tablets ; the officers and
prefects have a fixed ancestral hall. [4] They are distinguished
by their honourable origin ; an honourable origin is the
source of virtue. [5] The sacrifice to Heaven is limited to the
Emperor ; the sacrifices to the gods of the land belong to
the feudal nobles down to the officers and prefects.
4 That whereby the honourable are distinguished is that they
serve the honourable deities ; and the lowly serve the lowly
deities. It is proper that the great should have the great
deities, and the small the small deities. Hence he who

[1] Here probably thought of as the impersonal source of humanity—a
tacit acceptance of the Confucian cosmology.

[2] The Emperors.

[3] Prince Tsi, Shun's Minister of Agriculture, was the high progenitor
of the Chou dynasty, and by them made the representative of Heaven.
Heaven being impersonal, was unable to receive worship, and so each
dynasty made its ancestor the representative of Heaven, to whom worship
was offered together with Heaven. Another interpretation of this arrangement is that it was the result of a syncretism of ancestor worship and
nature worship.

[4] A fixed clan relationship and descent.

[5] The Commentary on the *Spring and Autumn* by Ku-liang quotes this
sentence and those following.

possesses the empire [1] serves seven generations [2] ; he who possesses one state [3] serves five generations [4] ; he who has territory which sends forth five chariots [5] serves three generations ; he who has territory of two chariots serves two generations [6] ; he who eats from the labour of his hands does not achieve the establishment of an ancestral temple.   That which distinguishes those whose accomplishments are great is that they transmit great blessings to their descendants : those whose accomplishments are small transmit small blessings.

At the great sacrifice,[7] on the upper side of the altar there is water [8] in the wine vessel ; in the three-legged flesh vessel there is raw fish ; in front [9] there is the meat soup [10] —this is honouring the first food and drink.   In the seasonal sacrifice,

The Rites honour the ancient and follow one's liking.

---

[1] The emperor.

[2] Seven generations of ancestors.   The text says " ten generations ", but those early writers who quote this passage, the Commentary of Ku-liang, the *Ta Tai Li*, and the *Historical Record*, have " seven generations ", and so we follow them.   The emperor has seven shrines for the worship of seven generations of ancestors in the ancestral temple ; one shrine for the high progenitor and shrines for the six proximate generations of ancestors.   Cf. *Li Ki*, xx, 5.

[3] A duke or marquis.

[4] Of ancestors.

[5] A place of 10 *li* (3⅓ miles) sent out one chariot, without about seventy-five foot-soldiers.   " Five chariots " would refer to a " prefect ", 大夫.

[6] He establishes two shrines to two generations of ancestors.   This is the " officer ", 士.

[7] The triennial worship of the early ancestors.

[8] Used because water is more ancient than wine, hence a more primitive form of worship.   In China, as everywhere, the rites were conservative, and illustrate the most ancient customs.

[9] On the side next the worshipper.

[10] Made without salt, as in extremely ancient days.

on the upper side of the altar there is water in the wine vessel,
but wine and spirits are used [1] ; in front there are two
varieties of panicled millet, but rice and spiked millet is
5 eaten. At the monthly sacrifice, the meat soup is
tasted, but other viands are eaten—this is honouring the
original [2] but following one's own liking. Honouring the
original is called elegant ; following one's own liking is called
doing that which is reasonable. When both accord, the
ceremony becomes beautiful, and returns to uniformity with
the primitive. This is called the most excellent of all.[3] For
it is for one and the same reason that the wine vessel on the
upper side of the altar contains water, the three-legged meat
dish contains raw fish, the meat dish contains the meat soup.[4]
It is for the same reason [5] that at a great marriage the father
does not give the marriage cup to his son, that in the great
temple the impersonator of the dead is offered food,[6] that
when first dead the corpse is not even put in a cheap coffin.[7]
It is for the same reason that in the imperial chariot [8] there

---

[1] Water is offered, but wine is used in the accompanying banquet.

[2] The ancient or original kind of food.

[3] What is both in accord with antiquity and satisfies man's present likings
is the most excellent form of conduct or ritual.

[4] To be like ancient times. Probably these are extremely ancient
ritual forms.

[5] To " honour the original " ; more recent customs were different and
not followed ; as for example the ancient custom was not to encoffin, but
to bury the dead on a mat, hence when first dead, the corpse is not
encoffined at all.

[6] At the ancestral sacrifice a youth of the line of the dead impersonated
him.

[7] Only washed and dressed, and put on a mat.

[8] Used to go to the sacrifice to Heaven, the chariot of state.

should be plain screens, that in the sacrifice to Heaven, the emperor should wear a sackcloth cap, and that in mourning apparel the hemp girdles should at first be worn loose. It is for the same reason that in the three years' mourning,[1] **6** the crying is without interruption, that in the Pure Temple,[2] one singer lines out an ode and three others follow, that only one bell is hung,[3] that the " fu " drum is beaten as in ancient times, that the vermillion string passes through the hole in the lute.[4]

All rites and rules of proper conduct (*Li*) begin in accumulating rules ; they are perfected in becoming beautiful and end in producing joy. Hence when they have reached **7** perfection, men's emotions and sense of beauty are both fully expressed. The rite is of the second degree when either the emotion or the sense of beauty overcomes the other. It is of the lowest degree when it reverts to the state of emotion and returns to its primitive state.

The perfection of Rites and conduct.

Li is that whereby Heaven and Earth unite,[5] whereby the sun and moon are bright, whereby the four seasons are ordered, whereby the stars move in the courses, whereby rivers flow, whereby all things prosper, whereby love and hatred are tempered, whereby joy and anger keep their proper place. It causes the lower orders [6] to obey, and the upper orders to be illustrious ; through a myriad changes

Li is a cosmological principle.

---

[1] For parents ; actually only 25 or 27 months.
[2] The ancestral temple of the Chou emperors.
[3] In that temple.
[4] Hole in lute through which strings pass to the nuts.
[5] *Li* is here equated to the *Tao*, the principle whereby Heaven and Earth unite to produce all things.
[6] Of men.

it prevents going astray. But if one departs from it, he will be destroyed.[1] Is not *Li* the greatest of all principles ? When it is established grandly, it becomes the centre of all, and the whole world will not be able to subtract from or add to it. Its source and aim accord with one another. Its end and beginning reach each other. It is most beautiful, but preserves the distinctions.[2] It can be most closely scrutinized, and will be found to be explicable. When the country follows it, there is good government and prosperity ; when it is not followed there is anarchy and calamity. He who follows it is safe ; he who does not follow it is in danger. He who follows it will be preserved ; he who does not follow it will be destroyed. The small-minded man cannot fathom this.

Li submerges unorthodoxy and makes the Sage.

The principle of *Li* is truly deep ; if the discussions of " hardness and whiteness " or " likeness and unlikeness " [3] enter, they are submerged. Its principle is truly great ; if unauthorizedly made laws or depraved doctrines enter, they are destroyed. Its principle is truly high ; if tyrannous, remiss, insolent people who despise the common people and think they are exalted, enter, they fall. For when the plumb-line [4] is truly laid out, one cannot be deceived as to whether

---

[1] The quotation by the *Ritual of the Senior Tai* stops here.

[2] Between superior and inferior, etc.

[3] Cf. p. 49, notes 3 and 4.

[4] Lit. " string and ink." Chinese carpenters ink a string, fasten one end to a sharpened nail stuck in a board, and hold the other end taut ; then snap the string to make a straight mark along the board—this is the instrument referred to ; but for the sake of Western readers who may not be familiar with this instrument, I have called it a plumb-line, which instrument may also be denoted.

a thing is crooked or straight; when the balances [1] are truly suspended, one cannot be cheated in weight; when the compass and square are truly applied, a person cannot be cheated as to squareness or roundness; when the superior man has investigated into *Li*, he cannot be cheated as to what is false. For the plumb-line is the extreme of [8] straightness; the balances are the extreme of equableness; the compass and square are the extreme of squareness and roundness: the rules of proper conduct (*Li*) are the utmost of human morality (*Tao*). Moreover those who do not follow the rules of proper conduct (*Li*) neither are satisfied with it, are people without a direction in life; they who follow the rules of proper conduct (*Li*) and are satisfied with it are gentlemen who have a direction to their life. To be able to meditate deeply in the rules of proper conduct (*Li*) is to be able to reflect; to be able to keep from deviating from the rules of proper conduct (*Li*) is to have the power to be firm. He who is able to think deeply and to be firm and adds to that a love of *Li*, is a Sage. For as heaven is the utmost in height, the earth is the utmost in depth, the boundless [2] is the utmost in breadth, so the Sage is the utmost in morality (*Tao*). Hence the student who resolutely studies *Li* becomes a Sage; without especially studying it, he is a person without direction.

---

[1] Lit., " steelyard "—a wooden stick suspended near one end, with the article to be weighed hung on a hook on the short end, and balanced by an iron bob hung from a string on the longer end, which is moved along the arm of the steelyard until it balances, its place then indicates the proper weight. By suspending this instrument improperly, incorrect weight results.

[2] The four directions, east, west, south, and north.

Observance of *Li* is the greatest thing in character.

The man who observes the rules of proper conduct (*Li*) considers wealth and things as that which proper conduct uses ; he considers the division into the noble and base as the adornment of society [1] ; he considers the many and the few as different classes [1] ; he considers the embellishment or the simplification of conduct as the important thing.[2]

The embellishment and simplification of ceremony.

A rite (*Li*) [3] is embellished when its beauty is great, but its emotional content is small. A rite (*Li*) is simplified when its beauty is small and its emotional content is great. A rite reaches the mean when its beauty and emotional content are related as inner and outer, when the visible actions and the inner emotions go along together and revolve around each other. Hence the superior man when dealing with superiors reaches the grand heights [4] ; when dealing with inferiors he makes it [5] very simple ; but when dealing with equals he keeps to the mean.[6] Walking, fast riding, galloping, and furious galloping, are not exempt from this.[7] This is the **9** superior man's terrace and his palace.[8] If a man keeps

[1] Produced by the rules of proper conduct.

[2] To know in proper conduct.

[3] A piece of ritual conduct, whether in the temple or at court, or merely in meeting a friend on the street.

[4] Of *Li* ; he reaches its embellished state.

[5] *Li.*

[6] Of ritualistic conduct. *Li* was extended to the proper greeting of people, the proper honorific appellation in conversation, such as speaking of oneself as " the stupid one ", etc., a form used to superiors only ; or such embellishment could be omitted entirely, as when dealing with inferiors ; or only a moderate amount used, as in dealing with equals. The important thing is to use the right amount.

[7] From the application of the rules of proper conduct ; they reach to the whole of life.

[8] The limits of his actions ; he is always in the realm of the rules of proper conduct as if it were his home. Cf. p. 119 for a similar statement.

within this boundary, he is a scholar or superior man ; if he goes beyond this, he is an ignorant fellow. Then he who walks up and down, makes a circuit within these boundaries,[1] and indirectly gains its order is a Sage. For he who is dignified is so because he has created habits of observing the rules of proper conduct (*Li*) ; he who is great is so because he has made broad his observance of the rules of proper conduct (*Li*) ; he who is exalted is so because he has magnified the rules of proper conduct (*Li*) ; he who is illustrious is so because he has completely observed the rules of proper conduct (*Li*).[2] The ode says :—

> " Every rite (*Li*) is according to rule,
>   Every smile and word is as it should be "—

this expresses my meaning.[3]

The man who observes the rules of proper conduct (*Li*) sedulously cares for life and death. Birth is the beginning of man ; death is the end of man ; when the end and beginning [4] are both beautiful, the way (*Tao*) of man is complete. Hence the superior man respects the beginning [5] and venerates the end [5] ; to make the end and previous life [6] alike is the practice (*Tao*) of the superior man and the beauty of the rites for proper conduct (*Li*) and justice (*Yi*). Then to dignify his previous

Li cares for life and death.

---

[1] Of *Li* ; he who covers the entire territory of *Li*.

[2] The quotation by Sze-man Ch'ien in the *Historical Record* ends here.

[3] *Book of Odes*, II, VI, v, 3. Also quoted on p. 45.

[4] I.e., the whole of life.

[5] Of man.

[6] " Previous life," 始, is the same word previously translated " beginning ". Hsüntze changes from one meaning to the other unconsciously.

life and make mean his death [1] is to respect him when he
has knowledge and disrespect him when he has no knowledge
—this is the way (*Tao*) of the evil man and shows a rebellious
mind.[2] The superior man would consider it a shame to treat
a low grade of slave or an infant according to a rebellious mind ;
how much more to treat thus him whom he honours [3] or loves.[4]
Hence in death, this [5] is the way (*Tao*). Once dead, a person
cannot be resurrected again. The minister most honours
his prince by *Li* ; the son most honours his parents by it ;
because of that it should be completely observed. For to
serve the living without loyalty and faithfulness or without
any sense of what is respectful or beautiful is what is meant
by shabby treatment. The superior man despises savage
treatment and is ashamed of shabby treatment. Hence for
the emperor the inner and outer coffins have seven thicknesses ; for the feudal nobles five thicknesses ; for the
prefects three thicknesses ; for the officers two thicknesses.
10 Besides they each have more or less coverings of cloth
laid over the corpse in its coffin and presents, generously or
stingily presented ; they each have a great ornamented
flabellum,[6] adornments, and things of that sort, to reverence
and beautify the dead, to cause their life and death, their end

---

[1] A criticism of Micius, who advocated inexpensive burials.
[2] Rebellious against the right Way.
[3] His prince.
[4] His parent.
[5] By the rules of proper conduct.
[6] A wooden frame, with cloth sides, ornamented with clouds and figures,
carried with the coffin and set at each corner of the grave to represent his
palace.

and previous life, to be alike. This likeness is sufficient to make people willing to do it. This is the Way (*Tao*) of the ancient Kings, the last thing that a faithful minister or a filial son can do.

The funeral [1] of the emperor stirs the whole continent, and is the business of the feudal nobles [2]; the funeral of a feudal noble stirs all through the states and is the business of the prefects; the funeral of a prefect stirs a whole state, and is the business of an officer of the first class; the funeral of a first-class officer stirs a whole region, [3] and is the business of his friends; the ordinary man's funeral is the business of his clan or fellow-villagers and stirs his district [4] or village [5]; the funeral of a criminal [6] who has suffered capital punishment cannot be the common business of his clan or fellow-villagers, but is the business of his wife and son; his inner and outer coffin can be only three inches thick; his burial clothes and grave cloths can only be three in number; his coffin cannot be ornamented; his funeral cannot be by day, but at dusk he should be buried beside the road, and those who go to the burial must wear ordinary clothes. Contrary to other 11 burials, there should be no term of weeping, no mourning

---

[1] This word includes all that pertains to a funeral, from the ceremonies of dressing the corpse to the burial. These ceremonies last months in the case of the Emperor and less for others; but from the time of death to the actual burial may be years.

[2] The relatives manage the funeral and leave the son free to mourn.

[3] The "region" was composed of five "districts", and was supposed to contain 12,500 families.

[4] A "district" was supposed to contain 2,500 families.

[5] A "village" was supposed to be 25 to 50 families.

[6] The term for "criminal" is the same now used by Christians for "sinner"

badges, or sackcloth clothing, without the near and distant
relatives waiting for a month [1] ; everything as ordinarily,
everything as in life. When he is buried, it should be as if
there were no one to mourn for, and the ceremonies should
stop after the burial [2]—this is called the greatest shame. [3]

Funeral
ceremonies.

The man who observes the rules of proper conduct (*Li*) is
careful in worship and mourning ; but he does not allow
them to overcome him. [4] When the floss is put to the nostrils, [5]
and when people are waiting for the breathing to stop, then
the loyal minister or the filial son knows his loss. But if he
had made all preparations for the encoffining, he would have
no longer had any hope. His tears fall down and he is in
fear, yet his feeling of hope for life has not ended, his grasping
for life [6] has not stopped. When death has occurred, then
only does he act and make preparations. Hence, although
the household is prepared, a day must pass and then only
can the dead be encoffined ; three days, and then go into
mourning. After that the messengers who inform the distant
set out and those who make preparations get to work. For

[1] Before the funeral.

[2] No mourning or worship of the departed.

[3] This description of a criminal's burial is an intentional reproduction
of the kind of funeral that Micius recommended for everyone ; it is thus a
criticism of him. Micius wanted to economize and prevent the great waste
of time and money in funerals. Confucius forbade his disciples giving Yen
Huei a sumptuous funeral, but they did so nevertheless ; by the time of
Hsüntze sumptuous funerals seem to have been looked upon as a necessity.
Cf. *H.*, p. 137 ff.

[4] He does not allow his emotions to overcome his feeling for what is
right and proper, so that he cannot perform the appropriate ceremonies.

[5] To see if the dying man is still breathing.

[6] For the dying.

the funeral should not be later than seventy days, or if hurried, not less than fifty days after.[1] Why is this ? That the distant may come; that everything may be obtained; that all matters may be attended to. When the loyal have come, when the elapsed time is great, when the ceremonial articles are prepared, then on the first of the month they divine the day,[2] and on the last of the month they divine the burial-place, and then only bury the dead.[3] At this time the content of meaning of the ceremonies stops. Who would succeed in continuing it ? When the meaningful ceremonies continue who would succeed in stopping them ? For the three months' burial is for the sake of the living, to beautify the dead, not immediately leaving the dead in order to comfort the living.[4] This is the meaning of the most exalted affectionate thoughts.

THE REGULAR PRINCIPLE OF FUNERAL RITES (*Li*) 12

At every turn beautify it[5]; in every move, remove it[6] farther away; with the lapse of time return to the ordinary course of life. For the way (*Tao*) of death is thus; if it is not made beautiful, it becomes ugly; if it is ugly, there is no mourning; if it is near, it becomes wearisome; if wearisome, then it becomes distasteful; if distasteful, then it

Funeral rites give a standard of normal emotional observance.

---

[1] He is speaking of the funeral of an officer.

[2] Of the burial.

[3] This order of first picking the day and then the site for the grave is the opposite of that pursued to-day.

[4] To let the feeling of sorrow die down gradually.

[5] In dressing the corpse, encoffining, etc.

[6] The first rites, washing the body, etc., are performed in the death room; the next in the great entrance way of the house, the encoffining in the reception hall, etc.

becomes neglected; if neglected, then it is not done reverently.[1]
Suppose on one morning I should lose both parents, and the
mourners in the funeral should not mourn nor be respectful,
then I should be loathed by the birds and beasts. The
superior man would feel shame at that, hence at every turn
he beautifies death, thereby to lessen its ugliness; at every
move, he removes it farther away, thereby reverence con-
tinues to be felt; with the lapse of time he returns to the
ordinary course of life, thereby to tranquillize life. The rules
of proper conduct (*Li*) cut off that which is too long and
stretch out that which is too short; they diminish that which
is too much and increase that which is insufficient; they
attain to the beauty of love and reverence, and they strengthen
the excellence of character and right moral feeling (*Yi*). For
beautiful adornment and ugliness, music and weeping, contentment and sorrow are opposites; yet the rites (*Li*) unite
them and use them, at the right time they arouse them and
in turn bring them forward. For beautiful adornment,
music, and contentment, are that whereby a tranquil life is
supported, and that which brings good fortune. Ugliness,
weeping, sorrow are that whereby anxiety is nourished, and
that which brings ill-fortune. For the rites provide for
beautiful adornment, but do not go so far as to be fascinating;
they provide for coarse mourning clothes, but do not go so
far as to be stingy and neglectful; they provide for music
and contentment, but do not go so far as licentiousness or

---

[1] Reverence is the great virtue in performing rites (*Li*). The first sentence
in the *Book of Rites* is : " In everything be respectful ", and the commentator
says, " This sentence sums up the whole of the rites and rules of proper
conduct (*Li*)."

laziness ; they provide for weeping and sorrow, but do not go so far as an undue degree of distress and self-injury. This is the middle path of the rites (*Li*). Hence the change in the feelings and appearance [1] should be sufficient to differentiate whether the occasion is a happy or sad one ; it should make plain whether the person honoured is noble or inferior,[2] near or distant,[3] and it should stop there. Anything beyond this is evil. Although it may be difficult,[4] the superior **13** man despises it. For to limit one's food and eat only so much, to limit one's necessities and be bound by that, to observe high thinking with the result of making oneself sick and lean, are the way (*Tao*) of an evil man, not the ceremonies of the rules of proper conduct (*Li*) and justice (*Yi*). It is not the feelings of a filial son that inspire the person who acts thus.[5]

Hence pleasure, agreeableness, sorrow, and weariness are the expression of the feelings of good or bad fortune, sorrow or joy, shown in the features. Singing, jesting, weeping, and wailing are the expression of the feelings of good or bad fortune, sorrow or joy, shown in the voice. Meat, grain, wine, fish, pork, and congee, greens, beans, water, and broth [6] are the expression of the feelings of good or bad fortune, sorrow or joy, shown in food and drink. Caps, crowns, embroidered garments, woven silk garments, and coarse mourning clothes,

Li is the beautiful expression of emotion.

[1] Of the host or guest, in acting according to the rules of proper conduct.

[2] Death does not level all men for the Confucian. His principle is to treat the dead as if living, hence the noble dead have noble ceremonies ; the inferior dead have inferior ceremonies.

[3] In relationship.

[4] He should not vie in going beyond the customary ceremony just because it is difficult to do so.

[5] Cf. *Li-Ki*, I, I, iv, (6), 32–24.

[6] The last five are the food of a son mourning for his parent.

sackcloth badges, loose woven cloth, and straw sandals are the expression of feelings of good or bad fortune, sorrow or joy, shown in clothing. Large houses, deep

14 temples, elevated beds, fine rush mats, low tables and mats,[1] and thatched roofs, lean-to houses, firewood for chairs, clods for a pillow,[2] are the expression of the feelings of good or bad fortune, sorrow, or joy, shown in dwellings. These two kinds of feelings certainly have their origin in human life. If they are cut down or extended, enlarged or made shallow, added to or diminished,[3] thus made to fit the situation, completely expressed, glorified and beautified, to make the origin and aim, end and beginning all harmonize, so that they can become a pattern for all [4] generations—these are the rules of proper conduct (*Li*).

Without following these rules and without much self-cultivation, were a person a superior man, he could not know how to act. Hence I say, the original nature of man is the beginning and material; acquired characteristics are the beautification and glorification of the original nature. Without original nature, there would be nothing to which to add acquired characteristics; without acquired characteristics, the original nature could not become beautiful of itself. When original nature and acquired characteristics unite in character-

---

[1] Used for feasts—like the Japanese to-day.

[2] At the death of his father, the filial son was supposed to live in a lean-to thatched shed like a primitive man, during the period of mourning.

[3] These opposites refer to different people. In the case of the unworthy son, his natural sorrow being so little, it needs to be deepened; but the worthy son needs to have his feelings controlled so that he will not injure himself from the violence of his passion.

Lit., " ten thousand."

development, then only the name of Sage becomes inseparable from that man ; and therefore the benefit of the whole empire comes to him.[1] Hence it is said : Heaven and Earth unite and all things are born ; the *Yin* and the *Yang* meet and mutations begin ; original nature and acquired character- istics unite and the country is ruled. Heaven can bring things to birth, but cannot discriminate things ; the Earth can support man, but cannot rule men ; under the canopy of heaven the ten-thousand things bring humankind to birth, but wait for the Sage and then only are separated in their proper classes and uses. The ode says :—

" He has attracted and pacified all spirits,

   Even the spirits of the River [2] and the loftiest mountain "

—this expresses what I mean.[3]

Funeral rites (*Li*) are the beautification of the dead by the living ; they are sending off the dead very similarly to in their life. Hence we should treat the dead like the living, the absent like the present ; their end and their previous life should be alike. When first dead, bathe the head and body, tie the hands, and put food in the mouth, as it was in life. If you do not wash the hair, then wet it and comb it three times only ; if you do not bathe the body, then wet a towel and wipe the body three times only. Fill the ears and put in the ear plugs.[4] Provide raw rice for food, put dry bones in the mouth,[5] contrary to what is done in life.

Funeral rites are treating the dead like the living.

15

---

[1] He becomes emperor.

[2] The Yellow river.

[3] *Book of Odes*, IV, I, i, 8. When the Sage rules even the most important of the spirits are at rest and favourable.

[4] Made of white floss silk.

[5] Of the corpse ; jade was also used for this purpose.

Arrange the three suits of underclothing; wrap the girdle around without fastening it. Arrange the face covering; bind up the eyes; tie up the hair, but do not put on the hat nor the hairpin.[1] Write his name, and put it upon his tablet,[2] so that his name is not seen, but only the coffin containing the body is visible. Arrange the sacrificial articles and the hat with a flaring rim, but use no fillet to confine the hair. The earthern water and wine jars should be empty and not filled. There should be a fine bamboo mat but no bed. The wooden articles[3] should not be completely carved out; the pottery articles should not be completed; the thin articles[4] should 16 not be usable. The pipes and organ should be prepared but not sound in harmony; the lyre and lute should be strung, but not tuned. The carriages for carrying these articles are buried, but the horses are sent away and informed that they are not to be buried. The articles used in life[5] should be prepared to put into the grave, as if he were moving his house. Only a few things should be taken, not all of them: a show should be made of doing it, but it should not be done thoroughly. The carriages for sacrificial articles

[1] This was before the custom of cutting the hair or shaving the head came into vogue.

[2] Not the tablet permanently worshipped. The tablet here meant was a wooden one (now a scroll of silk is used) to provide a resting place for the spirit of the deceased until the permanent tablet is prepared.

[3] For burial with the dead; they were originally intended for the use of the spirit; at the present time paper imitations are burned; but Hsüntze reinterprets these ceremonies as treating the dead as if in life—it is like moving house. He does not believe in the existence of these spirits of the dead.

[4] Made of bamboo or reeds.

[5] Articles of personal use, such as bow, arrows, plates, bowls, etc.

should be hurried to the grave and buried, but the metal rein ends, the reins, the horse collars do not go into the grave. This shows that these things are not to be used.[1] This is the manner (*Tao*) of moving house, but these things are plainly not for use. This is all for the sake of emphasizing sorrow. For things used in life are adorned, but not completed; things for the dead are showy, but not useful.[2]

All rites (*Li*), if for the service of the living, are to beautify joy; or if to send off the dead, they are to beautify sorrow; or if for sacrifice, they are to beautify reverence; or if they are military, they are to beautify majesty. In this all the Kings were alike, the ancient times and the present are the same. But we do not know whence they came. Hence

---

[1] The absence of some things necessary for life, such as a carriage without horses or harness, shows that the burial of these things is not because the man's spirit is to use them. These articles were originally buried for the use of the spirit, but as civilization progressed, the rite was preserved but its meaning was changed—here Hsüntze is changing its meaning. Conservative Confucianism stuck to the ancient funeral rites; Hsüntze reinterpreted them in harmony with his enlightened view of the non-existence of spirits.

[2] In this sentence " things used in life " and " things for the dead " both refer to articles for burial with the dead, the distinction being that some are actual articles and others only imitations of articles. The *Book of Rites* says: " In the Chou period people used both (things used in life and things prepared especially for the dead), because they did not know whether the dead had knowledge or no knowledge, hence they used both things used in life and things prepared especially for the dead (to bury in the grave)." The 士 喪 禮 says, " The ' things used in life ' are the bow, arrows, the plough, the ditching spade, two earthenware dishes, two tubs, the wash-basin and the like. The articles for the nature spirits and the spirits of the dead are of the sort of things in which wooden articles are not completely hewn out, bamboo articles are not completely useful, and pottery articles are not completed."

the appearance of a tomb and its tumulus is like a house.[1]
The appearance of the coffin is like the carriage screen and
17 cover; it is like the carriage screen.[2]   The appearance
of the coverings for the hearse and the feathery ornaments
on it are like a door curtain or a bed curtain.[3]   The matting
and framework for keeping the dirt off the coffin is like the
plaster on the thatch and the screen in front of the door.[4]
Hence funeral ceremonies are for nothing else than to make
plain the meaning of death and life, to send off the dead
with sorrow and reverence, and at his end to provide for storing
his body away; for burial is reverently storing his body away.
Sacrifice is reverently serving his spirit [5]; engraving his
eulogy to hand it on to posterity is reverently passing on his
18 fame.   Service of the living is beautifying their life;
sending off the dead is beautifying their end; when the end
and the previous life are both attended to, the way (*Tao*) of
the Sage is completed.   Slighting the dead and over-
emphasizing the living is obscurantism [6]; slighting the living

---

[1] Ancient tombs seem to have been modelled on the primitive dug-out:
two stones were put up to represent a door; they also had a tunnel.   One
theory is that in primitive days, the individual was buried in his house
(which was a dug-out in the loess), and the family moved to another.

[2] The coffin and the carriage screen had the same carvings on them.
The meaning of this sentence is not plain, nor have the Chinese commentators cleared it up; there appears to have been some primitive error.
The idea in this section is the same as in the preceding paragraph, that
the funeral ceremonies are treating the dead, as if he were alive; even his
coffin, etc., are similar to things used in his life.

[3] The meaning of this sentence is not clear.

[4] All are for keeping dirt from going in.

[5] Traditional phraseology; not meant literally.

[6] There is a biting play on words here; the word " obscurantism " can
also be translated " Micianism "

and over-emphasizing the dead is to be misled; killing
the living to send off the dead [1] is murder. The method
and manner of the rules of proper conduct (*Li*) and justice
(*Yi*) is to send off the dead very similarly to in their life;
to cause death and life, the end and the present existence
both to be suitably treated, and to love goodness—the
Confucian does this.

Why [2] are there three years of mourning? Ceremonies
were established in accordance with the strength of
the emotions in order to beautify the ceremonies relating
to social relations, to friends and strangers, to kindred and
those who are not related, and to the noble and base. They
cannot be added to or diminished. Hence it is said, whatever
happens, they are the unchanging methods of mourning.
A bad wound remains for a long time; a severe hurt heals
slowly; three years of mourning arises because ceremonies
were established in accordance with the strength of the
emotions. Therefore it is the extremity of the greatest
distress. Mourning garments, a rush staff, living in a hovel,
eating rice gruel, using firewood for chairs, and clods for
a pillow, is the expression of the greatest distress. The
three years' mourning is finished in twenty-five months, [3]

Why three years of mourning for parents?

[1] Immolating the living with the dead   this custom, though disapproved
by all educated men, never quite died out.

[2] Beginning here down to the point where mourning for the prince is
taken up (p. 242), this section is the whole of chapter xxxv of the *Book of
Rites* (with the exception of one sentence at the end). It fits in so well
with the argument of this book that it seems plainly to be Hsüntze's
composition.

[3] In China, years are reckoned by what year it is "going on to"; ages
are reckoned thus; three years is just over two years, until it is "going
on to" three years. The period of mourning is now 25 or 27 months.

but the sorrow and distress is not yet ended; the thinking about and longing for the dead is not yet forgotten; yet the ceremonies (*Li*) stop at this point.[1] Why should they not terminate at the funeral and the time for returning to ordinary life [2] be at that time? Every living thing that is born between heaven and earth has knowledge. Now if one of the larger birds or beasts should lose its mate, after a month or season it would certainly return and go about its old haunts. Then it would certainly walk back and forth, howl, now move and now stop, embarrassed, and not knowing what to do, before it can leave the place. Even the small ones, such as the grey finch, will twitter a moment before it can leave the place. But among living creatures there is none with greater intelligence than man. Hence man's sorrow for his parents remains unexhausted even till death. But suppose we consider a stupid, mean, immoral, depraved man: if in the morning there were a death, by evening he 19 would have forgotten it; so if he were allowed to give rein to his feelings, he would not be equal to a bird or beast. How could he live with his neighbours without stirring up trouble? But suppose we consider a cultivated gentleman; for his three years of mourning, which is completed in twenty-five months, would be like a team of four horses passing over a crevice [3]; even if the time of mourning were extended, he would never reach its end. Accordingly the early Kings and Sages established a mean,

[1] Mourning dress is put off after the last sacrifice in this 25 or 27 month period.

[2] End of mourning.

[3] A fast team passing over a crevice in the road; swiftly gone by.

and regulated the period of mourning, all to make it sufficiently long to perform a beautiful series of actions, and then only is it to be laid aside.

Then how is the period determined ? There is a break Other in the mourning for the nearest relatives at a full year.[1] relatives. Why is that ? Heaven and Earth have then already made a complete mutation ; the four seasons have then already gone through their changes ; everything in the world has begun its processes anew. Hence the early Kings, in conformity to this, made the period of mourning like it. Then why three years ? To magnify it ; because they wanted to double the time ; hence they made it two full years. And what is the explanation of nine months' mourning [2] and less ? So as to make it not as much as that for parents. For three years' mourning should be considered the magnification of mourning ; the five and three months' mourning [3] should be considered the simplification of mourning ; the year and nine months are between these two. Looking above, Heaven gives us an example ; looking below, Earth gives us a pattern ; between we take our model from man. The harmony and unity that should characterize man, who lives in society, are thus completely shown. For the three years of mourning is the most beautiful thing in human practices (*Tao*) ; this is what is called the greatest exaltation of human actions. In this all the Kings agree, the ancient and the present are the same.[4]

---

[1] A change in mourning garments at this time.
[2] Mourning for an uncle.
[3] For a great-uncle or cousin.
[4] The quotation by the *Book of Rites* ends here.

Why does the mourning for a prince take three years ? The prince is the lord of rule, the source of law and custom, the one towards whom right feelings [1] and attitudes [2] should be completely expressed : Cannot one rightfully follow him [3] and exalt him to the highest ? The ode says :—

" The generous and respectful prince,
The father and mother of the people."

This prince certainly held the doctrine that he was the
20 father and mother of the people. [4] A father can beget a child but cannot feed it ; a mother can feed it but cannot instruct it [5] : the prince can both feed the people [6] and is also good at instructing them. [7] Is three years enough ? A wet-nurse gives me food and drink, and I mourn three months for her ; a foster-mother clothes me, and I mourn nine months for her ; my prince does both : is three years enough for him ? If the prince's government [8] is obtained, there is prosperity ; if it is lacking, there is calamity : this is the greatest of accomplishments. If it is obtained, there is peace ; if it is lacking, there is danger : this is the extreme of right feeling. [9] Since both of these extremes are reached, three years of service [10] for him seems not enough ; but should

[1] Faithfulness and sincerity.

[2] Respectfulness.

[3] Treat him as a parent.

[4] Cf. *Book of History*, V, I, 1, 3, for a similar statement.

[5] China is a land of almost universally ignorant women.

[6] By giving them government posts or by his granaries in famine and poverty, and by his government generally.

[7] By his edicts and laws.

[8] His means of giving food and clothing.

[9] The prince's care for his subjects.

[10] Mourning.

I go on without end ? Instead of the spirits of the land we worship the tutelary god [1] ; instead of the spirits of the grains we worship the god of agriculture [2] ; in the sacrifice to Heaven all the Kings are included with High Heaven [3] and are sacrificed to.

Why three months after the encoffining to the burial ? To magnify it ; to make it important. The early Kings [4] feared that in taking up and moving what was most exalted and most dear, in leaving the house and going to the grave-yard,[5] the performance would not be beautiful ; therefore they lengthened the period to make the number of days sufficient for adequate preparation. Hence for the emperor it is seven months ; for the feudal nobles five months ; for a prefect three months ; all so that the period may be long enough for taking the business in hand : that the business may be sufficiently well in hand so that it may be completed ;

Why three months from the encoffining to the burial ?

[1] Kou Lung, 句 龍, who was made equal with or taken to represent all the gods of the land. The Emperor, as Son of Heaven, has power to dispose of gods as well as mortals, and appointed deceased individuals to represent objects or places that were worshipped so as to have someone to receive the sacrifice. The point is that instead of many gods of the land we only worship one ; instead of many gods of the grain we worship only one, showing that these sacrifices are inferior to the sacrifice to Heaven, as other things were inferior to the prince.

[2] Hsi or Tsi, 棄, was taken to represent these spirits.

[3] This term, 上 天, may be translated " God " ; but in view of Hsüntze's impersonal view of Heaven, I have translated as above. The Kings were taken to represent Heaven and so were included in the worship of Heaven which became both a sacrifice to Heaven and to the ancestors of the officiating Emperor. This is Hsüntze's interpretation of the much-discussed sacrifice to Heaven.

[4] Who established the rites.

[5] Lit., " mound " or " hill "—Chinese graves are on the hills.

that it may be completed well enough so as to permit it to be beautiful; that it may be beautiful enough so as to be perfect: to permit things to be wholly perfect is the right Way (*Tao*).

21

The emotions produced in him who performs sacrifice [1] by his memories, ideas, thoughts, and longings, cause him to change countenance and pant [2]; it cannot be that such feelings should never come to him. For at the time when men are joyful and harmonious, the thoughts of a loyal minister and a filial son change, and these feelings come to him. That which causes them to come is a very strong impulse. If such feelings come in vain,[3] then the emotions produced by his memories and ideas [4] are disappointed and not satisfied, and that which the rite (*Li*) could have satisfied is lacking. For this reason the early Kings established ceremonies for the purpose of honouring the honoured and loving the beloved to the utmost. Hence I say: Sacrifice is because of the emotions produced by memories, ideas, thoughts, and longings; it is the extreme of loyalty, faithfulness, love and reverence; it is the greatest thing of the rites (*Li*) and of beautiful actions.[5] If there were no Sages, no one could have understood this. The Sage plainly understands it; the scholar and superior man accordingly perform

---

[1] Sacrifice to the spirits of the deceased.

[2] The effect of strong emotion.

[3] Because there is no sacrificial ritual to give it expression.

[4] Of the departed.

[5] Hsüntze's reinterpretation of sacrifice. We must remember that in China sacrifice was an elegant form in which food and praise were offered to the departed.

it [1]; the official observes it; among the people it becomes
an established custom. Among superior men it is considered
to be a human practice (*Tao*); among the common people
it is considered to be serving the spirits.

Hence the bells, drums, pipes, stone chimes, lyres, lutes,
reeds and organs, the Shao,[2] the Hu [3] of the Hsia dynasty,
the So [4] of King Wu, the Hsiao-chien-hsiang [4] of Duke Huan
are that whereby the superior man adapts himself to the
situation in beautifully expressing his joy. Mourning
garments, a rush staff, living in a hovel, eating rice gruel,
using firewood for a chair and clods for a pillow—this is the
way the superior man has of adapting himself to the situation
in beautifully expressing his sorrow and distress. Armies
have their regulations; criminal law has its degrees of crime,
all to suit the crime—this is the way the superior man
adapts himself to the situation in appropriately expressing 22
his hatred. Divination, finding the lucky days,
fasting, cleaning the temple,[5] spreading out tables and
mats, offering animals and grain, praying for blessings, as
if the deceased enjoyed the sacrifice; taking the offerings
and offering them all as if the deceased tasted them; offering
the three-legged wine-cup without washing it [6]; for the one
who sacrifices to have a wine bottle ready as if the deceased

---

[1] Sacrifice to the dead.

[2] Emperor Shun's music.

[3] T'ang's music.

[4] Names of pieces of music.

[5] The ancestral temple, where the deceased were worshipped.

[6] Not washing the wine cups to offer a second cup of wine to the deceased; using fresh cups instead.

drank from his goblet; when the guests leave, for the host to bow them off, change to his mourning clothes and sit down and cry, as if the spirit of the departed had left—this is sorrow, reverence, serving the dead as if serving the living, serving the departed as if serving those who are present, an appearance without the inner reality, imagery become a ritual.

BOOK XX

ON MUSIC

Now " music is the expression of joy." [1] Men's feelings **1** make this inevitable. For [2] man must needs be joyous; if joyous, his feelings must needs be expressed in sound, and bodied forth in movement and rest, [3] and the fact that

[1] A quotation from the *Book of Music* (in the present *Book of Rites*) used as a text. *Li-Ki, Ch.* xvii, II, 19.

The Chinese character for " music " and for " joy " is the same, 樂, though pronounced differently for the two different meanings.

This section is quoted in the " Book of Music " in the *Book of Rites* (*Li-Ki*, XVII, iii, 27–30 incl.). (See *H.*, p. xxii, note 1, for the manner of composition of the *Book of Rites*.) The first sentence (in quotation marks) is quoted from the older and original part of the " Book of Music ", and this quotation, together with Hsüntze's discussion, are added towards the end of the " Book of Music ". Hsüntze's text shows some roughnesses of reading which are smoothed out in the " Book of Music ", which fact would tend to show that Hsüntze was the author of this section. In addition, Hsüntze's characteristic references to Micius, which are omitted in the " Book of Music " (indeed the first part of this book is a rebuttal of Micius' attack on music, taking up each item of Micius' attack in order) would show that it originated with Hsüntze, but from the middle of p. 250 on may be spurious.

Yang Liang, the T'ang dynasty commentator on Hsüntze, has not commented on this book, though he has commentated on every other book of Hsüntze (except Book XII, the Way of the Prince), even on what are plainly spurious books—probably his copy of Hsüntze's works did not contain this book. He says that Hsüntze " contains doublets, and is torn, tattered, and parts missing, and shows mistakes from inaccurate copying ". (Quoted from his preface, A.D. 818.)

[2] Sze-ma Ch'ien's *Historical Record* (" Book of Music ", f. 32) also quotes four paragraphs, beginning here. Minor differences of text indicate that he probably quoted it from the *Book of Rites*, not directly from Hsüntze.

[3] Singing and dancing were an integral part of ancient Chinese music.

man directs (*Tao*) sound together with movement and rest
to express the changes in his disposition is completely
expressed in that statement. Hence man must needs be
joyous; if joyous, then he must needs embody his feelings;
if they are embodied, but without conforming to any
principles (*Tao*), then they cannot avoid being disordered.[1]
The early Kings hated this disorder, hence established the music
of the " Ya " and " Sung "[2] to conform it to principle (*Tao*),
so as to cause its music to produce joy and not to degenerate,
so as to cause its beauty to change but not stop, so as to
cause its indirect and direct appeals, its manifoldness and
simplicity, its frugality and richness, its rests and notes,
to stir up the goodness in men's minds, and to prevent evil
feelings from gaining any foothold. This is the manner
in which the early Kings established music. But Micius
attacks it[3]; what is to be done now ?

For when music is performed in the ancestral temple, the
prince and minister, the ruler and ruled hear it together,
and they cannot fail to be harmonious and reverent; when
it is performed in the inner apartments of the house, father
and son, older and younger brothers hear it together. and
cannot fail to be harmonious and affectionate; when it is
performed before the elders of the village or clan, old and
young hear it together, and cannot fail to be harmonious
and obedient. For music discriminates and unites[4] in order

[1] This word connotes political disorder, ill-government, and decadence,
together with unorthodoxy.

[2] Two of the divisions of the *Book of Odes*.

[3] One of Micius' books was entitled " Against Music "; his objections are
answered seriatim by Hsüntze here.

[4] The metaphor is from music to morality.

to establish harmony ; it compares and distinguishes in order
to beautify its measures ; it is performed in harmony in
order to create beauty, so that it leads everything in
one direction (*Tao*), so that it controls all changes—this
is the manner in which the early Kings established music.
But Micius attacks it ; what is to be done now ?

For when I hear the music [1] of the " Ya " and " Sung ", my
purposes are broadened. When I see the dancers grasp
their shields and pole-axes,[2] practise the lowering and raising
of their heads, the bending and straightening of their bodies, my
deportment becomes dignified. From the way in which
they move in groups and adapt themselves to the music,
the arrangement of the ranks is made correct, and their
advancing and retreating are together. For music, when
the dancers step forward, is of attacking and dealing death ;
when they step back it is of courtesy.[3] The meaning of
attacking, dealing death, and of courtesy are the same ;
when the dancers step forward to attack and deal death,
none fail to obey ; when they step back and act courteously,
none fail to accord. Hence music is the greatest unifier **2**
in the world, the bond of inner harmony, the inevitable
consequence of human emotion. This is the manner in which
the early Kings established music. But Micius attacks it:
what is to be done now ?

Music harmonizes and unites the people.

---

[1] " Music " includes instrumental and vocal music, the words as well
as the tune, and also the dancing which accompanies and expresses it—
it is a much broader term than the English " music ", and is much closer
to the ancient Greek concept of " music ".

[2] Used in military dances ; yak tails were used in peaceful dances.

[3] Lit., " bowing and yielding the precedence."

Music turns
the people's
hearts to
virtue.

Music is that whereby the early Kings beautified joy.
Armies and halberds are that whereby the early Kings
beautified anger ; so both the joy and the anger of the early
Kings got their proper expression. For this reason, when
they rejoiced, the whole empire chimed in : when they were
angry, tyrannous and misgoverned states feared. In the
Way (*Tao*) of the early Kings, the rules of proper conduct
(*Li*) and music were exactly that in which they excelled.[1]
But Micius attacks it. Hence I say : Micius in regard to the
correct doctrine (*Tao*) is like a blind man regarding white
and black, or like a deaf man regarding harmony and noise,
or as if a person wishes to go to Ts'u [2] and sought it in the
north.

The New
Music.

Now sound and music enter deeply into people; their
influence is rapid. For the early Kings carefully made
it beautiful. When music is moderate and even, the people
are harmonious and do not degenerate ; when music is
reverent and dignified, the people are tranquil and not in
turmoil. When the people are harmonious and tranquil,
the armies are strong, cities are secure, and enemy countries
dare not attack. Then the people will all be safe in their
dwellings, and happy in their villages, to the point of being
satisfied with their rulers. Therefore their fame will be
bright ; therefore their glory will be great ; in the whole
empire none of the people will be unwilling to have this

---

[1] The quotation in the " Book of Music " stops here ; it omits the three
sentences naming Micius. It follows this quotation from Hsüntze with a
saying of one of Confucius' disciples, which is plainly an addition to the
Book. The quotation in the *Historical Record* also stops here.

[2] A state in the south of China.

prince for their leader. This was the beginning made by the Kings.

When music is pretty and fascinating, it is dangerous ; then the people degenerate, are negligent, mean, and low. If they lose self-restraint and are negligent, turmoil will begin ; if they are mean and low, they will wrangle. If they are in turmoil and wrangle among themselves, then the armies will be weak, cities will be attacked, and enemy states will be dangerous. In this situation the people will not be safe in their dwellings nor happy in their villages, and they will not be satisfied with their rulers. Hence the casting aside of the rules of proper conduct (*Li*) and music, and the arising of unorthodox ditties, are the source of anger, loss of territory, insult, and disgrace. Therefore the early Kings honoured the rules of proper conduct and music, and despised unorthodox ditties. In the " Arrangement of Officials "[1] it is said : " The preparation of the laws and edicts, the examination of odes and essays, the elimination of licentious music, and obediently to do each at its proper time, so that barbarian or popular ditties do not confuse the Odes—this is the business of the Chief Instructor." [2]

Micius says : Music is what the Sage-Kings attacked, and wherein the Confucians err. The superior man thinks otherwise. Music is that wherein the Sages rejoiced,[3] and that which can turn the people's hearts to goodness. Its

---

[1] A title given by Hsüntze to what is now a section of Book IX, cf. p. 139.

[2] Might the quotation as an authority of a part of what is genuinely Hsüntze's writing indicate that this paragraph is not genuine ? But this paragraph is thoroughly in his style and in accordance with his teaching.

[3] " Rejoice " and " music " are the same character in Chinese.

influence is great ; it changes people's customs. Hence the
early Kings directed them by the rules of proper conduct
(*Li*) and music, and the people were peaceful. Now if the
people have the feelings of liking and hatred, but not the
reactions of joy and anger, then there will be disorder.
The early Kings hated this disorder, hence they cultivated
their characters, and corrected their music, and the whole
country obeyed them. For mourning clothes and the sound
3 of crying cause people's hearts to be sad ; to wear armour,
head-ornaments, and a helmet, and to sing among the ranks,
makes people's hearts reckless. Pretty and fascinating
appearance, the music of Cheng [1] and Wei [2] make men's
hearts licentious ; straight girdles and proper clothes,
posturing the Shao,[3] singing the Wu [4] make men's hearts
dignified. Hence the ear of the superior man does not listen
to licentious sounds ;   his eyes do not look at
licentiousness ; his mouth does not utter evil words.
Of these three things the superior man is careful. " Whenever [5] evil and depraved sounds influence men, their rebellious
temper responds ; when the rebellious spirit has embodied
itself,[6] then disorder begins. When correct music influences

[1] A state in present Honan.

[2] An important feudal state in present Chihli and Honan. Cf. with this
geographical classification of music the similarly geographic Greek classification of music as Lydian, Phrygian, etc.

[3] Shun's music.

[4] Wu's music.

[5] Here begin a series of reminiscences or quotations from the " Book of
Music " (*Li-Ki*, XVII, ii, 14). I shall indicate by quotation marks the extent
of these reminiscences. The quotations are not verbatim, but altered here
and there.

[6] In the countenance, etc.

men, the obedient temper responds to it ; when the obedient temper has embodied itself, then tranquillity and good government begins. There is a correspondence between the singing and the response " ; good and evil embody themselves. Hence the superior man is careful where he goes and whom he approaches. The superior man directs (*Tao*) his will by the bells and drums ; he makes his heart rejoice by the lyre and lute ; " he [1] is moved by the shield and the pole-axe [2] ; his mind is beautified by the feathers and yak's tail [3] ; he is made obedient by the stone chimes and flutes." Hence " the [4] fine and distinct notes are like Heaven, the large and grand notes are like Earth ", the lowering and raising of the head, and the turning around are like the " four seasons ". " For [5] when music plays ", the will " is clear ", the rules of proper conduct (*Li*) are cultivated and the character is perfected ; " the ear and eye are acute, the body and mind are tranquil, the customs and habits are altered, the whole country is peaceful," beautiful, good, and joyous. " Hence it is said : Music is the expression of joy. The superior man rejoices to attain to its course (*Tao*) ; the inferior man rejoices to satisfy his desires. If a person controls desire by the right Way (*Tao*), then he rejoices without disorderliness. If he forgets the right Way (*Tao*), then he

[1] Another quotation : *Li-Ki*, XVII, ii, 16.

[2] Military dances.

[3] Dances of peace.

[4] Another quotation or rather reminiscence. *Li-Ki*, XVII, ii, 17. Is this paragraph and all the subsequent matter in this Book spurious ? It is unlike Hsüntze to quote and paraphrase another work as in this section.

[5] Another quotation, altered, *Li-Ki*, XVII, ii, 18. The *Historical Record* also quotes it.

rejoices without disorderliness. If he forgets the right Way (*Tao*) for desire, then he errs and is not joyful." Hence music is that whereby joy is conformed to principle (*Tao*). "Metal,[1] stone, silk, and bamboo" are the things which induce (*Tao*) virtue. When music is played, the people turn towards it. Hence music is the greatest power in ruling. But Micius attacks it.

Music and *Li* embrace the whole heart of man. Moreover "music [2] is unchanging" concord. "The rules of proper conduct (*Li*) are unvarying principles. Music unites; the rules of proper conduct (*Li*) distinguish.[3] The ' union ' of the rules of proper conduct (*Li*) and music embraces the whole ' heart ' of man. To exhaust the source and extreme of change is the nature of music. To display sincerity and take away falseness is the law of the rules of proper conduct (*Li*)." Micius attacked it; he almost met with punishment, but the wise Kings had already passed away, and no one corrected him. Stupid people learn his doctrines and endanger themselves. The superior man

4 is clear about music, but he is born in an evil generation which hates goodness and will not listen to him. Alas! It cannot be done![4] Students avoid studying music and there is no way to attend to it.

Music reflects the universe. "Sound [5] is the form of music." The drum is the great pair [6]; the bells are the perfect ruler; the stone chimes

---

[1] Another quotation. *Li-Ki*, XVII, xii, 19.

[2] Another quotation, partly improved. *Li-Ki*, XVII, iii, 1, 2.

[3] Distinguish the classes of society.

[4] An exclamation like that in the *Gloss* (cf. p. 320). Is this section by the author of the *Gloss*, a close disciple of Hsüntze?

[5] Another reminiscence. *Li-Ki*, XVII, ii, 25.

[6] Two faces of the drum, hence a pair.

discriminate and regulate ; the organs of 36 reeds and 13 reeds respectively are reverent and harmonious ; the flageolet of 6 holes and the flute of 3 holes give volume ; the ocarina [1] and the bamboo flute [2] are like mist rising from the sea ; the lute with many strings [3] is easily excellent ; the lute with 7 strings is beautiful ; the vocal parts show the greatest clarity ; dancing shows forth the Way (*Tao*) of Heaven ; together, the drum is the leader of the music. [4] Hence the drum is like Heaven ; the bells are like Earth ; the stone chimes like water ; the organs, the flageolet, and flute are like the stars, the sun and the moon ; the hand drum, [5] the tub clapper, [6] the " fu " drum, the bell-frame, the notched sounding board, [7] and the time marker, [8] are like the ten-thousand things. How do we know the meaning of dancing ? The dancer's eyes do not look at himself ; his ears do not listen to himself, yet he controls the lowering and raising of his head, the bending and straightening of his body, his advancing and retreating, his slow and rapid movements ; everything

[1] An egg-shaped porcelain wind instrument with six to eight holes, blown through the apex—giving a whistling sound. Another explanation is that it was struck like a bell.

[2] It gave a sound like children crying.

[3] It has 50, 25, 15, or 5 silken strings.

[4] Very characteristic of Chinese music in which rhythm often predominates over every other element of music.

[5] Furnished with buttons tied to strings on each side and twirled—now used by pedlars.

[6] Wooden, made like a tub with a handle in the middle and a clapper on the side, which hit when twirled.

[7] A hollow wooden image of an animal used to make music by running a stick across its ridged back.

[8] A wooden instrument. These instruments correspond to the " percussion instruments " in a modern orchestra.

is discriminated and regulated. He exerts to the utmost all the strength of his body to keep time to the measures of the sounds of the drum and bell, and has no rebellious heart. All his purposes are summed up and earnest.

* * * * *

5

The District Gathering shows that the Way of the Kings is easy.

When [1] I watched the district [2] gathering, I know that the Way (*Tao*) of the Kings is very easy. [3]

The host in person goes [4] and invites the guests and their attendants ; and all the guests follow him. When they arrive at the gate, [5] the host makes an obesiance to the guests together with their attendants, and all the guests enter ;

---

[1] This section is part of Book XLIII of the *Book of Rites*, and is prefaced there by the words, " Confucius said ". It seems displaced in Hsüntze, as it barely mentions the subject of music, and comes after a series of paragraphs which are of doubtful authorship. It also interrupts the course of the argument in the *Book of Rites*. Seemingly it was a separate pamphlet ; the compiler of the *Book of Rites* took it to be from Confucius, and added it to that classic ; another editor, possibly Liu Hsiang, took it to be from Hsüntze, and added it to his works. Considerations of style seem to show that it is not from Hsüntze's pen. It has been included here because of its intrinsic interest, showing how Hsüntze's doctrine of *Li* worked in actual practice.

[2] Anciently the largest territorial division of the state, containing nominally 12,500 families and presided over by a prefect. This is a description of the triennial district gathering, under the superintendence of the Prefect himself. In the principal school or college of the district he assembled the gentlemen of accomplishments and feasted them ; at the same time selecting, especially from among the younger men, those who were to be the most useful to him in various departments of government service.

[3] This district gathering probably represented ancient customs and ceremonies, especially because it was held in the country, which is naturally conservative.

[4] To the houses of the guests, when everything is ready, to lead the principal guest to the feast—still a Chinese custom.

[5] The outer gate of the place where the feast is to be held.

thus the meaning of the distinctions between noble and inferior are exhibited.

Thrice they bow, and arrive at the steps. After the precedence has been thrice offered to them, the guests ascend and bow. When the host presents the guests with wine,[1] and receives wine from them in return,[2] the ceremonies of declining and yielding are numerous; but towards the attendants the ceremonies are fewer. The host goes to greet all the guests; they ascend and receive wine. Kneeling, they offer some in sacrifice; they rise and drink it; but without pledging the host in return, they descend—thus the opulence and simplicity of the ceremonies are distinguished.[3]

The chorus enters, ascends, sings three pieces, and the host offers them wine. The reed organists enter, play three pieces, and the host offers them wine. After an interval, the chorus sings three pieces, then they perform three pieces together. The musicians announce that the music is ended, and go out. Two men raise their horn goblets. Then they appoint a presiding officer to see that everything is done correctly. Thus I know they can be harmonious and joyful, and yet not be disorderly.

The guests pledge the host; the host pledges the attendants; the attendants pledge all the guests; the young

---

[1] The wine was not made from grapes, but from some cereal, possibly rice.

[2] The ceremony is as follows: The host pours out wine and offers it to the guests. The guests respond and the host again replies. The guests urge the host to drink. This is done to three guests only. With the attendants the urging to drink is omitted. Towards the guests at large the pledge to the host is omitted. So the ceremony is both made fulsome and simple.

[3] The proper distinction is made between the different parties by the multitude or paucity of observances paid to them.

and old pledge each other according to their age ; finally they pledge the keepers of the vases and the cup-washers. Thus I know that they can show brotherly deference to their elders, and not neglect any one.

After this they descend and take off their shoes,[1] then re-ascend, sit down, and drink goblets of wine without any limit as to number. The festival of drinking wine, if in the morning, does not use up the morning ; if in the evening, neither does it use up the evening. When the guests leave, the host bows and escorts them away. The ceremonies now come to an end. Thus I know that they can enjoy the feast without confusion.

The noble and inferior are thus exhibited ; the opulence and simplicity of the ceremonies are distinguished ; they are harmonious and joyful without disorder ; they show brotherly deference to their elders and do not neglect anyone ; they enjoy the feast without confusion—those five characteristics are enough to correct one's person and pacify a state. When that state is peaceful, the country will be peaceful. Hence I say : When I watch the district gathering, I know that the Way (*Tao*) of the Kings is very easy.[2]

---

[1] A custom like that of the modern Japanese.

[2] There is another paragraph added to this book, a criticism of a disordered and erring generation's customs. Since it does not belong to the subject of the book, and seems spurious, I have omitted it.

BOOK XXI

THE REMOVAL OF PREJUDICES

Everything that men suffer is from being prejudiced [1] by one false thing : and so the great principles are hidden from them. Good government consists in returning to the principles of the Classics ; other doubtful principles lead into error. In the world there are not two Ways (*Tao*) ; the Sages had not two minds. But now the dukes have a strange [2] government ; the hundred schools of philosophy have strange doctrines ; so that right and wrong are uncertain, good and bad government are uncertain. The result of sincerely following a wrong doctrine is that although the prince of an erring country or the member of an erring school of philosophy seeks to be right, yet he considers himself the judge of right and wrong. He is averse to the Way (*Tao*),[3] and in error, and others mislead him to follow the doctrines that he follows. He keeps his practices to himself and only fears that others will hear of his evil acts. He is partial to his own ideas, and inquires into strange arts ; and only fears that others will hear of the good qualities

All evil is from being prejudiced.

---

[1] Lit., " blinded," or " beclouded ", from a word meaning " to cover and screen ", and so throughout this chapter. The subject and text of this book is a reference to *Analects* XVII, vii, where Confucius speaks of the six " becloudings ". Hsüntze, however, does not follow Confucius' classification of the things that hinder a man from knowing the truth, but has his own classification.

[2] Unorthodox, unlike that of ancient times.

[3] The Confucian doctrines as found in the Classics.

of his beliefs.[1] Thus his government departs from right principles, and his overvaluation of himself is not checked. Is not this being prejudiced by one false thing and losing just the thing for which he is seeking ? If a person does not pay attention, when white or black is in front of his face, his eyes will not see it ; when somebody beats a drum thunderously beside him, his ear will not hear it   How much more the man who purposely causes his senses to dis-regard things ? Of those men who follow a principle (*Tao*), the prince who brings his country into disorder is at one extreme of evil ; the man of an erroneous school of philosophy is at the other extreme of evil— isn't it too bad !

Anything unorthodox can bring prejudice.

What brings prejudice ? Desire can bring prejudice ; that can bring prejudice ; the beginning can bring prejudice ; he end can bring prejudice ; distance can bring prejudice ; nearness can bring prejudice ; the profound can bring prejudice ; the superficial can bring prejudice ; the ancient can bring prejudice ; the present can bring prejudice. Everything that is unorthodox cannot help from bringing prejudice— this is the universal affliction of the mind.

Examples of good and evil kings.

In ancient times examples of some princes who were prejudiced were Ch'ie of the Hsia dynasty, and Chou of the Yin dynasty. Ch'ie was prejudiced by Mo-hsi and Sze-kuang,[2] and did not know Kuan Lung-feng.[3] So his mind was misled and his actions were thrown into confusion.

---

[1] Keeping the good to himself.
[2] Two concubines.
[3] Prime minister.

Chou was prejudiced by Ta-ki [1] and Fei-lien,[2] and did not know Wei Tze-Ch'i.[3] So his mind was misled and his actions were thrown into disorder. Hence all the officials lost their loyalty and sought their own ends ; the people hated his evil and rejected him. The worthy and the good left and retired into private life. This is how he lost the country and made vain the name of his dynasty in the ancestral temple. Ch'ie died at Mt. Ting [4] ; Chou's head was tied to the crimson pennon.[5] He was not able to judge men, and no one admonished him. This is the misfortune which comes from being prejudiced.

T'ang the Completer established himself by observing what Ch'ie of the Hsia dynasty had done, therefore he made his mind the ruler of his actions and carefully controlled them. This was why he was able for a long period to employ Yi Yin [6] and did not depart from the right Way (*Tao*). This is why he took the place of the kings of the Hsia dynasty and held the empire. King Wen observed Chou of the Yin dynasty, therefore he made his mind the ruler of his actions and carefully controlled them. This is why he could continuously use Lü Wang,[7] and did not depart from the right Way (*Tao*). This is why he took the place of the kings of the Yin dynasty and held the empire. None of the worthies

---

[1] A concubine.

[2] An official.

[3] Half-brother ; upright and opposed Chou ; later founded the feudal state of Sung ; 1112–1079 B.C.

[4] Far from the capital.

[5] He was decapitated and his head tied to a pennon.

[6] His prime minister.

[7] His prime minister.

of distant parts of the country failed to count it an honour to come to them[1]; hence their[1] eyes saw perfect colours; their ears heard perfect sounds; their mouths tasted perfect flavours; they themselves lived in a perfect palace; their names received the perfect appellation.[2] When they were born the whole empire sang; when they died all on the continent wept. This is what is called the extreme of exaltation. The ode says:

> "The phoenix is dancing livelily;
>
> Its wings are like a shield;
>
> Its voice is like a flute;
>
> Both male and female are present;
>
> They delight the Emperor's heart"—

this is the happiness of not being prejudiced.[3]

Examples of good and evil ministers and officials.

Of ancient officials who were prejudiced there were Tang Yang[4] and Hsi Ts'i.[5] Tang Yang was prejudiced by his desire for power, and so he drove out T'ai-tze.[6] Hsi Ts'i was prejudiced by his desire for a dukedom, and so had **4** Sung-seng[7] condemned to death. Tang Yang was killed in Sung; Hsi Ts'i was killed in Tsin: they expelled

---

[1] Referring to these good emperors.

[2] The appellation of Emperor.

[3] Quotation from a lost ode. The phoenix was a fabulous bird which only came to earth when there was a Sage. In the time of Yao these felicitous birds were thought to have come to build nests in his palace garden.

[4] Tang Yang was an official of King K'ang of the state of Sung. He advised his king to kill officials right and left in order to make himself feared.

[5] Hsi Ts'i was a son of Duke Hsien of the state of Tsin (676–651 B.C.) by a concubine. He had the heir of the dukedom killed.

[6] The prime minister of the state.

[7] Older brother of Hsi Ts'i.

a worthy prime minister and had a filial older brother condemned to death. They suffered punishment by death,
but did not know that this was the misfortune which comes
from being prejudiced. For from ancient times until the
present day there never has been anyone who was avaricious,
mean, rebellious, striving for power, and was not in danger
of disgrace and destruction. Pao Shou, Ning Ts'i, and
Hsi P'eng [1] possessed the qualities of humanity and wisdom,
and were not prejudiced, so they could support Kuan Chung, [2]
and their reputation, fortune, happiness, and emoluments
were equal to that of Kuan Chung. Duke Chao and Lü
Wang [3] possessed the qualities of humanity and wisdom
and were not prejudiced; hence they were able to support
Duke Chou, and their reputation, fortune, happiness and
emoluments were equal with that of Duke Chou. It is said :
Recognizing the worthy is what is meant by having clear
perception ; supporting the worthy is what is meant by being
a man of ability. The happiness of the person who strives
to do this and forces himself to do it will certainly last long—
this expresses my meaning. This is the happiness of not
being prejudiced.

In ancient times the travelling scholars were prejudiced— Examples of
these were the erring schools of philosophy. Micius [4] [5]
good and evil
philosophers.

[1] Officials of Ts'i under Kuan Chung.
[2] Prime minister of Ts'i under Duke Huan ; one of the great model
prime ministers.
[3] Officials of King Wen.
[4] Advocated that utility was the criterion of right and wrong—
utilitarianism. He held that the ruler and ruled should work together,
and neglected the distinctions of class by which the ruled should serve the
ruler.

was prejudiced towards utility and did not know the elegancies of life. Sungtze [1] was prejudiced towards desire and did not know virtue. Shentze [2] was prejudiced towards law, and did not know the worthy man. Shentze [3] was prejudiced towards power and did not know wisdom. Hueitze [4] was prejudiced towards words and did not know reality. Chuangtze [5] was prejudiced towards Nature, and did not know man. For if we consider life (*Tao*) from the standpoint of utility, it will merely be seeking for profit. If we consider life (*Tao*) from the standpoint of desire, it will merely be seeking for satisfaction. If we consider life (*Tao*) from the standpoint of law, it will merely be an art. If we consider life (*Tao*) from the standpoint of power, it will merely be convenience. If we consider life (*Tao*) from the standpoint of words, it

[1] 宋子 Believed that desires naturally seek little, and so by giving rein to them they would be controlled.

[2] 慎子 Taught that there can be many worthies in a government, but only one prince ; a state can get along without worthy officials, but not without a prince, i.e. with law there can be good government even if there are no worthy officials. Hence there is no necessity for incentives for officials, such as honouring the worthy and employing the able.

[3] 申子, not the same as the preceding. This philosopher is only mentioned in this one place by Hsüntze. He was from Honan ; he was the prime minister of Marquis Chao of the state of Han (358–333 B.C.). " Whenever the worthy get power and ability, they control their inferiors by law ; when the ruler does not know men of authority and ability, he waits for one who has the talent and wisdom, and then only is there good government." He believed that the ruler should only delegate his power to a man of talent and wisdom.

[4] Leader of the Neo-Micians. He stressed dialectic, and often reasoned from mere words, instead of from principles.

[5] Taught that good and bad government were the results of the law of cause and effect, and did not know that it rested with human efforts. He himself refused to take high office, even when it was offered him.

will merely be dialectic.   If we consider life (*Tao*) from the
standpoint of Nature, it will merely be cause and effect.
These different presentations are all one aspect of life (*Tao*).
Now the right Way of life (*Tao*) is constant and includes
all changes ; one aspect is insufficient to express the whole.
Those who have partial knowledge perceive one aspect of
the Way (*Tao*), but they cannot know its totality.   So they
think it sufficient, and gloss things over.   On the one hand
they confuse themselves, and on the other they mislead others.
The rulers prejudice their inferiors ;   the inferiors prejudice
their superiors.   This is the calamity which comes from being
prejudiced and hindered from knowing the truth.

Confucius possessed the qualities of benevolence (*Jen*) Confucius.
and wisdom, and was not prejudiced ; hence his scholarship
and mastery over all teachings were sufficient to make him
equal with the ancient Kings.   He possessed the whole **6**
of the right Way (*Tao*) ; he brought it to people's notice,
and he used it ; he was not prejudiced nor unable to carry
it out.   Hence his virtue was equal with that of Duke Chou ;
his reputation is abreast of that of the three Kings [1] ; this
is the happiness which comes from not being prejudiced.

The Sage knows the afflictions which befall the mind The Sage
and sees the calamities which come from being prejudiced criterion.
and hindered from knowing the truth.   Hence he
considers neither desire nor hate, neither beginning nor
end, neither nearness nor distance, neither the universal
nor the superficial, neither the ancient nor the present.
He is equally able to dispose of all things, and keeps the

[1] Yu, T'ang and Wen and Wu (Wen and Wu are counted as one).

balances level.[1] For this reason all the sects are not able to prejudice him, nor do they confuse his perception of the organizing principles of life.

The criterion is the *Tao*.
What can be considered to be the weight used in the balances ?[2] It is the Way (*Tao*).[3] Hence one's mind dare not be ignorant of the right (*Tao*). If one's mind is ignorant of the right (*Tao*) then it cannot will to do the right (*Tao*), and can only will to act contrary to the right (*Tao*). What man desires to obtain license to do what he does not will, and to prohibit what he wills ? If he selects men according to a mind which does not will to do right (*Tao*), then he will necessarily be like vicious (un-*Tao*) men, and not be like virtuous (*Tao*) men. If he discusses virtuous (*Tao*) men with vicious (un-*Tao*) men according to a mind which is unwilling to do right (*Tao*)—this is the origin of disorder.[4] Then how is he to know the right (*Tao*) ? When a man's mind knows the right (*Tao*), then only can he will to do the 7 right (*Tao*). When he can will to do the right (*Tao*), then only can he do the right (*Tao*) and abstain from doing the wrong (not-*Tao*). If he picks men according to a mind which is willing to do the right (*Tao*), then he will be like virtuous (*Tao*) men and unlike vicious (un-*Tao*) men. To

[1] He rightly judges the value of things.

[2] The weight on the balances against which things are weighted, i.e. the standard of weight or truth. The instrument implied here is the steelyard, which has a movable bob used to balance the article to be weighed. Lit., " What is called the bob ? "

[3] The right way of life, or *Tao*. *Tao* may take the connotation of any of the words, " right," " way," or " life ". For Hsüntze *Tao* is defined by *Li* and *Yi*.

[4] Bad government, calamity, erroneous doctrine.

discuss the wicked (not-*Tao*) with virtuous (*Tao*) men according to a mind willing to do the right (*Tao*) is the important thing in good government. What harm is there in not knowing virtuous men ? The important thing in good government is knowing virtuous (*Tao*) men.

How can a person know the right (*Tao*) ? By the mind. How does the mind know ? By emptiness, unity or concentration, and unperturbedness. The mind never ceases to store away impressions, yet there is that which may be called emptiness.[1] The mind has always a multiplicity,[2] yet there is that which may be called a unity.[3] The mind is always in motion, yet there is that which may be called quiescence or unperturbedness.[4]

How know the *Tao* ?

Emptiness.

Concentration.

Unperturbedness.

A man from birth has the capacity to know things ; this capacity to know things has its collected data [5] ; these collected data are what are meant by stored away impressions. Moreover he has that which may be called emptiness. That which does not allow what is already stored away to injure that which is about to be received is called the mind's emptiness. The mind from birth has the capacity for knowledge ; this knowledge contains distinctions ; these distinctions consist of at the same time perceiving more than one thing. To perceive more than one thing at the same time is plurality. Yet the mind has that which may be called a unity. That which does not allow that impression to harm

Emptiness.

Unity.

---

[1] 虛, receptiveness to new impressions, lack of prejudice.
[2] Multiplicity of objects of the mind.
[3] 壹, unity of mind or concentration.
[4] 靜, the quality of not being disturbed by emotion.
[5] The apperceptive mass, or the items of memory.

this impression is called the mind's unity.[1] When the mind

Unperturbed-
ness.

sleeps, it dreams ; when it takes its ease, it indulges in reverie ; when it is used, it reflects. Hence the mind is always in motion. Yet it has that which may be called unperturbedness. That which does not permit dreams [2] to disturb one's knowledge is called the mind's unperturbedness.[3]

To know the
Tao brings
true great-
ness.

If a person is seeking for the right way of life (*Tao*), but does not know it, he should make his mind empty, unified, and unperturbed, and act in that way. Cause him who is seeking for the Way (*Tao*) to make his mind empty, and then

8 he can receive it ; cause him who is serving the right (*Tao*) to make his mind unified, and when his mind is unified, he can do the right in its entirety ; cause him who desires the right (*Tao*) to make his mind unperturbed ; when his mind is unperturbed, he can arrive at the truth. He who perceives the right (*Tao*) and gets at the truth of it, he who perceives the right (*Tao*) and does it, can be said to embody the right (*Tao*). He who makes his mind empty, unified, and unperturbed can be said to follow right principle and to be illustrious in virtue. There is nothing visible which does not disclose its qualities to him ; there is nothing that he sees which he cannot discuss ; in discussing he never errs. He sits in his chamber and sees the world ; he lives in the present and discusses the ancient and the distant. He looks through all things and sees their nature ; he investigates good and bad government and arrives at their laws.[4] He

---

[1] Lit., 壹, which means both " unity " and " concentration ".
[2] Unrealities.
[3] Or " passionlessness ".
[4] How to get good and avoid bad government.

understands the whole of Heaven and Earth, and regulates all things ; he governs according to the great principle and the universe is rectified. He is very great—who knows his limits ? He is very splendid—who knows his virtue ? His character is very intricate—who knows its form ? He is brilliant, equal with the sun and moon ; his greatness fills the whole world. This is what is meant by being a truly great man.

The mind is the ruler of the body and the master of the spirit. It gives commands and all parts of the body obey. It itself makes prohibitions ; it itself gives commands ; it itself makes decisions ; it itself makes choices ; it itself causes action ; it itself stops action. The mouth can exert itself forcibly and make the silent speak ; the body can exert itself forcibly and make the bent straight ; the mind cannot exert itself forcibly and change one perception ; if it does this, then it would be in error and must resign its lordship. Hence I say : The mind must bear what it chooses. It cannot prevent the results of its action appearing of themselves. The mind's objects are confused and extensive ; its essence is a unity. The ode says : **9**

The mind rules, but must be empty, concentrated, and unperturbed.

> " I pick and pick the mouse ears,[1]
>   But I cannot fill my shallow basket.
> Alas for the man of my heart !
>   I have let him go to his place among the
>   official ranks of Chou." [2]

[1] Burr-weed.
[2] *Book of Odes*, I, i, iii, 1. This ode speaks of a wife who could not even fill her shallow basket with weeds because of sorrow for her absent husband.

A shallow basket is easy to fill; mouse-ears are easy to get; but she cannot do it because her mind is wandering to her husband among the Chou officials. Hence I say: When the mind is divided, it possesses no knowledge; when it is upset, it is not quick-witted; when it is wandering, it is in doubt. But when it is not so, it can be used to help investigate and all things can be embraced and known.

Concentration.

A person who fits into his niche is admirable. A person cannot be of two sorts, so the wise man picks one sort and concentrates on it. The farmer may be expert on the farm, but he cannot be considered a farm-sage; the merchant may be expert at the market, but he cannot be considered a market-sage; the workman may be expert with tools, but he cannot be considered a tool-sage. There are men who do not have these three kinds of ability, but who can cause these three businesses to be properly governed. We say that they are expert in the principles of life (*Tao*), not 10 expert in things. The man who is expert with things judges one thing by another thing; the man who is expert in the principles of life (*Tao*) comprehends all things and judges them. Hence the superior man concentrates on the principles of life (*Tao*), and uses them to assist in investigating things. When a man concentrates on the principles of life (*Tao*), he can be correct; when he uses them to assist in investigating things, he can get at the truth; when he investigates and discusses according to an upright mind, he can put all things in their proper place.[1]

---

[1] He makes no mistakes.

In ancient times when Shun governed the country, he did not need to issue proclamations, nevertheless all things were brought to a prosperous issue.[1] He dwelt in unity of mind and was solicitous of it—his glory was full and running over. He cultivated the subtleties of this unity—it gave him glory, but men did not know why. Hence the Classic of the Way (*Tao*) says[2] : " The carnal mind is anxious ; the virtuous (*Tao*) mind is subtle." If a man becomes as intelligent as a superior man, only then can he know the sources of anxiety [3] or subtlety.

The mind of man is like a tub of muddy river water [4] : place it upright and do not jar it, and the muddiness will sink to the bottom, and the clear water will be on top ; then it will be clear enough to mirror the beard and eyebrows, and to show the condition of the complexion. But if a little wind crosses its surface, the mud at the bottom rises and the clear water at the top is disturbed, until a person cannot see in it whether he is standing upright ! The mind is like that. Hence if it is guided by principle and nourished by purity, nothing can overturn it. Then it is sufficient to determine right and wrong, to decide what should be disliked and what suspected. But if a little thing leads the mind astray, on the one hand this man's aplomb is changed and on the other hand his mind is turned upside down ; then he is not even able to decide matters in general.

*Unperturbed-
ness—The
tub of water.* 11

[1] He was able to use worthy officials who did all things well.

[2] This sentence is now in the *Book of History*, II, II, ii, 15, and forms part of the advice Shun gives Yu.

[3] Or danger.

[4] Lit., " water " ; he refers to the river water used everywhere in China which is muddy but settles upon standing.

Concentration—Only one expert of each sort.

For there were many who liked to write, but tradition only gives one Ts'an Chie [1] as concentrating on it and making it his speciality. There were many who liked agriculture, but tradition gives only Hou Tsi [2] as concentrating on it and making it his specialty. Many liked music, but tradition gives only K'uei [3] as concentrating on it and making it his speciality. Many liked justice (*Yi*), but tradition gives only Shun as concentrating on it and making it his speciality. [4] Ch'ui [5] made the bow and Fou Yu [6] made arrows, but Yi [7] was expert at archery. Hsi Chung [8] made the carriage and Hsiang Tu originated the team of four horses, but Ts'ao Fu was expert at driving. From ancient times until to-day there have not been two men who could be said to be experts.

Unperturbedness—control of the

12

emotions.

Tzentze [9] said : If in a room a person watches whether he can hit a rat, how can he sing with me ? [10] In a cave there was a man whose name was Ch'i. [11] He was fond of pondering and loved thinking. But when the desires of the ear or eye came to him, they destroyed his train of thought ; when he heard the sound of mosquitoes or gnats,

---

[1] The historiographer of Hwangti, who is supposed to have invented writing.

[2] Shun's Minister of Agriculture, later made god of agriculture.

[3] Shun's Director of Music.

[4] Because of his determinedly just and right attitude to his father and older brother in spite of their actions.

[5] Shun's Minister of Works, who improved the bow.

[6] Unknown.

[7] A famous archer and rebel in the Hsia dynasty, ca. 2169 B.C.

[8] Improved the carriage ; lived in the time of Yu.

[9] A famous disciple of Confucius.

[10] Because his attention is divided.

[11] Unknown. Probably a hypothetical case.

it disturbed his concentration. So he shunned the desires
of the ears and eyes and got away from the noise of mosquitoes
and gnats, and lived at leisure, thinking in quietude, and
then thought to become wise. When such a man thinks
about virtue (*Jen*) [1] in this fashion, can he be said to have
abstruse knowledge ? [2] Mencius was afraid of disgrace
and divorced his wife—this can be called being forced to
act thus. Yiutze [3] scorched his palm to prevent nodding—
this can be called repressing oneself ; it does not come
up to love of thinking. When a person shuns the desires
of the ears and eyes and when the sound of mosquitoes and
gnats disturbs his concentration, this can be called anxiety ;
it cannot be called abstruse knowledge. For he who has
abstruse knowledge is the Wise Man. [4] Why should the
Wise Man need to be forced or repressed or anxious ? [5] For
what is foul is visible without ; what is pure is visible within.

The Sage gives reign to his desires and satisfies his passions, **13**
nevertheless he is controlled by principle ; so why need he The Sage.
be forced or repressed or anxious ? For the acting out of
the right Way (*Tao*) by the benevolent (*Jen*) man is without

---

[1] Attempts to think out virtue for himself. *Jen* is here that virtue
which springs from within as contrasted to an external standard of virtue.

[2] Implying the answer, No. The term here translated " abstruse
knowledge ", 微, is the same translated " subtle " in the quotation from
the Classic of the Way above.

[3] A disciple of Confucius. Because of his eagerness to keep awake to
study he placed a hot coal so that if he should nod he would burn
himself.

[4] Lit., 至 人 ; a Sage, but of the second grade ; the Wise Man has reached
the wisdom of a Sage ; the Sage has both wisdom and character. This
is the only place where Hsüntze mentions the 至 人.

[5] With the Sage, love of study of the *Tao* comes of itself.

effort [1] ; the performance of the right Way (*Tao*) by the
Sage is without forcing himself. The thoughts of the
benevolent (*Jen*) man reverence the thoughts of the Sage.
To rejoice at this is the way (*Tao*) of the man of a
controlled mind.

Unclearness invalidates judgments.

Whenever in observing things there is doubt and the
mind is uncertain, then things are not apprehended clearly.
When my thoughts are unclear, then I cannot decide whether
a thing is so or is not so. When a person walks in the dark,
he sees a stone lying down and takes it to be a crouching tiger ;
he sees a clump of trees standing upright and takes them
to be standing men. The darkness has perverted his clear-
sightedness. The drunken man crosses a hundred-pace
wide aqueduct and takes it to be a half-step wide ditch ;
he bends down his head when going out of a city gate, taking
it to be a small private door—the wine has confused his
spirit. When a person sticks his finger in his eye and looks,
one thing appears as two ; when he covers his ears and listens,
a tiny sound is taken to be a big noise—the circumstances
have confused his senses. So in looking down from
a mountain, a cow looks like a sheep ; but whoever wants
a sheep does not go down and lead it away—the distance
has obscured its size. In looking from the foot of a mountain,
a ten-fathom tree looks like a chop-stick ; but whoever
wants a chop-stick does not go up and break it off—the
height of the mountain has obscured its length. When the

---

[1] Lit. 無 爲, non-action, Laotze's famous term. This paragraph is an
expansion of what is implied in Confucius' saying of himself, " At seventy,
I could give rein to the desires of my heart, but without transgressing the
rule." *Analects*, II, iv, 6.

water moves, the shadows dance ; men cannot decide whether they are beautiful or ugly—the state of the water is confused. When the blind man lifts up his head and looks, he does not see the stars ; people do not because of that decide whether there are or are not any stars—the man is misled by his blindness. If there were a man who would make judgments under such circumstances, he would be the most stupid person in the world. This stupid man in making judgments would be using doubtful premises to make decisions. When he uses doubtful premises to make decisions, he could not be correct. If he could not be correct, how could he be without fault ?

South of the mouth of the Hsia river [1] there was a man called Chüan Chuh-liang.[2] In disposition he was stupid and very fearful. When the moon was bright, he was walking in the dark. He bent down his head and saw his shadow, and thought it was a devil following him. He looked up and saw his hair and thought it was a standing ogre.[3] He turned around and ran. When he got to his house he lost his breath and died. Wasn't that too bad ? Whoever says there are demons,[4] it must be because they make that judgment when they are suddenly startled or at a time when they are not sure or confused. This is when people think that a thing exists but it does not exist, or that it does not exist but it does exist, and in these circumstances make a judgment.

14

Seeing spirits and worshipping them.

---

[1] In northern Shensi ; south of this river would be the heart of ancient China. It is a veiled reference to ancient China.

[2] Unknown. A hypothetical instance ?

[3] A kind of demon.

[4] The spirits of the dead are primarily meant by 鬼, but by extension all spirits are included in the argument.

For when a person has been affected by dampness and contracted rheumatism, and when the rheumatic beats the drum and boils a suckling pig,[1] then there will necessarily be the waste resulting from a worn out drum and a lost pig, but he will not have the happiness of recovery from his sickness. So although he is not south of the mouth of the Hsia river, he is no different from that man.

Scientific knowledge can never be completed, hence fruitless.

That wherewith a person knows the nature of man [2] also enables him to know the laws of the material world. If he seeks to know the laws of the material world by using that wherewith he knows the nature of man, there is nothing to hinder him; but in a lifetime he cannot go all over them. In studying these laws, although he lived a myriad years, it would not be enough for his to embrace the changes of all things—he would be the same as a stupid man.

15 Though he studied until he was old and his children grown, he would be the same as a stupid man. If he did not know his mistake, he could be truly called a failure. For the true student studies resolutely until the end.

Completion of knowledge only gained by following the Way of Kings as the authority, which is the end of all knowledge.

What is the end? The end is until there is no deficiency. What may be called "until there is no deficiency?" The Way (*Tao*) of the Sage-Kings. The Sage fulfils the duties of the natural relationships; the King fulfils the ideal of government. When both are fulfilled, it is sufficient to make him the culmination of the world. Hence the student takes the Way (*Tao*) of the Sage-Kings as the judgments of an authority; he takes the government of the Sage-Kings as his law. He makes their methods his methods, in order

[1] An offering to the spirits to cure him.
[2] The mind.

to seek to be in the same class with them ; he strives to be like them and imitates their character. To strive for this Way (*Tao*) is the duty of every scholar ; to become of a class with this is to be almost a superior man. He who knows this Way (*Tao*) is the Sage. For although a man has knowledge, unless he cares for this Way (*Tao*), he is as bad as a robber. Although he is brave, unless he maintains this Way (*Tao*), he is as bad as a thief. Although he is skilled at investigation, unless it is to distinguish this Way (*Tao*), he is as bad as a rebel. Although he has many abilities, unless it is to cultivate his powers to this Way, he is as bad as a sharper. Although he has fine debating powers, unless it is to speak of this Way (*Tao*), he is a garrulous talker.

It is said : There are two kinds of people in the world : the Wrong criticizing the Right, and the Right criticizing the Wrong. That is to say, those who agree with the practices of the Kings, and those who do not agree with the practices of the Kings. In this country there are those who do not take this Way (*Tao*) for their standard ; can such people distinguish right and wrong, or try [1] the crooked and the upright ? If this were the case, that the Wrong **16** were to distinguish right and wrong, if the Wrong were to try [1] the crooked and upright, if the Wrong were to discriminate good and bad government, if the Wrong were to regulate the ways (*Tao*) of men, although they had the ability to do so, it would be of no benefit to men ; it could not fail to injure men. If, like the upright, they were to correct evil speech and examine strange arguments, they would confuse right and wrong ; like the strong they would practise

The Way of the Kings is the only standard of Right and Wrong.

---

[1] In court.

extortion and their mouths would be greedy of gain; they would be shameless and allow outrageous acts; they would be without uprightness, and disdainful in manner; they would make wanton decisions and benefit only those close to them; they would not love courtesy; they would not respect the rules of proper conduct (*Li*) and temperateness; they would love to overthrow others—this theory produces a disordered age and wicked men. Then theories of government for the country would become many. It is said: The superior man despises splitting words and considering that to be investigation, talking about things and considering that to be discrimination. The superior man despises shallow knowledge and violent aspirations, whatever does not agree with the rule of the King—this expresses what I mean. To do that [1] is of no benefit in getting things done; to seek it is of no benefit in obtaining what one wants; worry and distress over it is of no good. Then reject it and discard it. Do not allow it to hinder yourself; do not permit it in your breast for an instant. Neither desire it in the past nor grieve for it in the future; do not be anxious for it nor hold to it in your mind. Resolve upon your action at the moment; when the affair comes, respond to it; when the situation arises, adapt yourself to it; whether there be good or bad government, you will be illustrious and wise.

* * * * *

The secretive prince.

17 The [2] prince who is open and above-board does not consider

[1] Such a wrong theory of government as above spoken of.

[2] This paragraph may have been added later; it does not pursue the argument of this chapter; it is possibly spurious, but in Hsüntze's vein, and an expansion of what he says elsewhere.

that he succeeds by being secretive or fails through letting things be known. The secretive [1] prince does not consider that he succeeds by making things manifest or fails by being retired.[2] Hence slander comes to the ears of the prince who is secretive, and straight talk is unknown to him; small-minded men come near to him and superior men kept distant. The ode says:

"To think that to be obscure is to be wise,
Is because you are as secretive as a fox" [3]

this speaks of the ruler being in the dark and the subordinates being dangerous to him. Straightforward talk comes to the prince who is open and slander is unknown to him; superior men come near to him, and little-minded men keep distant. The ode says:

"Below he is illustrious;
Above It is awe-inspiring" [4]

this speaks of the ruler being illustrious and the subordinates being influenced accordingly.

---

[1] Who keeps his plans secret and his person inaccessible.

[2] Keeping away from the people and being secretive.

[3] From an ode now lost.

[4] *Book of Odes*, III, i, ii, 1. The word translated "illustrious", 明, means literally "bright"; that for "awe-inspiring", 赫, means "glowing hot". "He" refers to King Wen, the founder of the Chou dynasty: "It" refers to Heaven, who gave King Wen the Decree of Heaven whereby he was enabled to develop his state to the leadership of the empire. The meaning is that although King Wen was illustrious, it was because of the superior illustriousness of Heaven, who nourished and influenced King Wen. The ode is in praise of King Wen and his wife.

BOOK XXII

ON THE RECTIFICATION [1] OF TERMS [2]

When the later Kings [3] formed the terminology, in the names of punishments they followed the Shang dynasty, The sources of terms. in the titles of nobility they followed the designations of the Chou dynasty, [4] and in ceremonial terms they followed the Ritual (*Li*). [5] In the case of miscellaneous names given to things they followed the established customary designations of the Chinese people. Because of them, when people of distant districts with different customs indirectly meet, they can communicate.

In miscellaneous psychological terms the essential factor Some psychological terms defined. at birth is man's original nature. That which at birth is produced by the concord of the *Yin* and *Yang*, whose essence is suitable for the stimulus and response relation, which is not produced by training, but exists spontaneously, is called original nature. The love, hate, joy, anger, sorrow, and pleasure of original nature are called the emotions. When the mind selects from among the emotions by which it is moved—this is called reflection. When the mind reflects and can act accordingly—this is called acquired training.

[1] For this phrase, cf. *Analects*, XII, iii. Hsüntze has here taken up a task left by Confucius—the rectification of terms.

[2] Or names, 名, and so throughout this book.

[3] The great Kings of the Chou dynasty. " King " in this book (and often elsewhere) means a righteous King or Sage.

[4] The founders of the Chou dynasty apportioned fiefs and gave the titles of nobility according to those previously current in the state of Chou.

[5] Yang Liang explains the Ritual as the *I-Li*.

2 When reflection is practised and a man's powers are trained, and then only is it formed—this is called acquired character. To act for the sake of righteous gain is what is meant by having a proper occupation. To act correctly according to justice (*Yi*) is good conduct. That in man by which he knows is called knowledge; that knowledge which corresponds to reality is called wisdom. That in man which can be carried out is called his ability. That which corresponds to what really can be done is called ability. An injury to original nature is called a defect. What one meets at the moment is called destiny. These are miscellaneous psychological terms; these are terms fixed by the later Kings.

The benefit of established terms is to make the people virtuous; otherwise there will be disorder.

For when the Kings had regulated names, when they had fixed terms and so distinguished realities, and when this principle (*Tao*)[1] was carried out and hence their will was everywhere known, they were careful to lead the people and so the people were unified. Therefore distinguishing words, and making unauthorized distinctions, thus confusing the correct nomenclature,[2] causing the people to be in doubt and bringing about much litigation was called great wickedness.[3] It was a crime like that of using false credentials or false measures.[4] For their people did not dare to make

[1] The principle of regulating terms.

[2] Especially in litigation. It seems that Teng Sih or others made trouble by sophistically making distinctions in the legal terms of what was punishable as certain crimes.

[3] This statement is echoed in the *Li-Ki*, Book III, iv, 16, " Those who distinguished words or corrupted the laws, who confounded the terminology and made unauthorized distinctions . . . were put to death."

[4] Crimes punishable by law.

strange terms a pretext for confusing the correct nomenclature, hence their people were guileless. Since they were guileless, they could easily be moved to action ; since they were easily moved to action, they produced achievements. Since **3** their people did not care to make strange terms a pretext for confusing the correct nomenclature, they were united in virtue (*Tao*) and law-abidingness, and respectful in following orders. In this way their example spread. Their example spread and they produced achievements—this was the extreme of good government. This was the benefit of being careful in preserving the terms which had been agreed upon.

Now the Sage-Kings are dead, terms are carelessly preserved, strange nomenclature arises, terms and realities are confused, and what is right and wrong is not clear, so that even an official who guards the laws or a scholar who chants the Classics is all confused. Should a King arise, he would certainly follow the ancient terms and reform the new terms. Then he could not but investigate the reason for having terms,[1] together with the means through which similarities and differences are found, and the fundamental principles in applying terms to things.

A new King must reform the terms by three criteria.

That various forms, when absent, are understood by others, is because in the case of different things, terms and realities are mutually bound together.[2] When the distinction between noble and base [3] is not evident, when similarities and

I. The reason for having terms.—

---

[1] Each of these three criteria is later explained by the text.

[2] A difficult sentence which can be variously translated. It seems to mean that by the use of a name or term, the image of an absent article can be called up in another person's mind.

[3] Different social classes.

Terms mark the distinction between noble and base, like and different.

differences are not distinguished, in this situation a man's mind would certainly suffer from the misfortune of not understanding, and a person's occupation would certainly suffer from the calamity of being hindered or of failure. On that account the man who has knowledge separates what is different; he regulates nomenclature in order to point out the reality, on the one hand in order to make plain the noble and base, and on the other to distinguish similarities and differences. When the distinction between the noble and base is evident and similarities and differences are distinguished, under those circumstances a man's mind will not suffer from the misfortune of not understanding, and his occupation will not suffer from the calamity of being hindered or of failure. This is the reason for having terms.

2. The means of discovering similarities and differences— The senses and

Then by what means are similarities and differences found ? The means are the senses given by Nature. Whenever anything is judged to be the same sort or the same emotion, it is because the perception of the senses given by Nature is that the thing is the same. Hence for example, the reason that similarities are universally recognized to be such everywhere is because their agreed upon names have become universal, and so they can be recognized. Form and colour are distinctions made by the eyes. " Clear " and " confused " sound, harmony, musical time, and other sounds [1] are distinctions made by the ear. Sweet and bitter, salty and fresh, peppery and sour, and other flavours are distinctions made by the mouth. Perfumes and smells, fragrant and putrid, the smell of fresh meat and fetid smells, the smell

---

[1] Noises ?

of the mole-cricket [1] and the smell of decayed wood, and
other smells are distinctions made by the nose. Pain and [5]
itching, cold and heat, smooth and rough, light and heavy,
are distinctions made by the body. Doing things from a
liking to do them and forcing oneself to do things ; joy and
anger, sorrow and pleasure, love, hatred, and desire are
distinctions made by the mind.

The mind also gives meaning to impressions.[2] It gives *the mind ;*
meaning to impressions, and only then, by means of the ear, *it gives*
sound can be known ; by means of the eye, forms can be *impressions.*
known. But the giving of meaning to impressions must
depend on the senses given by Nature, each noting [3] its
particular kind of sensations, and then only can knowledge
be had. When the five senses [4] note something but do not
comprehend it, and the mind tries to give it a meaning
but has no explanation ; nobody would differ, everyone
would call this ignorance. These are the means by which
similarities and differences are found.

Then in accordance with that, names are given to things. *3. The*
When things are alike, they are named alike ; when *fundamental*
different, they are named differently. When a simple *principles in*
term [5] would be sufficient to convey the meaning, a simple *applying*
term is used ; when a simple term is insufficient, then a *things—*
compound term [6] is used. When simple and compound *should*
express the
meaning.

[1] A term from the Ritual.

[2] Tung Chung-shu gives this unusual meaning to this character. Cf.
胡適, 中國哲學史大綱, p. 333.

[3] The figure is that of a Chinese storekeeper, who sits in the back of the
store and records each transaction as it occurs.

[4] Ear, eye, nose, mouth, and body.

[5] A term composed of one character only, e.g. " horse ".

[6] A term composed of two or more characters, e.g. " white horse ".

concepts do not conflict, then the general term [1] may be used; although it is a general term, there is no harm in using it. The person who apprehends different realities uses different terms for them; hence he who refers to different realities should never use other than different terms; thus there could not be any confusion. Likewise he who refers to the same reality should never use other than the same term.

Classes of terms.

For although all things are manifold, there are times when we wish to speak of them all, so we call them "things". "Things" is the most general term. We press on and generalize; we generalize and generalize still more, until there is nothing more general; then only we stop. There are times when we wish to speak of one aspect, so we say "birds and beasts". "Birds and beasts" is the greatest classifying term. We press on and classify; we classify and classify still more, until there is no more classification to be made, and then we stop.

Terms made by common agreement.

There are no terms assuredly appropriate of themselves. There was an agreement and things were named. When the agreement had been made and had become customary— that is called an appropriate designation. That which is different from what is agreed upon is called an inappropriate designation. Terms have no corresponding realities appropriate of themselves. There was an agreement [2]

---

[1] The class or common term, e.g. " horse ".

[2] Hsüntze says nowhere who agreed; the Kings simply ratified a general agreement. But the Kings probably only fixed such terms as those of nobility and ceremony; this convention that the Kings fixed the terms is extended to all terms by a literary fiction.

and things were named ; when the agreement had been made and had become customary—these were called terms appropriate to realities. But terms are really felicitous ; when a term goes to the point, is easily understood and is not contrary to the reality—this is called a 7 felicitous term.

There are things which have the same form but two places [1] ; One or two realities ? or they may have different forms but the same place.[2] When things can be separated, when their forms are alike but their places different, although they may be indistinguishable —they are called two realities. When the form changes, but the reality cannot be separated, though it looks different,[3] we call it transformation. When there is transformation but no separation—these are called one reality. By this method realities are investigated and their number is determined. This is the fundamental thing in regulating terms. When a later King fixes terms, he must investigate these matters.

" To [4] receive an insult is no disgrace " [5] ; " a Sage does Three types of fallacies illustrated. 1. not love himself " [6] ; " to kill robbers is not to kill

[1] E.g. two similar horses in different places.

[2] E.g. grub and moth, young and aged person.

[3] Different as the grub and moth look different, but are the same insect. Here he is dealing with differences of time ; above with differences in space.

[4] Here Hsüntze proceeds to apply these logical distinctions to contemporary philosophy and make a classification of fallacies.

[5] Cf. p. 206 f. A teaching of Sungtze.

[6] A teaching of Yangtze or Chuangtze—it is the opposite of the saying quoted by Hu Shih, op. cit. Probably the argument is that the Sage love men (in Chinese 人 means " others " as well as " men ") hence not himself. Hu Shih quotes the Neo-Mician 大 取 篇, " The love of all men

men " [1] ; these are fallacies in the use of terms with the result of confusing the terms. Investigate the reason for having terms, observe of what sort the terms are, and then you will be able to stop this confusion. " Mountains and abysses are on the same level," [2] " the desires seek to be few," [3] " the flesh of domestic animals is not included in what is considered good tasting ; the great bell is not included in music " [4]—these are fallacies in the use of realities with the result of confusing the terms. Investigate the means through which similarities and differences are found, and see what fits the reality, and then you will be able to

8 stop this confusion. " Even if you do not go and see, the centre pillar exists," [5] " an ox-horse is not a

does not abstract from oneself ; oneself is included in the number of those who are loved : if oneself is among those who are loved, then one will love himself ; and the natural order will be to love oneself and love men (others)." But this argument is not the same as the quotation of Hsüntze here ; it seems rather to be a rebuttal of it. The aphorism quoted by Hsüntze would seem to come more naturally from Yangtze.

[1] A teaching of the Neo-Micians, found in 墨子小取篇, " Robbers are people (or men). . . . To love robbers is not to love the people. Not to love robbers is not failing to love people. To kill robbers is not to kill people (or men)." In this passage the word for " men " or " people " is one and the same, 人, and the argument turns on two meanings of it.

[2] A teaching of Huei Shih, the Neo-Mician. Cf. 莊子天下篇 " Heaven is as low as Earth, mountains and streams are level "—explained since the earth is round, there is no absolute up or down. Cf. 中國哲學 史大綱, p. 231.

[3] A teaching of Sungtze. Cf. p. 209 f.

[4] Possibly a teaching of the Neo-Micians. Yang Liang ascribes it to Micius, but it has not been traced.

[5] I have given the best translation I could for a cryptic phrase which no Chinese commentator pretends to understand ; I do not know who advocated the Berkeleian subjectivism against which such a proposition would be directed.

horse " [1]—these are fallacies in the use of terms with the result of confusing the realities. Investigate the agreements about terms ; use what these agreements acquiesce in, set yourself against what they refuse to countenance, and then you will be able to stop this confusion.

All heretical doctrines and flagitious teachings which are impudently fabricated and which depart from the correct doctrine (*Tao*) can be classed among these three fallacies. Hence the wise princes, knowing to which class they belonged, did not dispute about them. So the people were easily unified in the right Way (*Tao*), although the princes could not make them understand all the reasons for things. Hence the wise princes dealt with the people by authority, and guided them to the right way (*Tao*) ; they explained things in their proclamations, gave statutes in wise maxims, and restrained them by punishments. Hence their people were transformed into the right Way (*Tao*) as by magic. Why should they use dialectic ?

The wise prince guides the people by his proclamations and punishments.

Now the Sage-Kings are dead, the country is in disorder, wicked doctrines have arisen, the princes have no power to compel the people to do right, and no punishment to prevent them from following wrong, and so there is dialectic.

Names, designations, explanation, and dialectic.

---

[1] An argument based on an improperly formed term, " ox-horse ". The Neo-Mician 經 下 says : " That an ox-horse is not an ox is the same as saying it is ; both can be said " ; and the 經 說 下 says : " Hence it is said, that an ox-horse is not an ox should be denied ; that an ox-horse is an ox should also be denied. Then whether it is affirmed or denied, the statement ' that an ox-horse is an ox should be denied' should also be denied. For an ox is not two nor is a horse two, but an ox-horse is two. Then an ox is not a not-ox, and a horse is not a not-horse, but an ox-horse is ot an ox and not a horse. So there is no difficulty."

When the reality is not understood, its name is given [1];
when its name is given and the thing is not understood,
it is designated; when it is designated but not understood,
then it is explained; when the explanation is not understood,
then dialectic [2] comes into use. Hence the name, designation,
explanation, and dialectic are the great refinements which
make things usable and the primary things in the business
of being a King.

Literature,   The use of a term is to know the reality when one hears
the term. The beauty of terms is to string them together
and make literature. When both the utility and the beauty

names,   of terms are secured, that is called knowing terms. Terms
9 or names are that wherewith we designate many realities.

speech,   Speech is terms which combine many realities in order to
express one idea. In dialectic and explanation people should
separate realities from terms in order to make known the

the Tao.   law (*Tao*) of what one should do or should not do. Designation and giving names is the use of dialectic. Dialectic
and explanation is that whereby the mind delineates the
Way (*Tao*). The mind is the master-workman of the Way
(*Tao*).[3] The true Way (*Tao*) is the regular and necessary
principles which make order and good government.

The benefit   When a person's mind accords with the Way (*Tao*); when
of according   his teaching accords with his mind; when his speech accords
with the   with his teaching; when he rectifies terms and so designates
Way.   realities; when terms are founded on realities and are understood; when he discriminates differences and does not make

---

[1] To aid in understanding the doubtful article.
[2] Disputation, debate.
[3] Since its commands rule the personality and cause it to follow the Way.

mistakes ; when he classifies things without doing them any violence ; then he can listen to discussions and tell if they accord with a polished style ; he can argue and exhaust all possible reasoning ; by means of the right Way (*Tao*) he can distinguish wickedness as the plumb-line rules between crooked and straight. For this reason unorthodox doctrines cannot confuse him ; all the schools of philosophy cannot escape him.

To have the wisdom of having heard everything, but not the manner of an impetuous braggart ; to be doubly good and generous, but without the air of boasting of his virtue ; when his teachings are carried out, the country is upright ; when his teachings are not carried out, he is still wise in the Way (*Tao*) but retires into private life—this is the dialectic of the Sage. The ode says : *The dialectic of the Sage.*

10

> " Amiable and courtly,
>> Pure as a sceptre of mace or jade,
>> Of honourable reputation and great hopes,
>> My joyous young prince,
> You are the bond of the empire "—

this expresses what I mean.[1]

He has the moderation that comes from politeness [2] ; he obeys the principles of the elder and younger ; he does not speak of what is shunned or forbidden ; he does not utter imprecations ; he speaks from a benevolent (*Jen*) heart ; he listens with a receptive mind ; he disputes in a fair spirit ; *The dialectic of the Scholar or Superior Man.*

---

[1] *Book of Odes*, III, ii, viii, 6. A congratulatory ode addressed to the young King Ch'eng, son of King Wu. The purport of this quotation is that the Sage will have these virtues.

[2] Lit., 辭 讓, " declining honours and giving the precedence to others."

he is unmoved by the criticism or praise of the multitude ;
he does not pervert the ears and eyes of the onlooker ; he
does not corrupt the power of people of rank ; he does not
take pleasure in repeating the speech of the depraved [1] ;
hence he is able to dwell in the right Way (*Tao*) and not err ;
he may be oppressed but cannot be forced to act wrongly ;
it may bring gain, but he will not depart from the right ;
he respects fairness and uprightness and despises vulgar
striving—this is the dialectic of the scholar or superior
man. The ode says :

> " The long night is endless ;
>> My ever-flowing thoughts are nimble ;
> They do not disesteem the ancients ;
>> They do not vary from the rules of proper conduct
>> (*Li*) and justice (*Yi*) ;
> What care I for people's talk ? "—

this expresses what I mean.[2]

The speech of
the Superior
Man.

The speech of the superior man is deep but yet refined,
reaching down to people's understanding but yet systematic,
making distinctions but yet having unity. He corrects
his words and makes his speech appropriate, in order to
make clear his meaning. The terms he uses and his speech
are the messengers of his meaning. When they are sufficient
to be understood, he stops. To use them wrongly is wickedness. Therefore when his words are sufficient to point
out the reality, and his speech is sufficient to make his
11 end manifest, he stops. In anything more than that, he is
called slow of speech. This is what the superior man rejects

---

[1] Heretics.
[2] A lost ode.

and the stupid man picks up and considers as his treasure.
For the speech of the stupid man is hasty and coarse, or
else mysterious and unsystematic, babbling and bubbling.[1]
He sophisticates his words and makes his speech mysterious,
but has no depth to his meaning.   Hence he travels far but
does not come to any goal ;   he works hard but without result ;
he desires but does not obtain renown.   Reflect on the speech
of the wise man and it is easily understood ;   carry it out
and you will easily be at peace ;   hold to it and you will be
easily established ;   bring it to accomplishment and you
will certainly obtain your desire, and not meet with what
you hate ;   but the stupid man is the opposite of this.   The
ode says :

" Were you an imp or a water-bow,[2]
  Then you would be beyond reach,
 But when a person can be seen face to face and eye to eye,
  It does not take forever to see through him.
 I have made this good song
  To show how very shifty you are "—
this expresses my meaning.[3]

*   *   *   *   *

Every doctrine of self-control which depends on the removal
of desire has no way of guiding the desires and is hampered
by the presence of desire.   Every doctrine of self-control

Desire is innate ; control depends on the mind.

---

[1] Like boiling water.

[2] A fabulous creature, said to lie hid in the sand at the bottom of a
stream, and when the shadow of anyone on the bank appears in the water,
to spurt sand at it, after which the person is sure to die.

[3] *Book of Odes*, II, v, v, 8.   This ode bewails and exposes a slanderer
who had been a friend.

which waits for the lessening of desires has no way to curb the desires and is hampered by the numerousness of desires. The presence or absence of desire is one class of phenomena ; it is one of the elements of human nature, not the result of self-control or of disorderly conduct : the numerousness or fewness of the desires is a different class of phenomena ; it depends on the strength of the emotions, not on self-control or disorderly conduct. Desire does not depend on whether attainment is possible, but the person who seeks for anything 12 follows after what is possible.[1] That desire does not depend on whether attainment is possible is received from Nature ; that the person who seeks for anything follows after what is possible is brought about by the mind.[2] That which is received from Nature is one thing—desire ; it is controlled by the many desires of the mind, and certainly can hardly be compared with what Nature originally gave man.[3] What men desire most is life, and what they hate most is death. Yet there are men who follow after life and find death—it is not because they do not desire life and desire death ; it is because they cannot live and can die. For if a person's desire overpasses what his actions can obtain, the mind renounces it. If what the mind assents

[1] The contrast is between the faculty of desire, which is part of original human nature and does not consider the possibility or impossibility of its objects, and the particular desires, which are restricted by the mind to objects that are possible of attainment.

[2] The commentator Yang Liang catches the essence of Hsüntze's teaching exactly, " Human nature naturally has desires ; the mind is their controller." This sentence has found its way into the text in some editions, and is quoted by Hu Shih as original with Hsüntze.

[3] A corrupt sentence, the translation of which is doubtful.

to is in accordance with moral law, although the desires are
many, what harm are they to self-control ?   When a person's
desires are weak but his actions are extravagant, the mind
has caused it.   If what the mind assents to deviates from
the moral law, then although the desires be few, how would
that stop disorderly conduct ?   Hence self-control and
disorderly conduct depend on the assent of the mind, not
on the desires of the affective nature.   If you do not seek
for self-control where it is,[1] and instead seek for it where
it is not,[2] although you say, " I have it," you have lost it.

Human nature is the production of Nature ;   the emotional
nature is the essence of human nature ;   desires are the
reactions of the emotional nature.   The emotional nature
cannot escape from assuming that what a person desires
can be had.   The starting point of wisdom must be to consider
the desires necessary, but to guide them.   For although
a person be a doorkeeper,[3] his desires cannot be **13**
removed.   Although he were the Emperor, his desires cannot
be completely fulfilled.[4]   Although desires cannot be
removed, their pursuit can be temperate.   Although the
desires cannot be completely fulfilled, a person who seeks
for it can be as if almost completely satisfied ;   although
desire cannot be removed, if what he wants cannot be
obtained, the person who reflects will desire to restrain
his pursuit.   If the man who knows the Way (*Tao*) obtains

The Way is the best way to deal with desire.

---

[1] In the mind.
[2] In the emotions.
[3] A very lowly station.
[4] The text here has a sentence which interrupts and disagrees with the
argument and is probably a gloss : " Although desires cannot be completely
fulfilled, they can be almost completely fulfilled."

power and wealth, he can come near to satisfying all
his desires ; if he loses power and wealth, he can come
near to satisfying all his desires ; if he loses power and wealth,
he can restrain his pursuit—there is nothing else in the world
that is better than this !

Elimination
of desire is
fruitless.

No one fails to follow what he deems possible and reject
what he deems impossible—there is nothing better than
this in knowing the Way (*Tao*). But none of those who do
not follow the Way (*Tao*) do this. Suppose there were
a man who liked the south country ; but although it was
great, yet he desired it ; and he disliked the north, but
although it was small, yet he disliked it ; would it be probable,
because he could not obtain all of the south, that he
would leave the south and go north ? What people of to-day
desire is much, but yet they desire it ; what they hate is
little, but yet they hate it. Can it be that because they
cannot obtain all they desire, that they leave the Way (*Tao*)
whereby they obtain what they desire and take what they
hate ? [1] Therefore follow what agrees with the Way (*Tao*) ;
how could this bring loss and cause disorderly conduct ?
Desert what does not accord with the Way (*Tao*) ; how could
it bring gain and self-control ? Hence a wise man is only
concerned about the Way (*Tao*). What the minor schools
of philosophy wish for in their much-prized theories will
all fail.

Actions
should
correspond to
the standard
of the Way.

Men never get what they desire unadulterated ; in rejecting
what they hate, it never goes away unmixed. Hence men's

[1] He implies that the Confucian ethic enables one to satisfy his desires
by making the individual temperate ; while other philosophies which try
to eliminate desires are going against human nature and fail.

actions should always correspond to the standard. When 14
the steelyard [1] is not held properly, a heavy article
will cause it to swing up high and people will think it is light ;
a light thing will cause the steelyard to hang down low, and
people will think it is heavy. In this way people are misled
about weights. When the standard [2] is not right, calamity
is mixed with desire and people think it is happiness ; or
happiness is mixed with hatred, and people think it is calamity.
In this way, too, people are misled about calamity and
happiness. The Way (*Tao*) is the correct standard [2] in ancient
times and in the present. If you depart from the Way (*Tao*)
and pick your own inner standard, then you will not know
what calamity or happiness takes for a pretext to delude you.

If a trader barters one thing for one thing, people say, *Following the*
" He has neither loss nor gain." If he barters one for two, *Way is all*
people say, " There is no loss, but a gain." If he barters *gain.*
two for one, people say, " There is no gain, but a loss." The
schemer gets as much as he can ; the man who plans takes
all that he can : no one will exchange two for one because
they know the art of evaluating things. To start following
the Way (*Tao*) is like exchanging one for two ; how can there
be a loss ? To leave the Way (*Tao*) and pick one's own inner
standards is like exchanging two for one ; how can there
be any gain ? Such a man will exchange the desire of a
hundred years for the dislike of one moment, because he does
not know the art of evaluating things.

[1] Everything in China is weighed on the steelyard and ways of cheating
are common. The steelyard may be just but held improperly, and so false
weights occur ; or the iron bob which is used to balance the object to be
weighted may be of incorrect weight, and false weight will be indicated.

[2] Lit., " the correct steelyard bob."

Attempts to
satisfy desires
all end in
failure.

Moreover the person who has tried to see into man's hidden
parts, and put himself hard at work to investigate it, knows
that there is no one who in their purpose despises moral
principles, who does not value material things ; and that there
is no one who does not externally value material things
and is not inwardly anxious ; and that there is no one whose
actions deviate from moral principles who is not in dangerous
circumstances ; and that there is no one who is in dangerous
circumstances who is not inwardly fearful. When the mind
is anxious and fearful, though the mouth be holding meat,
it will not recognize the flavour thereof ; though the ears
hear bells and drums, they will not recognize the sound
thereof ; though the eyes behold fine embroidery, they will
not know the pattern thereof ; though the clothes be light
and warm, and he be sitting on a rush or fine bamboo mat,
the body will not recognize the comfort thereof ; for he may
enjoy the goodness of all things, yet he cannot be contented.
15 If he gains a respite and contentment, his anxiety
and fear nevertheless do not leave him. For though he
be enjoying the goodness of all things, yet he is greatly
anxious; though he be absorbing the benefit of all things, yet he
gains great injury. Thus fares he who seeks material things.
Is food life ? Is porridge old age ? For he desires to foster
his desires, but indulges his emotions ; he desires to foster
his nature, but he endangers his body ; he desires to foster
his enjoyment, but he attacks his mind ; he desires to foster
his fame, but he disorders his actions. Although this sort
of man be made a marquis and called a prince, he would be
no whit different from a common man or a robber ; although
he were to ride in a nobleman's coach or wear a crown, he

would be no whit different from a footless cripple. Then he could well be called one who makes himself the servant of material things.

If the heart is tranquil and contented, though the colours be below the ordinary, they can nourish the eyes; though sounds be below the ordinary, they can nourish the ears; coarse food and vegetable soup can nourish the taste; coarse cotton [1] clothes and coarse hemp sandals can nourish the body; a straw hut for a house, reed screens for doors, straw beds, ancient plain stands and mats [2] can nourish the form. For a person may be without the goodness of all things, yet he can foster his enjoyment; he may be without a position of high rank, but he can foster his fame. If such a man were given the empire, it would mean much for the empire, but it would mean little for his contentment and joy. Thus he could be called one who makes his personality important and makes material things his servants. The [3] superior man is cautious about untried doctrine, actions which have not been previously seen, and plans which have been unheard of among people.

Inner contentment can vanquish poor circumstances.

[1] In China every gentleman wears silk.
[2] Like that used by the Japanese to-day for eating and sitting.
[3] This last sentence may be spurious. Cf. *Doctrine of the Mean*, I, 3.

BOOK XXIII

THE NATURE OF MAN IS EVIL

The nature of man is evil; his goodness is only acquired **1**
training. The original nature of man to-day is to seek for Original
gain. If this desire is followed, strife and rapacity results, evil, hence
and courtesy [1] dies. Man originally is envious and naturally necessary.
hates others. If these tendencies are followed, injury and
destruction follows; loyalty and faithfulness are destroyed.
Man originally possesses the desires of the ear and eye;
he likes praise and is lustful. If these are followed, impurity
and disorder results, and the rules of proper conduct (*Li*)
and justice (*Yi*) and etiquette [2] are destroyed. Therefore
to give rein to man's original nature, to follow man's feelings,
inevitably results in strife and rapacity, together with
violations of etiquette and confusion in the proper way of
doing things, and reverts to a state of violence. Therefore
the civilizing influence of teachers and laws, the guidance
of the rules of proper conduct (*Li*) and justice (*Yi*) is absolutely
necessary. Thereupon courtesy results; public and private
etiquette is observed; and good government is the consequence. By this line of reasoning it is evident that the
nature of man is evil and his goodness is acquired.

[1] Lit., " declining and yielding," 辭 讓; if an honour is offered
you, make a show of declining it; if you are asked to take the precedence
make a show of yielding it to others—still the standard procedure in China.

[2] Lit., " the beauty of private and public etiquette."

Crooked
wood and
blunt knives;
the Sages
trained man's
nature by *Li*
and *Yi*.

Crooked wood needs to undergo steaming and bending to conform to the carpenter's rule [1]; then only is it straight. Blunt metal needs to undergo grinding and whetting; then only is it sharp. The original nature of man to-day is evil, so he needs to undergo the instruction of teachers and laws, then only will he be upright. He needs the rules of proper conduct (*Li*) and justice (*Yi*), then only will there be good government. But man to-day is without good teachers and laws; so he is selfish, vicious, and unrighteous. He is without the rules of proper conduct (*Li*) and justice (*Yi*), so there is rebellion, disorder, and no good government. In ancient times the Sage-Kings knew that man's nature was evil, selfish, 2 vicious, unrighteous, rebellious, and of itself did not bring about good government. For this reason they created the rules of proper conduct (*Li*) and justice (*Yi*); they established laws and ordinances to force and beautify the natural feelings of man, thus rectifying them. They trained to obedience and civilized men's natural feelings, thus guiding them. Then good government arose and men followed the right Way (*Tao*). Now the people who are influenced by good teachers and laws, who accumulate literature and knowledge, who are led by the rules of proper conduct (*Li*) and justice (*Yi*) become superior men. Those who give rein to their natural feelings, who take joy in haughtiness, and break the rules of proper conduct (*Li*) and justice (*Yi*), become small-minded men. By this line of reasoning it is evident that the original nature of man is evil, and his goodness is acquired.

Reply to
Mencius.

Mencius says, " The fact that men are teachable shows

[1] An instrument used to straighten crooked wood.

that their original nature is good." I reply : This is not so.
This is not understanding the nature of man, nor examining
the original nature of man, nor the part played by acquired
elements. Whatever belongs to original nature is the gift
of Nature. It cannot be learned. It cannot be worked for.
The Sage-Kings brought forth the rules of proper conduct
(*Li*) and justice (*Yi*). Men learn them and gain ability ;
they work for them and obtain results in the development
of character. What cannot be learned and cannot be worked for,
what is in the power of Nature only is what is meant by original
nature. That which can be learned and which gives men
ability, which can be worked for and which brings results
in the development of character, whatever is in the power
of man is what is meant by acquired character. This is
the distinction between original nature and acquired character.
Now according to the nature of man, the eye has the power
of seeing and the ear has the power of hearing. However,
when a person sees a thing, his quickness of sight is not
outside of his eye ; when he hears, his quickness of hearing
is not outside of his ear. It is evident that quickness of
sight and quickness of hearing cannot be learned.[1] Mencius
says : Now the original nature of man is good ; all have
lost and destroyed their original nature, hence it is evil.
I reply : When he says this, he is greatly mistaken. Now
considering the nature of man, as soon as he is born, he would
already have grown away from his first estate, he would
already have grown from his natural disposition. He would
already have lost and destroyed it. By this line of reasoning

[1] i.e., that they are innate. Hsüntze is struggling to express the
concept of " innate ".

it is evident that the original nature of man is evil and his goodness is acquired.

Evil
tendencies
are innate ;
virtue is
against
nature.

The doctrine that man's original nature is good implies that without growing away from his first estate, he becomes admirable ; without growing away from his natural disposition, he becomes beneficial. To say that man's original nature is admirable, his heart and thoughts are good, is the same as to say that the power of seeing is not apart from the eye and the power of hearing is not apart from the ear.[1]
3 So we say, if there is an eye, there is the power of seeing ; if there is an ear, there is the power of hearing. Now the nature of man is that when he is hungry, he desires repletion ; when he is cold, he desires warmth ; when he labours, he seeks rest. This is man's natural feeling. But now when a man is hungry and sees food, he dares not rush in ahead of others ; instead the eater yields to others. When working, he dares not seek rest, instead he works for others. The son yielding precedence to his father, the younger brother yielding to his older brother ; the son working for his father, the younger brother working for his older brother—these two kinds of actions are contrary to original nature and antagonistic to natural feeling. Nevertheless there is the doctrine (*Tao*) of filial piety, the etiquette of the rules of proper conduct (*Li*) and justice (*Yi*). If a person follows his natural feelings, he has no courtesy ; if he has courtesy, then it is antagonistic to his natural feelings. By this line of reasoning it is evident that man's original nature is evil and his goodness is acquired.

[1] It is to say that goodness is innate and natural.

A questioner may say: If man's original nature is evil, *Li* and *Yi* come from the then whence come the rules of proper conduct (*Li*) and justice acquired (*Yi*)? In answer I say: All rules of proper conduct (*Li*) training of and justice (*Yi*) come from the acquired training of the Sage, the Sage. not from man's original nature. The potter [1] pounds and moulds the clay and makes the vessel—but the vessel comes from the potter's acquired skill, not from the potter's innate character. The workman hews a piece of wood and makes a vessel; but the vessel comes from the workman's acquired training, not from his innate character. The Sage gathers together ideas and thoughts, and becomes skilled by his acquired training, so as to bring forth the rules of proper conduct (*Li*) and justice (*Yi*), and originate laws and regulations. So the rules of proper conduct (*Li*), justice (*Yi*), laws and regulations come from the acquired knowledge of the Sage, not from man's original nature.

The eye desires colour, the ear desires sound, the mouth desires flavours, the heart desires gain, the body desires pleasure and ease: these all come from man's original nature and feelings. Give man a stimulus and they come forth of their own accord; they do not need to be taught to man before they can come forth. But if a man is stimulated and the virtue we are seeking cannot of itself come forth, if it needs to wait to be taught and then only can come forth —this is what is meant by an acquired characteristic. This is the distinction between original nature and acquired **4** characteristics, the evidence of their dissimilarity.[2] So the

---

[1] This example and language is taken from the Tao Teh Ching, sect. 11.
[2] Cf. Laotze, *Tao Teh Ching*, sect. 18. "When the great Principle (*Tao*) is lost there is benevolence (*Jen*) and justice (*Yi*); knowledge and wisdom

Sages influenced men's nature and established acquired training. When acquired training had arisen, the rules of proper conduct (*Li*) and justice (*Yi*) were evolved, laws and regulations were made. Hence the rules of proper conduct (*Li*), justice (*Yi*), laws, and regulations were brought forth by the Sages. The Sage has his original nature in common with ordinary people; he is not different from ordinary people in this respect. He is different and superior to ordinary people in his acquired training.

Man's very desire to be good comes because his nature is evil.

It is the original nature and tendency of man to desire gain and to seek to obtain it. If brothers have property and are to divide it, if they follow their original nature and feelings of desiring gain and seeking to obtain it, thus they will mutually thwart each other and endeavour to seize the property. But reform them by the etiquette of the rules of proper conduct (*Li*) and justice (*Yi*), and they will be willing to yield to outsiders. So by following the original nature and feelings, brothers will quarrel; influence them by the rules of proper conduct (*Li*) and justice (*Yi*), and they will yield to strangers. Every man's desire to be good is because his nature is evil. So if he is mean, he wants to be generous; if he is in circumscribed circumstances he wants unhampered circumstances; if he is poor, he wants to be rich; if he is in a low social position, he wishes to be in an honourable position; if he has it not within himself,

appear, and there is great acquired training." Hsüntze and Laotze differ in that Laotze supposes man was anciently perfect, but has deteriorated; hence we must return to the ancient practices and to its simplicity. Hsüntze supposes man had always been innately evil, but under the influence of the ancient Sage-Kings, he was developed to a state of goodness now unrealized because of the lack of a Sage to influence the people.

he inevitably seeks it from without. For if he were rich, he would not desire wealth ; if he were in a high position, he would not want more power. If he has it within his power, he would certainly not seek it from without. By this line of reasoning we see that men's desire to be good comes from his original nature being evil.

Now the original nature of man is really without the rules of proper conduct (*Li*) and justice (*Yi*), hence he strives to learn and seeks to have it. By his original nature he does not know the rules of proper conduct (*Li*) and justice (*Yi*), hence he thinks and reflects, and seeks to learn these principles. Then only are they developed. So man is naturally without the rules of proper conduct (*Li*) and justice (*Yi*), he does not know the rules of proper conduct (*Li*) and justice (*Yi*). If man is without the rules of proper conduct (*Li*) and justice (*Yi*), there is disorder ; if he does not know the rules of proper conduct (*Li*) and justice (*Yi*), there is rebellion. So these virtues are evolved. Then rebellion and disorder are within man himself. By this line of reasoning it is evident that the original nature of man is evil and his goodness is an acquired characteristic.

Rebellion and disorder come from within man himself.

Mencius says, " The nature of man is good." I reply : This is not so. In whatever age or place on earth, in ancient times or in the present, men have meant by goodness true principles and just government. They have meant by evil partiality, a course bent on evil, rebellion, and disorder. This is the distinction between goodness and evil. Now if we sincerely consider the nature of man, is it firmly established in true principles and just government ? If so, then what use are the Sage-Kings ? What use are the

Man is clearly evil.

rules of proper conduct (*Li*) and justice (*Yi*)? Although there were Sage-Kings, the rules of proper conduct (*Li*) and justice (*Yi*), what could they add to true principles and just government?

The Sage-Kings reformed man.

Now that is not the situation. Man's nature is evil. Anciently the Sage-Kings knew that man's nature was evil, that it was partial, bent on evil, and corrupt, rebellious, disorderly, without good government, hence they established the authority of the prince to govern man; they set forth clearly the rules of proper conduct (*Li*) and justice (*Yi*) to reform him; they established laws and government to rule him; they made punishments severe to warn him; and so they caused the whole country to come to a state of good government and prosperity, and to accord with goodness. This is the government of the Sage-Kings, the reforming influence of the rules of proper conduct (*Li*) and justice (*Yi*).

Without the authority of the prince there would be universal disorder.

Now suppose we try to remove the authority of the prince, and be without the reforming influence of the rules of proper conduct (*Li*) and justice (*Yi*); suppose we try to remove the beneficent control of the laws and the government, and be without the restraining influence of punishments. Let us stand and see how the people of the whole country would behave. If this were the situation, then the strong would injure the weak and rob him; the many would treat cruelly the few and rend them. The whole country would be in a state of rebellion and disorder. It would not take an instant to get into this condition. By this line of reasoning, it is evident that the nature of man is evil and that his goodness is acquired.

The man who is versed in the ancient times certainly sees its evidences in the present; he who is versed in the principles of Nature can certainly give evidence of their effect upon man. Every debater prizes distinctions and has evidence to support them. So he can sit down and discuss them; he can rise and establish them; he can act and exhibit them. Now Mencius says: Man's nature is good. This is without discrimination or evidence. A person can sit and discuss it, but he cannot rise and establish it; he cannot act and exhibit it. Isn't this extraordinarily erroneous? For if man's nature were good, then we could do away with the Sage-Kings; we would put an end to the rules of proper conduct (*Li*) and justice (*Yi*). But if man's nature is evil, then we should follow the Sage-Kings and prize the rules of proper conduct (*Li*) and justice (*Yi*). For the carpenter's square and rule are produced because there is crooked wood; the plumb-line arose because things were not straight; princes were established, the rules of proper conduct (*Li*) and justice (*Yi*) became evident because man's nature is evil. By this line of reasoning, it is evident that the nature of man is evil and his goodness is acquired.

If man's nature were good, that would do away 6 with the Sage-Kings Li, and Yi.

Straight wood does not need to undergo the action of the carpenter's rule in order to be straight; its nature is straight. Crooked wood does need to undergo the action of the carpenter's rule; it needs to be steamed and then only will it be straight, because its nature is crooked. Now the nature of man is evil; he needs to undergo the government of the Sage-Kings, the reforming action of the rules of proper conduct (*Li*) and justice (*Yi*), then good government and order will issue, and actions will accord with virtue. By

Man's nature is shown to be evil because it needs to undergo reform.

this line of reasoning it is evident that the nature of man
is evil and his goodness is acquired.

Li and *Yi*
are not from
man's original
nature.

A questioner may say : Even if the rules of proper conduct
(*Li*) and justice (*Yi*) are accumulated acquired training,
they are from man's nature. For the Sage-Kings could
bring them forth. In reply I say : This is not so. The
potter pounds and moulds the clay and brings the piece
of pottery into being ; then from clay there comes to be
pottery. Can it be that this is the potter's nature ? The
workman hews a piece of wood and brings a vessel into being ;
thus from wood there comes to be a vessel. Can it be that
this is the workman's original nature ? Now the relation of
the Sage to the rules of proper conduct (*Li*) and justice (*Yi*)
is the same as that of the potter and the clay ; he brings
them into being ; thus the rules of proper conduct (*Li*) and
justice (*Yi*) are accumulated acquired training. How can
they be the original nature of man ? The nature of all men,
of Yao and Shun, of Ch'ie and Chih is the same. The nature
of the superior man and of the little-minded man is the
same. Now do we use the rules of proper conduct (*Li*) and
justice (*Yi*) to make men's nature ; do we accumulate
acquired training for that purpose ? Then why do we
prize Yao and Yu ? Why do we honour the superior man ?
What we prize in Yao, Yu, and the superior man is that
they could reform their original nature and create acquired
training. When their acquired training was created, they
brought forth the rules of proper conduct (*Li*) and justice
7 (*Yi*). Thus the relation of the Sage to the rules of
proper conduct (*Li*) and justice (*Yi*) and accumulated acquired
training is the same as that of the potter and the clay : he

brings the pottery into being. By this line of reasoning
how can the rules of proper conduct (*Li*) and justice (*Yi*)
and accumulated acquired training be of man's nature ?
What was low about Ch'ie, Chih and the little-minded man
was that they followed their nature and acted according
to their inclinations : they took joy in haughtiness and the
result was that they were avaricious for gain, striving and
grasping. Hence it is evident that the nature of man is
evil and his goodness is acquired.

Heaven was not partial to Tsen,[1] Ch'ien,[2] and Hsiao Yi,[3] nor
did it neglect the common multitude. Then why are Tsen,
Ch'ien, and Hsiao Yi alone truly and perfectly filial, and
why do they alone have the name of special filiality ? The
reason is that they observed the rules of proper conduct
(*Li*) and justice (*Yi*) to the utmost extent. Heaven was
not partial to the people of Ts'i [4] and Lu,[5] nor did it neglect
the people of Ts'in.[6] But the people of Ts'in are not as good
in the righteous relation between father and son and in the
proper reserve between husband and wife, as are the people

*Human
nature is
originally th
same every-
where.*

---

[1] Tsentze, the most important of the immediate disciples of Confucius.
His teachings stress filial piety. With this saying compare Laotze : " Heaven
treats men like straw dogs "—treats all alike.

[2] Min Tze-Ch'ien, another famous disciple of Confucius.

[3] Heir-apparent of one of the sovereigns of the Shang dynasty.

[4] The cultivated feudal state which produced Duke Huan and Kuan
Chung.

[5] The cultivated state which produced Confucius ; these were two centres
of Chinese culture.

[6] The more barbarous state which was later to conquer the whole of
China ; elsewhere it is criticized by Hsüntze for its lack of refinement and
scholarship.

of Ts'i and Lu in filial piety and reverential respect.[1] Why
is this ? The reason is that the people of Ts'in follow their
feelings and original nature, take pleasure in haughtiness,
and are remiss in observing the rules of proper conduct
(*Li*) and justice (*Yi*). How can it be that their nature could
be different ?

The man on the street has the power of knowing and practising virtue and of becoming a Sage.

"The man on the street can become a Yu "[2]—how about
that ? What gave Yu the qualities of Yu was that he
carried into practice benevolence (*Jen*), justice (*Yi*), obedience
to the laws, and uprightness. If so, then there is the means
of knowing and practising benevolence (*Jen*), justice (*Yi*),
obedience to law, and uprightness. Moreover, every man
on the street has the nascent ability of knowing the principles
of benevolence (*Jen*), justice (*Yi*), obedience to law, and
uprightness, and the means whereby he can carry out the
principles of benevolence (*Jen*), justice (*Yi*), obedience to
law, and uprightness. Thus it is evident that he can become
a Yu.

Now are the qualities of benevolence (*Jen*), justice (*Yi*),
obedience to law, and uprightness definitely without the
possibility of being known or of being carried out ? If so,
then even Yu could not have known benevolence (*Jen*),
justice (*Yi*), obedience to law and uprightness, nor could he
have been able to be benevolent (*Jen*), just (*Yi*), law-abiding,
or upright. Then is the man on the street definitely without
the power of knowing benevolence (*Jen*), justice (*Yi*),

---

[1] Reverent respectfulness is the attitude which should exist between
husband and wife.

[2] A saying found in Mencius, VI, ii, ii, 1.

obedience to law, and uprightness, and definitely without
the ability to be benevolent (*Jen*), just (*Yi*), law-abiding,
and upright ?   Then the man on the street, on the one hand,
could not know the righteous relation between father and
son, nor on the other hand could he know the standard
of correctness of prince and minister.   Now that is not so.
Every man on the street can on the one hand know **8**
the righteous relation between father and son, and on the
other hand he can know the standard of uprightness of
prince and minister.   Thus it is evident that the man on
the street possesses the power of knowing and the ability
to practise these virtues.   Now if the man on the street
uses his power of knowledge and his ability of acting on
the nascent ability of knowing benevolence (*Jen*) and justice
(*Yi*) and the means of becoming so, then it is clear that
he can become a Yu ; if he concentrates his mind on one
purpose, if he thinks and studies and investigates thoroughly,
daily adding to his knowledge and retaining it long, if he
accumulates goodness and does not stop, then he will become
as wise as the gods, a third with Heaven and Earth.   For
the Sage is the man who has attained to that state by
accumulative effort.

A person may say :   The Sage attains to that stage by
cumulative effort, but not everyone can cumulate his
efforts : why is that ?   I reply, He has the capability, but
he does not use it.   For the small-minded man can become
a superior man, but he is not willing to become a superior
man ; the superior man can become a small-minded man,
but he is not willing to become a small-minded man.   It
is not impossible for the small-minded man and the superior

Everyone has
the capacity
of becoming a
Sage, but not
everyone
exercises it.

man to exchange places ; nevertheless they do not exchange places. There is the possibility, but they do not use it. For it is true that the man on the street can become a Yu, but it is probably not true that the man on the street has the ability to become a Yu. Although he does not have the ability to make himself a Yu, that does not destroy the possibility that he could become a Yu. It is perfectly possible that he could govern the whole country, yet he may never have the ability to govern the whole country. It is never an impossibility that the labourer, the artisan, the farmer, and the merchant might exchange professions, yet they never can exchange professions. By this line of reasoning a person could probably not be able to be so and so ; yet although he could not, it does not remove the possibility of his becoming so and so. Then there is a great difference between whether a person has the ability and whether he has the possibility of being so and so. Thus the impossibility for them to exchange places is evident.

*   *   *   *   *

Shun says man is evil.

Yao [1] asked Shun, " How are the passions of man ? " Shun answered, " The passions of man are far from beautiful. Why do you ask ? When a man has a wife and children, his filial duty to his parents decreases ; when sensual desires are satisfied, then faithfulness between friends decreases ; when his desire for noble title and high salary is satisfied, then his faithfulness towards his prince decreases. Man's

---

[1] The remainder of the book discusses other subjects and does not seem to be part of Hsüntze's concatenated discussion of human nature ; it may be spurious, but it is in Hsüntze's manner.

passions! Man's passions are far from beautiful! Why
do you ask? Only the Worthy is not thus.

*   *   *   *   *

There are those who have the knowledge of the Sage; **9**
there are those who have the knowledge of the scholar or The
superior man; there are those who have the knowledge of the Sage, the
the small-minded man, and there are those who have the Superior Man,
Scholar, the
knowledge of the menial. To be able to speak much, polished small-minded
and in order, to discuss a matter for a whole day; through menial.
man, and the
a thousand turns and changes, altogether to be discussing
only one subject—this is the wisdom of the Sage. To speak
little, but to the point and sparingly, coherently, and according
to rule, as if a thread ordered the speech—this is the wisdom
of the scholar or superior man. His speech is flattering,
and his actions are rebellious, his actions and doings are far
wrong—this is the knowledge of the little-minded man.
With sharp retorts and triflingly clever, but without **10**
concatenation, with great cleverness in out of the way knowledge,[1] but without real usefulness, practised in quickly
making many distinctions but not going to the point, not
caring for right or wrong, not considering error or truth,
having for an object to overcome his opponent—this is the
knowledge of a menial.

There is superior courage, mediocre courage, and inferior Three grades
of courage.
courage. He who dares to stand erect for the best Way there
is in the world, who dares to act out the meaning of the
Way (*Tao*) of the former Kings, who on the one hand will not
follow a prince who governs wrongly and on the other hand
will not follow a people who would govern wrongly; who when

---

[1] Fortune telling, etc.

there is benevolence (*Jen*) [1] will not consider poor emolument a bar, nor when there is no benevolence (*Jen*) will he consider riches an attraction,[2] who when the country recognizes his talents, desires only that the country should rejoice with him, and who when the country does not recognize him, he will stand alone [3] between Heaven and Earth and not

11 fear—he is a man of superior courage. Respectful of the rules of proper conduct (*Li*) and of few desires, stressing the attainment of fidelity and laying no store by goods or wealth ; when a worthy man comes, being willing to resign and advance him ; but when an unworthy man is in office, daring to expel and remove him—this is courage of medium grade. Laying no store by his character but thinking wealth important, rejoicing in trouble and spreading it widely, evading the consequences of his actions, not caring for right or wrong, unstable in character, having for his object getting the best of others—this is courage of inferior character.

*   *   *   *   *

Fan-jo and Chü-shu were famous bows of antiquity. But if they had not been put in frames for straightening, they could not have been straight of themselves. The Ts‘ung of Duke Huan, the Ch‘ueh of Duke T‘ai, the Lu of King Wen, the Fu of Prince Chuang, Ho-lü's Kan-chiang, Mo-hsie, Chü-ch‘ueh, P‘i-lu : these were renowned swords of ancient times. But if they had not been ground, they could not have become sharp ; if somebody had not laboured on them,

---

[1] In the character of the ruler.
[2] To taking office.
[3] For his principles.

they could not have cut. Hua, Liu, Ch'i, Chi, Hsien-li, Lu-er : these were all famous horses of antiquity. But on the one hand they needed the control of a bit and reins, and on the other they needed the fear of the whip. Add to that the driving of Ts'ao-fu,[1] and then they could do the thousand *li* in one day. Thus although a man has fine natural qualities and knows how to discuss, he needs to seek a virtuous teacher and serve him as a disciple ; he needs to pick out good friends and attach himself to them. When he obtains a virtuous teacher and serves him as a disciple, then what he hears is the Way (*Tao*) of Yao, Shun, Yu, and T'ang. When he obtains good friends and attaches himself to them, then what he sees is conduct according to loyalty, faithfulness, reverence, and humility. His character daily advances in benevolence (*Jen*) and justice (*Yi*), and unconsciously he grows like those people. Now if he should live with people who are not virtuous, then what he would hear would be cheating, maliciousness, falseness, and hypocrisy. What he would see would be impurity, boasting, excesses, erroneous doctrine, and conduct that is avaricious of gain., His character would advance towards deserving capital punishment, and unconsciously he would become like these people. It is said : If you do not know a person, look at his friends. If you do not know the prince of a state, look to the right and left. Follow that and it will be sufficient ! Follow that and it will be sufficient !

---

[1] A famous legendary driver.

A GLOSS [1]

Critics say: "Hsun Ch'ing [2] was not as great as Confucius." This is not so. Hsun Ch'ing was harassed by disordered times, and constrained by severe circumstances; when on the one hand there were no worthy lords [3] and on the other there was the aggression of Ts'in. [4] The rules of proper conduct (*Li*) and justice (*Yi*) were not observed, and the humanizing and correcting influence of good teaching was not carried out. The virtuous (*Jen*) were removed from office and restrained, and the whole country was in darkness. Good conduct was completely cut into; the feudal nobles had subverted everything. At this time the wise were not given the opportunity to reflect, the able were not given the chance to rule well, and the worthy were not given the opportunity to be used. [5] Hence princes were blinded and had no vision; worthy men were obstructed and did not receive office. Consequently Hsun Ch'ing, who cherished the heart of a Sage, but which could not express itself as such, [6] hid it under a manner of feigning

---

[1] Probably by a disciple of Hsüntze. Found in 荀子二十卷二十四張

[2] Hsüntze. Here too 孫 is used for 荀 in the surname.

[3] Who would give Hsüntze control over his state to try out his theories of government.

[4] The state which finally gobbled up the whole of China.

[5] In high office.

[6] A Sage should, like Yu and Shun, become emperor.

to be mad, and so appeared to the country to be stupid.[1]
The ode says :

> " He was wise and sage,
>> Yet he had to protect his life "—

this expresses my meaning. This is why his reputation was
not bright, not many disciples came to him, and his glory
was not widespread.

To-day the student can get the discourses and teachings
which Hsun Ch'ing left behind, which are sufficient to be
the pattern and exemplar of human usages, which will make
superhuman him who observes them, and correct him who
has been in error. Consider his goodness and character
and you will see that Confucius did not surpass him. But that
generation did not investigate carefully and said, " He is
not a Sage." What was there to do ? The country was not
well governed and Hsun Ch'ing missed his time. His virtue
was like that of Yao and Yu, but his generation knew it but
little ; he did not use artful tricks and people misunderstood
him. His wisdom was not brilliant ; he followed the Way
(*Tao*) [2] and acted uprightly, so that he could be the fundamental principle of life.

Alas ! A Worthy ! Fit to be an emperor ! The world [3]
did not recognize him, but admired Ch'ie and Chou. They
killed the worthy and the good. Pi-kan [4] was disemboweled

---

[1] The disciple's explanation of why Hsüntze, who had all the virtue,
which according to theory should have made him emperor, failed to advance
to that post. Cf. *H.*, p. 282.

[2] The Confucian doctrine.

[3] Lit., Heaven and Earth.

[4] Cf. note 13, p. 217.

of his heart; Confucius was arrested at K'uang [1]; Chieh-yü fled from the world; the Viscount of Chi [2] had to pretend to be mad; T'ien-shang [3] caused a rebellion; Ho-lu [4] presumed to be powerful. Those who did evil became prosperous; the good suffered from calamity.

To-day the critics likewise do not investigate the facts, but credit only his reputation. The times had changed; what means had his fame of being born? He had no opportunity of ruling [5]; how could his merit have been brought to perfection [6]? His will was cultivated; his virtue was great; who can say that he was not a Worthy?

[1] Cf. *Analects*, IX, v.

[2] Cf. note 1, p. 218.

[3] Possibly T'ien Ho who dispossessed the dynasty of Kiang on the throne of Ts'i, 385 B.C.

[4] Ruler of Wu, 514–496 B.C. He usurped the title of King.

[5] No opportunity of being the prince of a state, where he could distinguish himself and raise his state to the leading position in the empire. The fit reward for virtue was thought to be the fame of rule.

[6] I.e. glorious rule.

CHINESE INDEX AND GLOSSARY

References are to the book and folio of the Chinese edition of Wang Hsien Ch'ien, 荀子集解; that numbering is indicated by the heavy numerals in the margin of this translation. "A" and "B" refer to the verso and recto sides respectively of the Chinese folio or page. "e" indicates that this character is found in an emendation of the text accepted for this translation. "G" refers to the "Gloss" added at the end of the book.

Some special meanings, which these characters sometimes take in Hsüntze's writings, are added.

Radical 1. ──

壹 I, 4B, 5B, 6A, B, 8B, 9A, 12A; II, 16B, 17B, 20A, 21A, 23A; IV, 17A, 18B, 22B, 23B, 24A; V, 4A, 7A, B; VI, 14A; VII, 24A, 25A, B, 26A; VIII, 1B, 2B, 5A, B, 10B, 11B, 12A, 13B, 14B, 16A, B, 17A, 18A, B, 19A, 20B, 21A, 22B; IX, 3B, 4B, 9B, 11A, B, 12A, B, 13A, 16A, B, 17B, 18A; XV, 1B, 2B, 3A, 9B, 10B, 12A, (XIX), 14B; XVII, 16B, 17A, 19B, 20A; XVIII, 1B, 2B, 4A, 6A, B, 9A, 11B, 12A, 17A, 18A; XIX, 3A, 4B, 5A, B, 6A, 9A, B, 10B, 12A, 14A, B, 16B, 19A, B; XX, 1B; XXI, 1A, B, 5B, 6A, 7A, B, 8A, 9B, 10A, 11A, 13B, 14B, 15A; XXII, 2B, 3A, 7A, 8A, 9A, 12A, 14A, B; XXIII, 6B, 8A, 9B, 12A. Concentration or unity. See *Doctrine of the Mean*, xx, 8. Legge translates by singleness.

Radical 2. Ｊ

中 I, 1B, 3B, 4B, 8A; V, 3B, 4A, 8A; VIII, 6A, 7B, 18B, 21A; IX, 1A, 3A, 4B, 10A, B, 17A, 18B; XV, 1B; XVII, 14A, 19B; XVIII, 2B, 8A, 11A, 12B, 14A, 16A; XIX, 2A, 8A, B, 9A, 12B, 14B, 19A, B; XX, 1B, 2A; XXI,

6A, 11B, 13A, 16B; XXII, 12B; XXIII, 4B, 10A, 11A. Proper; contrasted with 姦, wicked.

Radical 5. 乙

亂 II, 14A, 15A, 16A, 18A, 22A; IV, 16B, 19A, 21A; V, 2A, 3B, 7A; VII, 12B, 13B; VIII, 7B, 8A, 11A, B, 13A, 17A, 19B, 21B; IX, 2A, 3B, 11B, 12B, 14B, 16B; XV, 4B, 10A, 11A, 12A; XVI, 11B; XVII, 12A, 14A, 15A, 17B, 19B, 20A; XVIII, 1B, 3A, 4A, 5B, 6A, B, 13A, 14A, B, 16A, 18A; XIX, 1A, 7A, B, 19A, 20A; XX, 1A, 2A, B, 3A, B, 4A, 5B; XXI, 1B, 2A, B, 4B, 5B, 6A, B, 7B, 8B, 11A, 13B, 16A, B; XXII, 2B, 3A, 6A, 7A, B, 8A, B, 9B, 11B, 12B, 13B, 15A; XXIII, 1B, 2A, 5A, B, 10B; G 24A, B. Ill-governed and calamitous, general disorder; anarchy, decadent.

Radical 7.

貳 I, 6A, 9A; V, 4A, 5A, B, 7A; VII, 25A, 28A; VIII, 11B, 20B, 21A, 22B; IX, 8A; XV (XIX), 14B; XVII, 12A; XVIII, 17A; XIX, 3B, 7A; XX, 5A; XXI, 1A, 9A, B, 15B; XXII, 7A, 10A; XXIII, 3A. Wandering mind; see *Doctrine of the Mean*, xxvi, 7.

Radical 9. 人

仁 I, 10B, 12A ; II, 18Be, 23B ;
IV, 18A, 20A, 22A, 23B ; V, 2A,
4A ; VII, 24B, 27B, 28A ; VIII,
6A, 9A, 18B, 19B ; IX, 7B, 8A,
17B ; XV, 2A, B, 3A, 4A, 11A, B,
12A ; XVIII, 15B ; XXI, 4A, 5B,
12A, 13A ; XXII, 10A ; XXIII,
7B, 8A, 10B, 12A ; G 24A. Paternal
benevolence ; *see* XV, 11.

侯 IV, 15B, 23B ; VII, 24A, 26A ;
VIII, 14B, 16B, 19A, 22A, 23A ;
IX, 4B, 5A, B, 6B, 7A, B, 16B ;
XI, 14B ; XV, 2A, 4A, B, 11B ;
XVIII, 2A, B, 3A, 6B, 7A, B, 10B,
11A, B, 16A ; XIX, 3B, 9B, 10B,
20B ; XXI, 1B ; XXII, 15A ; G
24A. Marquis.

信 II, 15A, 18B ; IV, 12B, 17A, B ;
VII, 25B, 26A, 28A ; VIII, 5A,
9B ; IX, 7B ; XV, 5A, 9A ; XVI,
11B ; XVII, 20B ; XIX, 2A,
21B ; XX, 4B ; XXIII, 1A, 8B,
11A, 12A ; G 24B.

俗 I, 2B ; II, 20A ; IV, 18A, B,
19A ; V, 1B, 3B, 9A ; VI, 14B ;
VIII, 5A, 11A, 16B, 17A, B, 19A,
20B, 21A ; IX, 14B, 16A, B, 17B,
18B ; XVIII, 1A, 2A, 3B, 4A, B,
5A, 6B, 8A, 12A, 13A, B, 16B ;
XIX, 7B, 21B ; XX, 2B, 3A,
5B ; XXI, 5B ; XXII, 1A, B,
6B ; XXIII, 10B.

修 II, 13B, 14A, B, 17B, 20A ;
IV, 15B, 17B, 19A, 22B ; VI,
14B ; VII, 24B ; VIII, 4Ae, 5A,
10A, 11B, 13A, 21B, 22A ; IX,
4B, 5A, 7A, 14A, B, 15A, B, 16A,
17B, 18A, B ; XV, 11B, 12A ;
XVII, 16A, 17B ; XVIII, 3A,
16A ; XIX, 10B, 14A, 19A, 22A ;
XX, 2B, 3A, 5A ; XXI, 15B ;
G 24B. Self-cultivation.

備 I, 5A ; IV, 19A ; VIII, 6B ;
IX, 13A, 15A, 18A ; XVII, 12A,
14B ; XVIII, 3B, 7A, 8B, 9B, 13A ;
XIX, 7A, 11A, B, 18A, 20A, B ;
XX, 5A ; XXI, 3A. Perfect.

偽 IV, 19Ae ; VIII, 17B ; XVIII,
8B ; XIX, 7B, 14A, B ; XX, 3B ;
XXII, 1B, 2A ; XXIII, 1A, B,
2A, 3A, B, 4A, 5A, B, 6A, B, 7A,
12A. Acquired character(istic).
See XXII, 1.

儒 I, 10A, 11B ; II, 19A, 22B ;
VIII, 1A, 3A, 5A, 16A, B, 17A, B,
18B, 19A, 22A ; XVIII, 15A ;
XIX, 3A, e, 18A ; XX, 2B ;
XXII, 3A. A Confucian literatus ;

its opposite is 人.

Radical 12. 八

公 II, 17B, 24A ; IV, 15B, 16A,
20A, 23B ; V, 1B, 2A, B ; VII,
23B, 24A, 25A ; VIII, 1A, B, 2A,
3B, 4A, 8A, 14A, B, 15A, 16B, 21B,
22A ; IX, 1B, 3A, 4B, 7B, 16A, B,
18A ; XI, 12A, 14B ; XV (XIX),
12A ; XVII, 18B ; XVIII, 1B,
9A, 11A, 14A ; XXI, 2B, 4A, 6A ;
XXII, 3A, 10A, B ; XXIII,
11B. Duke.

兵 IV, 11B ; XV, title, 1A, B, 2A,
3A, 4A, 10A, 11A, B, 12A, (XIX)
12B, 13A, B ; XX, 2B.

Radical 18. 刀

分 I, 8A ; IV, 15A, 22A, B, 23A, B ;
V, 6A ; VI, 14A, 15A ; VII, 23A ;
VIII, 4B, 7B, 9A, 11A, 12B ;
IX, 1A, 2A, 3B, 12A, B ; X, 1A,
2A ; XI, 14B ; XV (XIX), 13A,
14A ; XVII, 13A, 20B ; XVIII,
3A, B, 9B, 14A, 15B, 16A, B ;
XIX, 1A, 3A, 14B, 19A ; XXI,
15B, 16A ; XXII, 4A, 8A ;
XXIII, 1B, 2A, 4B, 5A. Social
division, social distinctions ;
function.

利 I, 1B, 3A, 6A, 13A ; II, 15A, 16A,
17A, 18A, 23A ; IV, 11B, 13B, 14A,
15A, B, 17A, 18B, 19A, 23A ;
V, 5A ; VI, 13B ; VII, 24B,
26A ; VIII, 5A, 10B, 17A ; IX,
12A, 15A ; X, 2A ; XV, 1B, 2A,
3A, 5A, 9B, (XIX), 12B, 13A ;
XVIII, 1A, B, 3A, 8B, 14A, B, 16A ;
XIX, 3A, 5A, 22A ; XX, 5B ;
XXI, 4A, 5A, 15B, 16A ; XXII, 2A,
10A, B, 15A ; XXIII, 1A, B, 2B,
3B, 4A, B, 7A, 11B, 12A. Service-
ableness ; successful.

制 IV, 23A ; VIII, 1B, 14B,
16B, 17A, 18A, B ; IX, 3B, 8A, B,
12B, 16B, 17B, 19B ; X, 1B ;
XI, 14A, B ; XV, 9A, 10A ; XVII,
19A ; XVIII, 6B, 7A, B, 8A, B,
9A, 16A ; XIX, 1A, 7B, 19A, 21B ;
XX, 1A, 3B, 4A, B ; XXI, 8B,
10A, 13A, 15A, B, 16B ; XXII,
2B, 3B, 4A, 7A, 12A ; XXIII,
2A, 4A, 11B.

Radical 19. 力

功 I, 5B, 6A ; V, 2A, 7B ; VI, 14A,
15A ; VII, 27B, 28A ; VIII, 12A,
16A ; IX, 4A, 5B, 8A, B, 14B,
15A, 16A, 17A, 19A ; X, 1B, 2A ;
XV, 4B, 9B, 10A, (XIX), 12A ;
XVII, 13B, 14A, B, 15B, 19A ;
XVIII, 1B, 6A ; XIX, 14A, 16A,
B, 19B ; XXII, 3A, e, 11A ;
G 24B. Work ; merit of the 儒.

Radical 26. 卩

危 IV, 15A, B, 16B, 17A, 18A, 19A ;
V, 4B ; VII, 25B, 27A, B ; VIII,
10B, 21B ; IX, 5A, B, 16B, 17A,
19A, B ; XV, 4A, B ; XVII, 19A ;
XVIII, 1B, 2A, 14A, B ; XIX,
3A, 7B, 20A ; XX, 2B, 3B ; XXI,
4A, 10A, B, 12B, 13A ; XXII,
14B, 15A. Uneasy, anxiety,
insecure, tottering, threatening
to fall ; restless, unquiet ; its
opposite is 安 or 利.

卿 V, 1A ; VIII, 3A, 5A ; IX, 1B ;
XV, 1A, B, 2A, 4B, 9A, 10A, 11A,
B ; XVIII, 16A, G 24A.

Radical 28. 厶

參 XVII, 13B ; XXI, 8B ; XXIII,
8A.

Radical 30. 口

名 I, 3A, B, 4B ; II, 14B ; IV, 17B,
23A ; V, 1B ; VII, 28A ; VIII,
5B, 8A, 10A, B, 16B, 17A ; IX,
2A, 4A, 16B, 17A, B ; X, 1B ;
XV (XIX), 12A ; XVII, 19A ;
XIX, 14B, 15B, 17B ; XX, 2A ;
XXI, 3A, 4A, 6A, 11B ; XXII,
title, 1A, B, 2B, 3A, B, 4A, 6A, B,
7A, B, 8A, B, 9A, 10B, 11A,
15A, B ; XXIII, 7A ; G 24A,
B. Term ; concept ; nomenclature.

君 I, 1A, B, 2B, 3A, 4A, B, 5A, 6A, B,
8B, 9B, 11B, 12B, 13B ; II, 14A,
17B, 18A, 20B, 21B, 22B, 23A, B,
24A ; IV, 12B, 13A, B, 14A, 17A,
B, 18B, 19A, 22B ; V, 1B, 3B,
5B, 7A, 8B, 9A ; VI, 14B, 15B ;
VII, 23B, 24B, 27A, B, 28A, B ;
VIII, 2A, 3B, 5A, 6A, B, 7A, B,
8A, B, 9B, 10A, B, 11B, 16B, 21A,
B, 22B, 23A ; IX, 3A, B, 4A, B,
5A, 10B, 11A, B, 12B, 18A, B ;
X, 1B ; XI, 14A, B ; XV, 1A,
B, 2A, B, 3B, 4A, B, 8B, 10A, 11A,
B ; XVI, 11B ; XVII, 14A, B,
15B, 16A, B, 18B ; XVIII, 2B,
3A, B, 16B ; XIX, 1B, 3A, B, 7B,
8B, 9A, B, 12A, 13A, 14A, 19A, B,
20A, 21B ; XX, 1B, 2B, 3A, B,
4B ; XXI, 1B, 2A, B, 8B, 10A, B,
15A, 16B, 17A ; XXII, 8A, B,
10A, B, 11A, 15A, 16A ; XXIII,
2A, 5A, B, 6A, B, 7B, 8A, B, 9A,
10B, 11A, 12A ; G 24A.

命 IV, 15A, B; IX, 6A, 12B, 14A, 15A; XV, 9B, 10A, (XIX) 13B; XVII, 19A; XVIII, 16A; XX, 2B; XXII, 2B, 5B, 6B, 8A, B, 9A.

善 I, 3A, 5A, 7B, 12A; II, 13B, 14A, B, 15B, 22B; IV, 11B, 17B, 21B; V, 1B, 2A, 8A, 9A; VII, 25B, 26A, B; VIII, 6A, 11A, 12A, 13B, 16A, 21A; IX, 2A, 3A, 9A, 12B, 19B; XV, 1B, 4A, 9A, 10A, 11A, B; XVII, 19B; XVIII, 6B, 8B, 11B, 12A, B, 17A; XIX, 9A, 18A, 20A; XX, 1B, 2B, 3A, B, 4A; XXI, 12A, 14A; XXII, 6B, 7A; XXIII, 1A, B, 2A, B, 3A, 4B, 5A, B, 6A, B, 7A, 8A, 12A; G 24A, B.

Radical 32. 土

地 I, 2A, 4B, 8B, 13B; IV, 11B; VII, 25A; VIII, 3A, 6A, 16A, B, 17A, 19A, 21A; IX, 3B, 5A, B, 9B, 10B, 11A, B, 13A; XV, 1B; XVII, 13A, 14B, 15A, B, 16B, 17A, 18B; XVIII, 6B, 7A, 14A; XIX, 3A, B, 4B, 7A, 8A, 14A, B, 18B, 19A, B; XX, 3A, 4B; XXI, 2B, 8B; XXIII, 8A, 10B; G 24B.

Radical 33. 士

士 I, 4B, 7B, 11B; II, 18A, 20A, 21B; IV, 13B, 14A, 15B, 23B; V, 3B, 4A, 8B; VIII, 8A, B, 11B, 22A, B, 23A; IX, 1B, 4A, 5A, BE, 6B, 11B, 18A, B; XI, 14B; XV, 1B, 4B, 5A, 10A; XVIII, 8B, 11B, 16A, B; XIX, 3B, 8A, 9A, B, 10B, 21B; XXI, 15A; XXII, 10B; XXIII, 9A. Officer; baron.

Radical 37. 大

大夫 IV, 15B, 23B; VIII, 16B, 22A; IX, 1B, 5A; XI, 14B; XV, 10A; XVIII, 11A, 16A, B; XIX, 3B, 9B, 10B, 20B. High official; great officer.

太 — XIX, 5A, 7A. Primitive.

天 I, 2A, 8B, 12A, 13A; II, 18B, 19A, B, 23A; IV, 15A, B, 20A, 21A, 22A, 23A, 24A; V, 1B, 3A, 4A, 7A; VI, 12B, 13B, 14A; VII, 23B, 24A, B, 25A, B, 27B, 28A; VIII, 1A, B, 2A, B, 5A, B, 6A, 9A, 10A, B, 13B, 14A, B, 15B, 16A, B, 17A, 19A, 21A, 22A; IX, 2A, 3B, 6B, 7A, 8A, 10B, 11A, B, 12A, B, 13A, 16B, 17A, B, 18A; X, 1B; XI, 14B; XV, 1B, 2A, 10A, 11A, 12A, (XIX), 12A, 14B; XVI, 11B; XVII, title, 12A, B, 13A, B, 14A, B, 15A, B, 16A, B, 17A, 18B, 19A, B; XVIII, 2A, B, 3A, B, 4A, B, 5A, 6B, 8B, 9A, B, 11B, 12A, B, 13B, 14A, 15B, 16A, 18A; XIX, 1B, 3A, B, 4B, 7A, B, 8A, 9B, 10B, 14A, B, 18B, 19A, B, 20A, B; XX, 2A, B, 3A, 4B, 5B; XXI, 1A, 3A, 5A, B, 8B, 10A, 15A, B, 16B; XXII, 5A, 8B, 9B, 12A, B, 13A, 15B; XXIII, 2A, E, 5A, B, 7A, 8A, B, 10A, B; G 24A, B.

奪 II, 23B, 24A; VIII, 2A; IX, 5A, 11B, 18A, 19A; XV, 2A, 11A; XVIII, 2A, 4A, 14A; XXI, 8B; XXII, 10A; XXIII, 1A, B, 4B, 5B, 7A.

Radical 39. 子

孔 and other names of Confucius. I, 3AE; II, 14A; V, 1B, 2B; VI, 16A; VII, 23A, 24B, 27A; VIII, 4A, 14A, 17A; IX, 4B; XVIII, 13B; XXI, 5B; G 24A, B.

孝 IV, 16A; VII, 26A; VIII, 5A; IX, 4A, 12B, 15A; XV, 1A, 4A, 8B; XIX, 10B, 11A, 13A, 18A, 21A; XXI, 4A; XXIII, 3A, 7A, 8B.

學 I, title, 1ᴀ, ʙ, 2ᴀ, 3ᴀ, 7ʙ,
8ᴀ, ʙ, 9ʙ, 10ᴀ, 12ᴀ, ʙ; II, 21ᴀ,
22ᴀ, ʙ; V, 1ᴀ, ʙ, 3ᴀ, 8ʙ; VIII,
8ʙ, 17ᴀ, 19ʙ, 21ᴀ, 23ᴀ; IX, 1ʙ,
XVIII, 12ʙ, 18ᴀ; XIX, 8ᴀ;
XX, 3ʙ, 4ᴀ, 5ʙ; XXI, 15ᴀ;
XXII, 10ᴀ; XXIII, 2ᴀ, ʙ, 5ᴀ,
8ᴀ; G 24ᴀ.

Radical 40. 宀

安 I, 2ʙ, 7ʙ, 10ᴀ; II, 18ᴀ, 22ᴀ, ʙ,
23ʙ; IV, 11ᴀ, 13ʙ, 15ᴀ, ʙ, 17ᴀ,
ʙ, 18ᴀ, 19ᴀ, 20ᴀ, 22ᴀ, ʙ; V,
8ʙ; VI, 13ʙ; VII, 23ʙ, 25ᴀ, ʙ,
27ᴀ; VIII, 10ʙ, 11ʙ, 19ᴀ, 21ᴀ,
ʙ, 22ᴀ, ʙ, 23ᴀ; IX, 1ʙ, 4ᴀ, 5ᴀ,
9ʙ, 10ʙ, 14ʙ, 15ᴀ, ʙ, 16ʙ, 17ᴀ,
18ᴀ, ʙ, 19ᴀ, ʙ; XV, 4ᴀ, ʙ, 9ᴀ,
10ʙ, 11ᴀ; XVI, 11ʙ; XVII,
17ʙ; XVIII, 1ʙ, 2ᴀ, ʙ, 3ᴀ, 11ᴀ;
ʙ, 14ᴀ, ʙ; XIX, 2ʙ, 3ᴀ, ʙ, 7ʙ,
11ʙ, 19ᴀ, 20ᴀ, 21ʙ; XX, 2ᴀ,
ʙ, 5ʙ; XXI, 13ʙ, XXII, 11ᴀ,
14ʙ; XXIII, 2ᴀ, 7ᴀ, ʙ; G 24ʙ.
Comfort; its opposite is 危.

定 I, 13ᴀ; V, 2ᴀ; VI, 15ᴀ; VIII,
5ᴀ, 7ᴀ, 15ʙ; IX, 1ᴀ, 9ᴀ, 15ᴀ;
XV, 9ʙ; XVIII, 8ʙ, 9ᴀ; XX,
1ʙ; XXI, 11ᴀ, 13ᴀ, 14ᴀе;
XXII, 2ʙ, 6ʙ, 7ᴀ. Determine;
定 物, make judgments.

察 XVII, 13ᴀ, 18ʙ; XIX, 7ʙ;
XXI, 8ᴀ, 10ᴀ, 11ᴀ, 15ʙ, 16ʙ;
XXII, 3ʙ, 7ᴀ, 14ʙ; XXIII,
2ᴀ, 8ᴀ; G 24ᴀ, ʙ. Arrive
at the truth.

Radical 42. 小

小 人 I, 8ʙ; II, 14ᴀ, 17ʙ; IV, 12ʙ,
13ᴀ, ʙ, 14ᴀ, 17ᴀ, ʙ, 18ʙ, 19ᴀ;
V, 1ʙ; VII, 24ʙ; VIII, 8ᴀ, 21ᴀ,
ʙ; IX, 3ʙ; XVII, 15ʙ, 16ᴀ, ʙ;
XVIII, 4ʙ, 5ᴀ, 16ʙ; XIX, 7ʙ;
XX, 3ʙ; XXI, 17ᴀ; XXIII,
2ᴀ, 6ʙ, 7ᴀ, 8ᴀ, 9ᴀ. The mean-
minded man.

Radical 50. 巾

帝 VI, 11ᴀ, (XIX) 14ʙ; XVIII,
11ʙ; XXI, 3ʙ; G 24ᴀ.

師 II, 14ᴀ, 17ʙ, 22ᴀ, ʙ;
IV, 19ᴀ, ʙ; VIII, 5ʙ, 19ʙ, 20ᴀ,
ʙ; IX, 10ᴀ, 11ʙ, 13ʙ, 14ʙ, 15ᴀ,
ʙ; XV, 10ʙ, (XIX), 13ʙ; XVI,
11ᴀ; XVIII, 3ᴀ, ʙ, 16ᴀ, 18ᴀ;
XIX, 3ᴀ, ʙ, 21ʙ; XX, 2ᴀ, ʙ;
XXI, 9ʙ, 15ᴀ; XXIII, 1ʙ, 2ᴀ,
12ᴀ.

常 II, 16ᴀ; IV, 15ᴀ, ʙ, 18ᴀ, ʙ,
19ᴀ; VII, 28ᴀ; VIII, 21ʙ;
IX, 6ʙ, 7ʙ; XV, 4ʙ, 11ᴀ, 12ᴀ;
XVII, 12ᴀ, 15ʙ, 17ᴀ, 20ᴀ;
XVIII, 2ᴀ; XIX, 3ʙ; XXI,
5ʙ. Ordinarily, regular principle.

Radical 57. 弓

弟 II, 22ʙ; IV, 16ᴀ; V, 4ᴀ;
VIII, 2ᴀ, 4ʙ, 5ᴀ; IX, 4ᴀ, 11ʙ,
12ʙ, 15ᴀ; XV, 2ʙ; XX, 1ʙ,
4ᴀ, 5ᴀ, ʙ; XXII, 10ᴀ; XXIII,
3ᴀ, 4ᴀ, ʙ. Fraternal duty;
reverence to elders.

Radical 59. 彡

形 I, 7ᴀ, 8ʙ; IV, 13ʙ; V, 1ʙ, 2ʙ,
5ᴀ; VIII, 5ᴀ; XVI, 11ᴀ;
XVII, 13ʙ; XVIII, 6ʙ, 7ʙ, 9ʙ,
16ᴀ, 17ʙ; XIX, 17ʙ, 22ʙ;
XX, 1ᴀ; XXI, 3ᴀ, 8ᴀ, ʙ, 11ᴀ;
XXII, 3ᴀ, 4ᴀ, 5ᴀ, 15ᴀ, ʙ. Body.

Radical 60. 彳

微 I, 8ʙ; V, 2ʙ; VIII, 13ʙ, 16ᴀ;
IX, 13ᴀ; XV, 1ʙ, 10ᴀ; XXI,
10ᴀ, ʙ, 11ᴀ, 12ᴀ, ʙ. Abstruse
knowledge.

德 I, 4ʙ, 5ᴀ, 8ᴀ, 13ᴀ; IV, 15ʙ,
18ᴀ; VII, 26ᴀ, 28ᴀ; VIII, 7ᴀ,
10ᴀ, 11ᴀ, 22ʙ; IX, 2ᴀ, 6ᴀ, ʙ,
8ʙ, 16ᴀ; X, 2ᴀ; XV, 2ʙ, 11ʙ;
XVII, 16ᴀ; XVIII, 2ᴀ, 3ᴀ, 6ᴀ,
8ʙ, 9ᴀ, 16ᴀ; XIX, 3ʙе; XX, 3ʙ,
4ᴀ; XXI, 2ᴀ, 5ᴀе, 6ᴀ, 8ʙ;
XXII, 9ʙ; G 24ᴀ, ʙ.

Radical 61. 心

心 I, 5A, 6A, B, 8B, 12B, 13A; II, 14A, 16B, 17B, 18A, B; IV, 19B; V, 1B; VII, 24B, 28A; VIII, 15B, 21B; IX, 7A, 17A; X, 1B; XV, 2B; XVI, 11A; XVII, 16A; XVIII, 9B; XIX, 9B, 11A; XX, 1B, 2B, 3A, B; XXI, 1A, B, 2B, 3A, B, 6A, B 7A, B, 8B, 9A, B, 10B, 11A, 13A 16B; XXII, 1B, 5A, B, 9A, 10A, 12A, B, 14B, 15A; XXIII, 2B, 3B, 8A, 12A; G 24A, B. Mind.

志 I, 6A, 10A; II, 15A, 17A, B, 21B, 22A, 23B; IV, 15A, B; V, 2B, 3A, 8B; VI, 15A; VII, 27B, 28A; VIII, 5A, 11Be, 13B, 17B, 21A, B, 22A, B; XV, 2A; XVI, 11A; XVII, 14B, 15A, 16A; XVIII, 9B, 16A; XIX, 21A, B; XX, 1B, 3A, 5B; XXI, 7A; XXII, 2B, 3B, 4A, 10B, 11A, 14B; XXIII, 8A; G 24B.

忠 II, 14A, 18B; IV, 17B; VII, 28A; VIII, 5A, 11A; XI, 12A; XVI, 11B; XIX, 9B, 10B, 11A, B, 21A, B; XXI, 2B; XXIII, 1A, 8B, 12A.

思 I, 12B; II, 17B; IV, 14B; V, 2A; VIII, 6A; XV, 10B; XVII, 19A, B; XIX, 8A, 11B, 18B, 21A, B; XXI, 8A, 12A, B, 13A; XXII, 10B; XXIII, 3B, 5A, 8A.

性 II, 21A; IV, 17A, B, 18A; VI, 13B; VIII, 11B, 20B, 21A, 22A; IX, 18A; X, 1ae; XVIII, 8B, 14A; XIX, 3A, 14A, B; XX, 1A; XXI, 14B; XXII, 1B, 2B, 11Be, 12B, 13A, 15A; XXIII, title, 1A, B, 2A, B, 3A, B, 4A, B, 5A, B, 6A, B, 7A, B, 12A. Original nature; it is contrasted with 偽.

惡 I, 7B; II, 14A, 22B, 24A; IV, 13A, B, 17A, B, 18B; V, 1B, 2B, 3A, 5A; VII, 24A; VIII, 1A, 2A, 6B, 8A, 15A, 17B, 21B; IX, 1A, 3B, 5B, 18A; X, 1B, 2A; XV, 4A, 9A, 11A; XVI, 11A; XVII, 13B, 15B, 17A, 21A; XVIII, 2A, 3A, 4A, 5B, 6A, 8B, 9B, 14B, 15A, 17B; XIX, 1A, 3B, 7A, 12A, e, 13A, 22A; XX, 1A, 2B, 3A, 4A; XXI, 1B, 2A, 6A, 8B, 11B, 12A, 13A, 15A; XXII, 1B, 5A, 8B, 11A, 12A, 13A, B, 14A; XXIII, title, 1A, B, 2A, B, e, 3A, 4B, 5A, B, 6A, B, 7A; G 24B. Ugly.

情 II, 18B, 22A; IV, 21A, 23A; V, 7A, B; VI, 13B; VIII, 7A, 10A, 11B, 20B, 21A, 22A; IX, 18A; XV, 4A; XVI, 11B; XVII, 13B, 14A, B, 19B; XVIII, 14B, 17A, B, 18A; XIX, 3A, 7A, 8B, 12B, 13A, B, 14A, 18A, 19B, 20A, 21A, B; XX, 1A, 2A, B, 3B; XXI, 8B, 9A, 13A; XXII, 1B, 4A, 7B, 9Ae, 11B, 12B, 15A; XXIII, 1B, 2A, 3A, B, 4A, B, 7A, B, 8B, 11A. For the 六情 see XXII, 1.

感 XX, 1A, 2B, 3A; XXII, 1B; XXIII, 3B. Stimulus.

愛 XI, 14A; XV, 5A, 11A, 14A; XIX, 12A, 18B, 21B; XXII, 5A, 7A.

慮 I, 12B; II, 15A, 16B; IV, 15B, 16B, 17A, B, 21B, 22A, B; VII, 27A; VIII, 11B, 15B; IX, 6A, 7B; XV, 4A, 9B; XVII, 13A, 14B, 16A; XVIII, 4A, 9B, 14A, 16A, 17A; XIX, 8A, 13A; XXI, 15A; XXII, 1B, 2A, 11A, 13A; XXIII, 3B, 5A; G 24A. To cogitate; deep thinking; calm deliberation.

應 I, 13A; VII, 26A; VIII, 3A, 5A, 7A, 10A, 11B, 14A, 16B, 18B; IX, 8A; XVI, 11A; XVII, 12A, 19A, B; XVIII, 1A, 14B, 15B, 17B; XIX, 7B; XX, 2B, 3A; XXI, 16B; XXII, 1B, 12B; XXIII, 3A, 6B. Reaction.

Radical 62. 戈

成 I, 5A, B, 13A; II, 15B, 21B; IV, 17B, 19A; VI, 13B, 14B, 15A; VII, 24B, 25A; VIII, 1A, B, 2A, 14A, 16B, 20A, 21A; X, 1B; XV, 1A, 3A, 4A, 8B, 9A, B; XVII, 13A, B, 19B; XVIII, 16B, 18A; XIX, 5A, 6B, 11A, B, 12A, 15B, 19A, 20B, 21B, 22B; XX, 1B, 3A, 4A; XXI, 3A, 6A, 10A, 16B, 17A; XXII, 1A, 2A, B, 3A, 6B, 7A, 8B, 11A, 12A; XXIII, 2A, 3B; G 24A, B.

Radical 66. 攴

敎 I, 2A, 4Be; II, 15B; VII, 24A; VIII, 1B, 18A, 23A; IX, 1A, B, 15A, 16A, 17B; XVIII, 12A, B; XIX, 2B, 20A; G 24A.

敬 II, 18B; IV, 12B; VII, 24A, 25B, 28A; IX, 4A, 7A; XV, 9B, 10A; XVI, 11A; XVII, 16A; XIX, 3A, 9A, B, 10A, 12A, 16B, 17B, 21B, 22B; XX, 1B; XXI, 16B; XXIII, 7A, 12A. Attentive.

數 I, 7B, 10B, 12B; IV, 15B; V, 4B, 6A, 7A; VII, 24A; VIII, 11B; IX, 3B, 4B, 8B, 13B; X, 1A; XVII, 15A, B; XIX, 10A, 11A; XX, 5B; XXI, 5B; XXII, 3A, 7A, 11B, 14A, B.

Radical 67. 文

文 I, 8A; II, 23Be; IV, 16B, 21A; V, 1B, 3A, 6A, 8B, 9A; VI, 13B, 14B; VII, 24B, 25A; VIII, 1B, 2A, 13A, 14A; IX, 1B, 8B, 10B, 11A, 15B, 16B;

XV, 11A; XVII, 15B, 18B; XVIII, 9B, 13B, 18A; XIX, 1B, 3A, 5A, 6A, B, 7A, B, 8B, 9B, 10A, 11B, 12A, B, 13A, B, 14A, 16B, 18A, 19A, B, 20A, B, 21B, 22A, B; XX, 1A, B, 2A, 5B; XXI, 3A, 5A; XXII, 1A, 8B, 9B; XXIII, 1B, 2A, 3A, 4B, 7Ae, 9A, 11A. Sense of beauty.

Radical 72. 日

易 II, 16A, B; IV, 15B, 17B; V, 9A; VIII, 2A, 7B, 15B; IX, 15B; XVIII, 1B, 2A, B, 9A, 16B; XIX, 8A, 18A, 22B; XX, 2B, 3A, B, 4B, 5A, B; XXI, 8B, 9A, 11A; XXII, 3A, 6B, 8A, 11A, 14A, B.

明 I, 5A, 6A, B, 11B, 13B; II, 21B; IV, 15B, 17B; V, 4A, 7A; VI, 14A; VIII, 2A, 3A, 8A, 10B, 11A, 13A, 17B, 18A, 19B, 21A; IX, 3B, 5A, 7B, 8A, 13A; X, 2A; XV, 3A, 4A, 9A, 10A, (XIX) 14A; XVII, 13A, 16A, 17A, 18B, 20A; XVIII, 1B, 2A, 3A, B, 8B, 14B, 16A, 17B; XIX, 7A, 9A, 12B, 15B, 16A, B, 17B, 21B; XX, 3A, B, 4A, 5B; XXI, 4A, 8A, B, 10B, 11A, 12B, 13B, 14A, 17A; XXII, 3A, B, 4A, 8A, 9B, 14A, B; XXIII, 1B, 2A, B, 3A, 5A, B, 6A, B, 7A, B, 8A, B; G 24A. Wise; virtuous.

暴 I, 1B; IV, 14A; VII, 25A; VIII, 2A, 16B; IX, 16B, 17A, B, 18A, B, 19A; XV, 3B, 11A; XVIII, 3A, 6A, 16A; XIX, 7B; XX, 2A; XXIII, 1B, 5B; G 24A. Aggressive, tyrannous.

Radical 73. 曰

書 I, 7B, 8A, 9B, 10A, 11A; II, 24A; IV, 22A, B; VII, 24A; VIII, 13B, 17A, 18A; IX, 4A; XVII, 18A, 21A; XVIII, 2A, 6B; XIX, 15B; XXI, 11A. The *Book of History*.

Radical 74. 月

期 V, 2ᴀ; XIX, 19ᴀ, 20ʙ; XXII 1ᴀ, 4ᴀ, 8ʙ, 9ᴀ, 10ᴀ; XXIII 11ᴀ. Equivalent to 會, which is equivalent to 合, comprehend.

Radical 75. 木

本 VII, 24ᴀ; VIII, 3ᴀ, 5ᴀ, 19ʙ; IX, 4ᴀ, 11ʙ, 16ʙ, 19ᴀ; XV, 1ʙ, 4ʙ, 11ᴀ, 12ᴀ; XVI, 11ʙ; XVII, 12ᴀ, ʙ, 17ᴀ; XVIII, 1ʙ, 5ʙ; XIX, 3ᴀ, ʙ, 4ʙ, 5ᴀ, 7ᴀ, 14ᴀ; XX, 2ʙ, 3ʙ; XXI, 6ʙ; XXIII, 6ʙ, 8ᴀ. The fundamentals for life.

樂 I, 8ᴀ, 9ʙ; II, 17ʙ, 18ʙ, 19ᴀ; IV, 15ʙ, 22ᴀ, ʙ, 23ᴀ; V, 8ʙ, 9ᴀ; VII, 23ᴀ; VIII, 5ʙ, 10ᴀ, 13ᴀ, ʙ, 15ʙ; IX, 9ʙ, 10ʙ, 15ᴀ, 16ᴀ; XV, 10ʙ, 11ᴀ, ʙ; XVII, 13ʙ; XVIII, 8ᴀ, 11ʙ; XIX, 3ᴀ, 12ᴀ, ʙ, 21ʙ; XX, title, 1ᴀ, ʙ, 2ᴀ, ʙ, 3ᴀ, ʙ, 4ᴀ, ʙ, 5ᴀ, ʙ; XXI, 3ʙ, 11ᴀ, 13ᴀ; XXII, 1ʙ, 5ᴀ, 7ʙ, 15ᴀ, ʙ; XXIII, 10ʙ.

權 I, 13ᴀ; VI, 14ᴀ; VII, 27ʙ; IX, 17ʙ; XV, 9ʙ, 10ᴀ; XVII, 19ᴀ; XVIII, 4ᴀ; XXI, 3ʙ, 4ᴀ; XXII, 10ᴀ, 13ʙ, 14ᴀ, Standard.

Radical 76. 欠

欲 I, 12ʙ; II, 14ᴀ, 20ᴀ, 24ᴀ; IV, 12ᴀ, 13ʙ, 15ᴀ, 17ᴀ, ʙ, 18ʙ, 21ᴀ, ʙ, 23ᴀ; V, 3ʙ, 5ᴀ, 6ʙ, 7ᴀ; VII, 27ʙ; VIII, 8ʙ, 11ʙ, 21ʙ; IX, 3ʙ, 4ᴀ, 5ʙ, 8ᴀ, 17ᴀ; X, 1ᴀ, ʙ; XV, 9ᴀ, ʙ, 11ᴀ; XVIII, 17ᴀ, ʙ, 18ᴀ; XIX, 1ᴀ; XX, 2ᴀ, 3ʙ; XXI, 2ᴀ, 3ʙ, 4ᴀ, 5ᴀ, 6ᴀ, 12ᴀ, ʙ, 13ᴀ; XXII, 5ᴀ, 6ᴀ, ʙ, 7ʙ, 11ʙ, 12ᴀ, ʙ, 13ᴀ, ʙ, 14ᴀ, ʙ, 15ᴀ; XXIII, 1ᴀ, 3ᴀ, 4ᴀ, ʙ, 8ʙ, 10ʙ.

Radical 77. 止

正 I, 2ʙ, 4ʙ, 10ʙ; II, 14ᴀ, 22ᴀ, ʙ; IV, 17ʙ, 19ʙ, 22ᴀℯ; V, 1ʙ; VIII, 4ᴀ, 5ᴀ, 6ʙ, 12ᴀ, 17ᴀ, 22ᴀ; IX, 1ʙ, 16ᴀ, 17ʙ; XI, 14ᴀ; XV, 9ʙ; XVII, 14ʙ; XVIII, title, 1ʙ, 15ʙ; XX, 1ʙ, 2ᴀ, ʙ, 3ʙ; XXI, 1ʙ, 10ᴀ, 11ᴀ, 14ᴀ, 15ʙ, 16ᴀ; XXII, title, 2ᴀ, ʙ, 3ᴀ, 8ᴀ, 9ᴀ, ʙ, 10ʙ, 14ᴀ; XXIII, 1ʙ, 2ᴀ, 5ᴀ, ʙ, 7ʙ, 8ᴀ, 11ᴀ; G 24ᴀ.

Radical 78. 歹

死 I, 3ᴀ, 13ᴀ; IV, 14ᴀ, 16ʙ, 17ʙ; V, 2ᴀ, 3ᴀ; VIII, 17ᴀ; IX, 1ʙ, 19ᴀ; XV, 10ᴀ, 11ʙ; (XIX), 13ᴀ; XVII, 15ᴀ, 17ᴀ; XVIII, 4ᴀ, 5ʙ, 6ᴀ, 8ʙ, 9ʙ, 15ᴀ; XIX, 2ʙ, 3ᴀ, 9ᴀ, ʙ, 10ʙ, 11ʙ, 12ᴀ, 14ʙ, 16ʙ, 17ʙ, 18ᴀ, ʙ, 22ʙ; XX, 5ʙ; XXI, 2ʙ, 3ᴀ, 14ᴀ; XXII, 11ʙ, 12ᴀ.

Radical 79. 殳

殺 VII, 23ᴀ, 26ᴀ; VIII, 1ʙ, 5ᴀ, 15ʙ, 17ᴀ, 18ᴀ; IX, 11ʙ, 12ʙ; XI, 14ᴀ; XV, 9ʙ, 10ᴀ, (XIX), 13ʙ, 14ʙ; XVIII, 5ᴀ, ʙ, 6ᴀ, 18ᴀ; XIX, 8ʙ, 18ᴀ, 19ʙ; XX, 5ᴀ, ʙ; XXII, 7ᴀ; G 24ʙ. Simplification.

Radical 81. 比

比 IV, 16ᴀ; VII, 25ʙ; VIII, 6ᴀ, 10ᴀ, ʙ, 15ᴀ; XVIII, 1ʙ; XXII, 4ᴀ; G 24ʙ. 比 中 is equivalent to 順 中.

Radical 85. 水

法 I, 8ᴀ, ʙ, 9ʙ, 11ʙ; II, 21ʙ, 22ᴀ, ʙ, 24ᴀ; IV, 13ᴀ, 15ʙ, 16ᴀ, 19ᴀ, ʙ; V, 6ᴀ, 8ʙ; VI, 14ʙ; VIII, 3ᴀ, 5ᴀ, 8ᴀ, 11ʙ, 17ᴀ, 18ᴀ, ʙ, 19ʙ, 20ᴀ, ʙ, 22ʙ;

IX, 3ᴀ, ʙ, 8ᴀ, 9ᴀe, 10ᴀ, 16ᴀ, 17ʙ; XI, 14ʙ; XVIII, 14ʙ, 16ʙ; XIX, 8ᴀ, 18ᴀ, 21ʙ; XXI, 15ᴀ; XXII, 3ᴀ; XXIII, 1ʙ, 2ᴀ, 3ʙ, 4ᴀ, 5ᴀ, ʙ, 7ʙ, 9ʙ; G 24ᴀ. A set of principles; obedience to law; to imitate.

治 II, 14ʙ, 15ᴀ, 16ᴀ, ʙ, 17ʙ; IV, 15ʙ, 16ᴀ, 17ʙ, 21ᴀ; V, 7ᴀ; VI, 13ʙ, 15ᴀ; VIII, 5ʙ, 7ʙ, 8ᴀ, 9ᴀ, 11ᴀ, 13ʙ, 20ʙ, 22ʙe; IX, 2ᴀ, 3ᴀ, 11ᴀ, 14ʙ, 16ᴀ; X, 1ʙ; XI, 14ʙ; XV, 4ʙ, (XIX), 12ᴀ, 14ʙ; XVI, 11ʙ; XVII, 12ᴀ, 13ᴀ, ʙ, 14ᴀ, ʙ, 15ᴀ, 18ʙ, 19ʙ, 20ᴀ; XVIII, 1ʙ, 5ᴀ, ʙ, 6ᴀ, ʙ, 9ᴀ, 13ᴀ, 14ᴀ, 18ᴀ; XIX, 3ᴀ, ʙ, 7ʙ, 9ᴀ, 14ʙ, 19ʙ, 20ᴀ; XX, 1ʙ, 3ᴀ, ʙ, 4ʙ, 5ʙ; XXI, 1ᴀ, ʙ, 3ᴀ, 7ᴀ, 8ʙ, 9ʙ, 10ᴀ, 13ᴀ, 15ʙ, 16ᴀ, ʙ; XXII, 3ᴀ, 9ᴀ, 11ʙ, 12ʙ, 13ʙ; XXIII, 1ʙ, 2ᴀ, 5ᴀ, ʙ, 6ᴀ, ʙ; G 24ᴀ. Well-governed and prosperous; self-control.

Radical 96. 玉

王 I, 2ᴀ, 10ʙ; II, 17ʙ, 24ᴀ; IV, 13ᴀ, ʙ, 16ᴀ, 20ᴀ, 22ᴀ, 23ᴀ; V, 1ʙ, 2ʙ, 6ᴀ, ʙ, 7ᴀ, 8ʙ; VI, 15ᴀ; VII, 24ʙ, 25ᴀ; VIII, 1ᴀ, ʙ, 2ᴀ, 3ᴀ, ʙ, 5ᴀ, 6ᴀ, 8ᴀ, 11ʙ, 13ʙ, 14ᴀ, ʙ, 16ʙ, 17ᴀ, ʙ, 18ᴀ, ʙ, 22ʙ, 23ᴀ; IX, 1ʙ, 2ᴀ, 3ʙ, 5ᴀ, 6ᴀ, ʙ, 7ʙ, 8ᴀ, ʙ, 9ᴀ, 10ᴀ, 11ᴀ, 12ʙ, 13ᴀ, 16ʙ, 17ᴀ, 18ᴀ, 19ʙ; XI, title, 14ʙ; XV, 1ᴀ, ʙ, 2ᴀ, 4ᴀ, ʙ, 8ʙ, 10ᴀ, ʙ, 11ᴀ, 12ᴀ, (XIX), 12ᴀ; XVII, 15ʙ, 16ᴀ, 18ʙ, 19ʙ, 21ᴀ; XVIII, 2ᴀ, ʙ, 3ᴀ, ʙ, 6ᴀ, ʙ, 7ʙ, 8ᴀ, ʙ, 12ʙ, 13ᴀ, 14ᴀ, 16ᴀ, ʙ, 18ᴀ; XIX, 1ᴀ, 3ʙ, 10ʙ, 16ʙ, 19ᴀ, ʙ, 20ᴀ, ʙ, 21ʙ; XX, 1ᴀ, ʙ, 2ᴀ, 3ʙ, 5ᴀ, ʙ; XXI, 3ᴀ, 5ʙ, 6ᴀ, 15ᴀ, ʙ, 16ʙ; XXII, 1ᴀ, 2ʙ, 3ᴀ, 7ᴀ, 8ʙ; XXIII, 1ʙ, 5ᴀ, ʙ, 6ᴀ, 10ʙ, 11ᴀ; G 24ᴀ. To rule as lawful King.

Radical 104. 疒

病 IV, 13ʙ. Defective.

Radical 108. 皿

盡 I, 12ʙ; IV, 19ᴀ, 23ʙ; VII, 24ᴀ; VIII, 13ʙ, 21ᴀ, 22ᴀ; IX, 16ᴀ; XVII, 19ᴀ, ʙ; XVIII, 3ʙ, 9ʙ; XIX, 7ᴀ, 8ʙ, 9ᴀ, ʙ, 14ᴀ, 16ᴀ, 18ʙ, 19ʙ; XX, 1ᴀ, 4ʙ; XXI, 5ᴀ, ʙ, 8ᴀ, 9ʙ, 15ᴀ; XXII, 9ʙ, 13ᴀ, ʙ. Fully expressed.

Radical 109. 目

直 I, 1ʙ, 2ʙ, 3ʙ; II, 16ᴀ; IV, 12ʙ, 20ᴀ; V, 3ᴀ, 4ᴀ; VIII, 16ᴀ; XVIII, 1ʙ, 3ʙ, 5ʙ, 15ʙ; XIX, 7ʙ, 20ᴀ; XX, 1ᴀ; XXI, 15ʙ, 16ᴀ, 17ᴀ; XXII, 9ʙ; XXIII, 1ʙ, 6ᴀ, 10ᴀ.

相 II, 20ᴀ, 21ᴀ; IV, 13ᴀ, 16ᴀ, 20ᴀ; V, 1ᴀ, ʙ, 2ʙ, 3ᴀ, 4ᴀ, ʙe; VIII, 6ʙ, 7ᴀ, ʙ, 8ᴀ, 10ʙ, 11ᴀ; IX, 1ʙ, 3ʙ, 9ʙ, 14ʙ, 15ʙ, 17ʙ, 18ᴀ, ʙ, 19ʙ; X, 1ʙ; XV, 10ʙ; XVII, 13ʙ, 16ʙ, 17ʙ; XVIII, 1ᴀ, 6ᴀ, 16ᴀ; XIX, 1ᴀ, 7ᴀ, ʙ, 8ʙ, 11ᴀ, 13ᴀ, 19ᴀ, ʙ; XX, 3ᴀ, ʙ; XXI, 2ʙ, 4ᴀ, 6ᴀ, 16ᴀ, ʙ; XXII, 4ᴀ, 6ᴀ, 10ʙ; XXIII, 4ʙ, 5ʙ, 8ᴀ, ʙ.

Radical 113. 示

神 I, 2ʙ, 5ᴀ; II, 17ʙ; VIII, 13ʙ, 21ᴀ; IX, 11ᴀ, 13ᴀ; XV, 10ᴀ, 11ᴀ; XVII, 13ʙ, 18ʙ; XVIII, 11ʙ; XIX, 2ʙe, 14ʙ, 17ʙ; XXI, 8ʙ, 13ʙ; XXII, 8ʙ; XXIII, 8ᴀ; G 24ᴀ. 神明 gods, human spirit; godlike.

福 I, 2ʙ; VII, 26ᴀ; XVII, 14ᴀ; XXI, 3ʙ, 4ᴀ, ʙ, 6ᴀ, 14ᴀ; XXII, 14ᴀ; G 24ʙ.

禍 I, 2ʙ, 4ʙ, 5ᴀ ; II, 17ʙ, 23ᴀe ; VII, 26ᴀ ; X, 1ʙ, 2ᴀ ; XVII, 12ᴀ, 13ᴀ, 14ᴀ ; XVIII, 14ᴀ ; XXI, 3ᴀ, 4ᴀ, 5ʙ, 6ᴀ ; XXII, 4ᴀ, 14ᴀ ; XXIII, 11ᴀ.

禮 I, 7ʙ, 8ᴀ, 9ʙ, 10ᴀ, ʙ, 11ᴀ, ʙ ; II, 15ᴀ, ʙ, 17ʙ, 18ʙ, 22ᴀ, ʙ ; IV, 19ᴀ, 22ᴀ, ʙ, 23ᴀ ; V, 6ᴀ, 8ʙ ; VI, 15ᴀ ; VIII, 3ᴀ, 5ᴀ, 6ᴀ, 11ʙ, 13ʙ, 16ʙ, 17ᴀ, 18ᴀ, ʙ, 21ᴀ, 22ᴀ ; IX, 1ʙ, 2ᴀ, 3ʙ, 4ᴀ, ʙ, 5ᴀ, 8ᴀ, 11ᴀ, ʙ, 12ʙ, 16ᴀ ; X, 2ᴀ ; XI, 14ᴀ, ʙ ; XV, 4ʙ, (XIX), 12ᴀ ; XVI, 11ʙ ; XVII, 17ʙ, 18ʙ, 19ᴀ, 20ᴀ ; XVIII, 3ᴀ, 9ʙ ; XIX, title, 1ᴀ, ʙ, 3ᴀ, ʙ, 6ʙ, 7ᴀ, ʙ, 8ᴀ, ʙ, 9ᴀ, 11ᴀ, 12ᴀ, ʙ, 13ᴀ, 14ᴀ, ʙ, 16ʙ, 17ʙ, 18ᴀ, ʙ, 21ᴀ, ʙ ; XX, 2ᴀ, ʙ, 3ᴀ, ʙ ; XXI, 16ʙ ; XXII, 1ᴀ, 10ʙ ; XXIII, 1ʙ, 2ᴀ, 3ᴀ, ʙ, 4ᴀ, ʙ, 5ᴀ, ʙ, 6ᴀ, ʙ, 7ᴀ, ʙ, 11ᴀ ; G 24ᴀ. The rules of proper conduct ; a sense of what is proper. Not merely overt acts, but includes feelings and emotions, *see* II, 22. A metaphysical principle, *see* XIX, 7. Human emotion expressed and beautified so as to become a pattern for all.

Radical 115. 禾

積 I, 5ᴀ, ʙ, 7ʙ ; II, 22ʙ ; IV, 18ʙ, 19ᴀ, 21ᴀ ; VII, 24ʙ ; VIII, 10ᴀ, 17ʙ, 20ʙ, 21ᴀ ; IX, 1ʙ, 11ᴀ, 17ʙ, 18ᴀ, ʙ ; XVII, 15ᴀ, 18ʙ ; XVIII, 3ᴀ ; XIX, 4ʙ, 9ᴀ, 20ᴀ, 21ᴀe ; XX, 4ʙ ; XXI, 1ʙ, 6ᴀ ; XXII, 2ᴀ ; XXIII, 2ᴀ, 3ʙ, 6ʙ, 7ᴀ, 8ᴀ. Practise ; self-cultivation.

Radical 116. 穴

窮 II, 15ᴀ, 18ᴀ, ʙ, 20ᴀ, 22ʙ, 23ʙ ; IV, 15ᴀ, 17ʙ, 21ᴀ, 22ᴀ ; V, 4ᴀ ; VII, 26ᴀ, 28ᴀ ; VIII, 3ᴀ, ʙ, 9ʙ,

11ᴀ, 16ʙ, 17ᴀ ; IX, 3ʙ, 4ᴀ ; X, 1ʙ, 2ᴀ ; XIX, 8ᴀ, 18ʙ, 19ᴀ ; XX, 3ʙ ; XXI, 14ʙ ; XXII, 9ʙ, 11ᴀ ; XXIII, 10ʙ. Out of office ; the contrary of 通.

Radical 118. 竹

節 II, 15ᴀ, 17ᴀ ; IV, 18ᴀ, 21ʙ ; V, 6ᴀ, 8ʙ ; VII, 23ʙ, 24ᴀ, 26ᴀ, 27ᴀ ; VIII, 2ʙ, 5ᴀ, 11ʙ, 13ʙ, 18ʙ ; IX, 4ᴀ, ʙ, 17ʙ ; XV, 4ʙ ; XVI, 11ᴀ, ʙ ; XVII, 12ᴀ, 16ᴀ ; XIX, 2ʙ, 7ᴀ, 11ᴀ, ʙ, 12ʙ, 18ᴀ, ʙ, 19ᴀ, 21ᴀ, ʙ ; XX, 1ᴀ, ʙ, 4ʙ, 5ᴀ, ʙ ; XXI, 16ʙ ; XXII, 2ʙ, 10ᴀ, 11ʙ, 13ᴀ ; XXIII, 5ʙ. Self-restraint ; what is fitting to the circumstances, equivalent to 適 ; accord.

籍 VIII, 1ʙ, 2ᴀ, 14ᴀ ; IX, 19ᴀ ; XVIII, 2ᴀ, ʙ. Position, rank ; equivalent to 位.

Radical 119. 米

精 II, 18ʙ ; XVII, 13ᴀ ; XXI, 9ʙ, 10ᴀ, 11ʙ, 12ᴀ, ʙ, 13ʙ ; XXII, 1ʙ, 10ʙ. Concentration.

Radical 120. 糸

統 IV, 20ᴀ, 22ᴀ ; VI, 15ᴀ ; VII, 28ᴀ ; VIII, 13ᴀ, 18ʙ, 22ᴀ ; IX, 11ʙ ; XV, 12ᴀ, (XIX), 13ᴀ, ʙ ; XX, 3ʙ ; XXI, 15ᴀ. 統 類 general principles.

絕 I, 3ᴀ ; IX, 7ᴀ, 12ʙ. Line of succession run out.

經 I, 7ʙ, 9ʙ, 10ʙ ; VII, 28ᴀ ; VIII, 3ʙ ; IX, 3ʙ ; XX, 3ʙ ; XXI, 5ᴀ, 8ʙ, 10ʙ ; XXII, 9ᴀ.

綱 I, 8ᴀ ; VI, 15ᴀ ; XXII, 10ᴀ ; G 24ᴀ. 綱 紀 unifying principle.

Radical 123. 羊

義 I, 7B, 10B, 12A ; II, 16A, 17B, 18A, B, 22A, 24A ; IV, 14A, 15A, 16A, 18A, 19A, 20A, 22A, 23A ; V, 2A, 8B ; VI, 15A ; VII, 26A, 28A ; VIII, 2A, B, 3A, 5A, 6A, 9A, 17A, 18A, B, 19B, 21A ; IX, 1B, 3B, 7B, 8A, 11A, B, 12A, B, 17B ; X, 1B ; XV, 4B, 11A, B, e, 12A ; XVI, 11A, B ; XVII, 17B, 18B, 19A ; XVIII, 3A, 8B, 9B, 16A, B ; XIX, 1A, 3A, 9A, 11B, 12A, 13A, 17B, 18A, 21B ; XX, 1B, 5A ; XXI, 11A ; XXII, 2A, 10B, 11A ; XXIII, 1B, 2A, 3A, B, 4A, B, 5A, B, 6A, B, 7A, B, 8A, 12A ; G 24A. Class rights and their recognition ; equivalent to δικαιοσύνη.

羣 I, 4B, 13A ; IX, 12A, B, 17B ; X, 1B, 2A ; XV, 9B ; XVII, 20B, 21A ; XVIII, 14A, 17B ; XIX, 18A, B, 19A, B ; XXI, 2B. Form a social organization.

Radical 128. 耳

聖 I, 5A, 7B ; II, 21B, 22A ; IV, 13A, B, 22B ; V, 6A, B, 7B ; VII, 25A, 27B, 28A ; VIII, 8A, B, 12A, 13B, 19B, 21A ; IX, 12B, 13A, 17B ; XVII, 13B, 14A ; XVIII, 2B, 3B, 5A, 8B, 9A, 13A, 16A, B ; XIX, 8A, 9A, 14B, 18A, 19A, 21B ; XX, 2B ; XXI, 1A, 6A, 13A, 15A ; XXII, 3A, 7A, 8B, 9B ; XXIII, 1B, 2A, 3A, B, 4A, 5A, B, 6A, B, 8A, 9B ; G 24A.

職 IV, 15B, 23B ; VIII, 11A ; IX, 1B, 3A ; X, 2A ; XI, 12A, 14B ; XV, 10A ; XVII, 13A, B ; XVIII, 6A, 12B, 16A. Responsibilities.

Radical 130. 肉

能 I, 3A, B, 5B, 6B, 10A, 13A ; II, 14A, 18B, 24A ; IV, 15B, 17A, B, 18A, 22B, 23A, B ; V, 4A ; VII, 23B, 24A, B, 26A, B, 27B ; VIII, 1B, 2A, 3A, 6B, 7A, 8A, B, 10B, 11A, 12B, 16A, B, 17A, B, 18A, 19B, 20A, 21B, 22A ; IX, 1A, B, 3A, B, 4A, 6B, 8B, 9B, 12A, B, 14B, 16B, 17B, 18A ; X, 1B ; XI, 12A ; XV, 1B, 4B, 9B, (XIX), 13B ; XVII, 12A, B, 13A, B, 19B ; XVIII, 3A, B, 5A, 6A, B, 8B, 9B, 12A, B, 13B, 14A, 15A, 16B ; XIX, 1A, 7A, B, 8A, 11A, 14A, B, 18B, 19A, 20A, 21A, B ; XX, 1A, 5A, B ; XXI, 3A, 4A, 5B, 7A, 9B, 10B, 11B, 12A, B, 13B, 14B, 15B, 16B ; XXII, 1B, 2A, 7B, 8A, 9B, 10A, 14B, 15A ; XXIII, 2A, 3B, 6B, 7B, 8A, B, 10A, 11A, B ; G 24A, B. Ability, contrasted with 巧 skill.

Radical 131. 臣

臣 V, 3B ; VI, 14B ; VII, 24A ; VIII, 2A, 3A, B, 11A, 16B, 19A, 22B ; IX, 5A, 7B, 11B, 17B, 18B ; X, 1B ; XI, 12A, 14A ; XV, 1B, 2A, B, 4B, 9B, (XIX), 13B ; XVII, 18B ; XVIII, 4B, 6B ; XIX, 9B, 10B, 11A, 21A ; XX, 1B ; XXI, 2B, 3B ; XXIII, 7B, 8A. Vassal.

Radical 139. 色

色 I, 11B, 13A ; V, 1B, 2B ; VII, 28A ; IX, 8B ; X, 2A ; XVIII, 9B, 17B ; XIX, 13A ; XX, 3A ; XXI, 3A ; XXII, 4A, 9B, 15A ; XXIII, 1A, 3B ; G 24A. Sights, what the eye sees, as 聲 is what the ear hears ; complexion.

Radical 140. 艸

萬 IV, 22A; V, 7A; VII, 26B; VIII, 3A, 7A, 12A, 13B, 16B, 18B, 19A; IX, 9A, 11A, B, 12A, B, 13A, 16B; X, 1A; XVI, 11A; XVII, 13B, 14B, 18A, 19B, 20A; XVIII, 16B; XIX, 7A, 14A, B; XX, 1B, 4B; XXI, 2B, 6A, 8A, B, 9B, 10A, 14B; XXII, 1A, 6A, 14B, 15A, B; XXIII, 9B. 萬 物, all things between heaven and earth.

Radical 141. 虍

虛 VIII, 1B, 7B, 10A; XVII, 14A; XVIII, 11B; XIX, 15B; XXI, 2B, 7A, B, 8A. Emptiness.

Radical 144. 行

術 II, 16B, 17B, 18B; IV, 18A; V, 1B; VII, 25B, 26A, B, 27A, B, 28A; VIII, 17A; XV, 1B, 9A, 10A; XIX, 15A, 18A; XX, 1A, B, 2A; XXI, 1B, 2B, 5B, 6A; XXIII, 8A; G 24A. Principles; art.

Radical 145. 衣

衰 IX, 11A; XIX, 11A, 12B, 13B, 18B, 21B; XX, 2B; XXII, 13B; XXIII, 8B. Little; contrasted with 隆.

Radical 147. 見

規 I, 1B; VIII, 6B; XIX, 7B, 8A.
親 II, 14A; IV, 12B, 13A, 17A, B; V, 3B, 5B; VIII, 4B; IX, 2A, 7A, 8A, 12B, 18A, B; XI, 12A, 14A; XV, 1B, 3B, 11B; XVII, 18B; XVIII, 2A, 4A; XIX, 5A, 9B, 11A, 12A, B, 18A, B, 19A, 20B, 21B; XX, 1B, 5A; XXIII, 8B. Cherish regard for.

Radical 149. 言

詩 and other names of the *Book of Odes*. I, 2B, 6B, 8A, 9B, 10A, 11A, 12A; II, 14A, 15B, 22B; IV, 22A, B, 24A; V, 4B; VII, 26A; VIII, 6A, 8A, 10B, 11A, 13B, 17A, 18A, 21B; IX, 11A, 14A; XV, 4A, 10B, 11B; XVII, 15A, B; XVIII, 2A, 12B; XIX, 9A, 14B, 19B; XX, 1A, B; XXI, 3A, 9A, 17A; XXII, 10A, B, 11A; G 24A. The *Book of Odes*.

誠 II, 18A; IV, 13A; V, 8B; VII, 23A; VIII, 3B, 9B, 10A, 11A; IX, 17A; XI, 12A; XV (XIX), 14A; XVIII, 1B; XIX, 7B; XX, 3B; XXI, 1B; XXIII, 5A.

Radical 154. 貝

賢 II, 14A, 23A; IV, 17B; V, 4A, 8A; VII, 24B, 26B, 27A, B, 28A; VIII, 6B, 7A, 11A, 18B; IX, 1A, 2A, 4A, 8B, 10B, 12B, 17B; XI, 12A; XV, 4B; XVIII, 4A, 14A, 18A; XXI, 2B, 4A, 5A; XXIII, 8B, 11A, 12A; G 24A, B. Morally worthy.

賤 II, 19A; IX, 3B, 11B, 18B, 19A; XI, 12A, 14A; XV, 4B; XVII, 20B; XVIII, 2A, 4A; XIX, 1B, 8B, 9B, 12B, 13A, 18A; XX, 2B, 5A, B; XXI, 16B; XXII, 3B, 4A, 10B; XXIII, 4B, 7A. Esteem lightly.

Radical 158. 身

身 I, 4B, 8B, 11B; II, 14A, B, 18A, 20A, 22A, B; IV, 12B, 13A, 17B; V, 2B, 3A, 9A; VII, 25B, 26A; VIII, 8A, 10A, B, 11A, 14A, 17B; IX, 1B, 5A, 16A, 18B, 19A; XVIII, 4A; XX, 3B, 5B; XXI, 3A, 4A, 9B, 15A; XXIII, 10A, 11A, 12A; G 24A. Character.

Radical 160. 幸

辨 II, 22A ; IV, 17B, 18B ; V, 3A,
5A, B, 6A ; VI, 14B ; VIII, 8B,
11B ; IX, 15A ; XI, 14B ; XV
(XIX), 12A, 13B ; XVIII, 1B,
3B, 15B, 17B ; XIX, 14B, 19B ; XX,
1A, 5A, B ; XXI, 16A, B ; XXII,
2B, 4A, 8A, B, 9A, B, 10A, B ;
XXIII, 6A. Make distinctions.

辯 I, 11B ; II, 20B ; IV, 12B ;
V, 8B ; VI, 15A ; VIII, 6B, 8A,
9A, 11A, 20A ; XVII, 18B ;
XXI, 15B ; XXIII, 12A.
Dialectic.

辟 I, 11B ; IV, 14A, 19A ; VI, 15B ;
VII, 26A ; VIII, 10B ; XIX,
3A ; XX, 5A ; XXI, 5A, B, 8B,
16A, B ; XXII, 2B, 3A, 8A, 9A,
10A, B, 11A ; XXIII, 1A, B, 3A.
辟讓, courtesy, declining and
yielding an honour.

Radical 161. 辰

辱 I, 5A ; II, 23A ; IV, 13B,
15A, 16B, 17A, 19A ; VII, 27B ;
VIII, 10B, 21B ; XVIII, 14B,
15A, B, 16A, B ; XX, 2B ; XXI,
4A ; XXII, 7A.

Radical 162. 辵

達 II, 19A, B ; VIII, 5B ; XV,
10B ; XVIII, 6B ; XIX, 12A.
Successful.

道 I, 2B, 6A, 8A, 11A, B ; II, 17A,
B, 18B, 20A, 21B, 23A, 24A ;
IV, 17A, 18B, 20A, 22A, 23B ;
V, 1A, B, 6A, 7A, B ; VII, 25A, B,
26A, 27B, 28A ; VIII, 1A, 3A,
B, 6A, 7A, 10A, 11A, B, 13A, B,
14A, 16B, 19B, 22B ; IX, 2A, B,
5A, 6AB, B, 7A, B, 8A, 9B, 12B,
15B, 16A ; X, 1A ; XV, 1B, 2A,
4A, B, 9A, (XIX), 12A, B, 13B,
14A, B ; XVII, 13A, 15A, B, 17A,
19B, 20A, B, 21A ; XVIII, 1A,

B, 2A, 3A, B, 4B, 5A, 8B, 11B, 13A,
B, 16B ; XIX, 3B, 8A, B, 9A, B,
10B, 12A, 13A, 16A, 18A, 19B,
20B, 21B ; XX, 1A, B, 2A, 3A,
B, 4B, 5A, B ; XXI, 1A, B, 2A, 3A,
5A, B, 6A, B, 7A, B, 8A, 9B, 10A, B,
13A, 16A ; XXII, 2B, 3A, 8A, B,
9A, B, 10A, 11B, 12B, 13A, B, 14A,
B ; XXIII, 1B, 2A, 3A, 10A, 12A ;
G 24A. Way, physical or spiritual,
good or evil, the Confucian Way
or Doctrine ; method ; morality ;
consider.

過 I, 1B ; II, 23A, B, 24A ; IV, 13A,
17B ; VIII, 22B ; IX, 3A, 8A,
9A, 16B ; XV, 9A, 11A ; XVIII,
4A, 12A, 13A, 15A, 17A, 18A ;
XIX, 11B, 18B, 19A ; XX, 2B ;
XXI, 11A, 13B ; XXII, 9B,
12A, B ; XXIII, 2B, 4A, 6A ;
G 24A.

Radical 163. 邑

邪 I, 4B, 7B ; IV, 13B, 16B, 20A,
23A ; V, 3A, 8A ; VI, 12B ;
VII, 25B ; VIII, 3A, 17A ; IX,
16A ; XV, 3A ; XVII, 15A ;
XVIII, 5B, 7B, 15A, 18A ; XIX,
18B ; XX, 1B, 2B, 4B ; XXI, 15B ;
XXII, 8A, 9B ; XXIII, 5A, 6B,
7B, 11B, 12A.

Radical 170. 阜

陰 IX, 15B ; XVII, 13B, 15A, 16B,
17A ; XIX, 14B.

隆 I, 9B, 10A, 11B ; II, 14A, 23B ;
VII, 24B, 27B ; VIII, 3A, 6A,
11B, 17A, 18A, 20B, 22B ; IX,
4A, 16A, 17B ; XI, 14A ; XV, 4B ;
XVIII, 9A, 15B ; XIX, 3B, 5A,
7A, 8B, 9A, B, 11B, 14A, 19A, B,
20B ; XX, 5B ; XXI, 15B.
Magnify, exalt, embellish, its
contrary is 殺. 隆正, point of
reference.

陽 IX, 15B; XVII, 13B, 15A, 16B; XIX, 14B.

險 II, 22B; IV, 15B; VII, 23B, 27A; IX, 19A; XV (XIX), 13B; XVII, 17A, 19A; XVIII, 1B, 4A; XIX, 12B; XX, 2B, 5B; XXI, 17A; XXIII, 1B, 5A. Bent on evil; difficult to fathom. 心險 malignant feelings.

Radical 173. 雨

霸 V, 2A; VII, 23Ae, B, 24A; IX, 5A, B, 6B, 7B, 8A, 16B, 18B, 19B; XI, title. Lord Protector.

Radical 174. 青

靜 I, 8B; II, 15A; VII, 26A; IX, 4A, 18A; XX, 1A; XXI, 7A, B, 8A, 12A; XXII, 9A. Unperturbedness; see *Analects*, II, xxi; *Great Learning*, i, 2.

Radical 181. 頁

類 I, 4B, 8A, 12A; II, 22A; V, 3A, 8A; VI, 15B; VIII, 13A, 16B, 18A, B, 22A; IX, 3A, 8A, 11A; XVII, 14A; XVIII, 6A; XIX, 3A, 14A, 19B; XXI, 9B, 15A; XXII, 4A, 5A, 8A, 9B, 10B, 11A, B, 12A; XXIII, 9B, 10A. Analogy; come near the truth; imitate, equivalent to 法 species, classifications; make to fit the situation; classify by analogy.

Radical 184. 食

養 IV, 18B, 20A; VIII, 3A, 11A; IX, 1B, 3B, 9A, 10B, 12B, 13A, 14B, 15A, 17B; X, 1B, 2A; XV, 10B; XVII, 12A, B, 13B, 14A, B; XVIII, 11A, B; XIX, 1A, B, 2A, B, 3A, 20A; XX, 5B, 10A, 11A; XXII, 5A, 15A, B. Educate and nourish; essentials of life.

Radical 188. 骨

體 II, 18B, 21B, 23B; IV, 13B, 15A, B, 18B, 20A; IX, 17B; X, 1A; XVII, 15B, 19B; XVIII, 13B, 17A; XIX, 1B, 14B; XXI, 5B, 8A; XXII, 4A, 5A, 14B, 15B; XXIII, 3B. Deportment; embody.